Asset
Building
AND
Low-Income
Families

Also of interest from the Urban Institute Press:

Public Housing and the Legacy of Segregation, edited
by Margery Austin Turner, Susan J. Popkin, and Lynette Rawlings

Subprime Mortgages: America's Latest Boom and Bust,
by Edward M. Gramlich

Reshaping the American Workforce in a Changing Economy, edited
by Harry J. Holzer and Demetra Smith Nightingale

Making America Work, by Jonathan B. Forman

Asset **Building** AND Low-Income Families

Edited by **Signe-Mary McKernan** & **Michael Sherraden**

THE URBAN INSTITUTE PRESS
Washington, D.C.

THE URBAN INSTITUTE PRESS
2100 M Street, N.W.
Washington, D.C. 20037

Library of Congress Cataloging-in-Publication Data

Asset building and low-income families / edited by Signe-Mary McKernan and Michael Sherraden.
    p. cm.
  Includes bibliographical references and index.
  ISBN 0-87766-754-3 (alk. paper)
  1. Individual development accounts. 2. Poor—Finance, Personal. I.
McKernan, Signe-Mary. II. Sherraden, Michael W. (Michael Wayne), 1948-
  HG1660.A3A77 2008
  332.0240086'942—dc22

                                                            2008035508

ISBN 978-0-87766-754-3 (paper, alk. paper)

Printed in the United States of America

11 10 09 08   1 2 3 4 5

THE URBAN INSTITUTE is a nonprofit, nonpartisan policy research and educational organization established in Washington, D.C., in 1968. Its staff investigates the social, economic, and governance problems confronting the nation and evaluates the public and private means to alleviate them. The Institute disseminates its research findings through publications, its web site, the media, seminars, and forums.

Through work that ranges from broad conceptual studies to administrative and technical assistance, Institute researchers contribute to the stock of knowledge available to guide decisionmaking in the public interest.

Conclusions or opinions expressed in Institute publications are those of the authors and do not necessarily reflect the views of officers or trustees of the Institute, advisory groups, or any organizations that provide financial support to the Institute.

Contents

Acknowledgments

The research and writing for this book was funded by the Annie E. Casey Foundation and the Urban Institute. We thank them for their support but acknowledge that the findings and conclusions presented in this book are those of the authors alone, and do not necessarily reflect the opinions of these organizations.

The background reports and briefs drawn on for this book were funded by the U.S. Department of Health and Human Services, Office of the Assistant Secretary for Planning and Evaluation; the Ford Foundation; and the Annie E. Casey Foundation. We are grateful for their support of the Opportunity and Ownership Project and the Center for Social Development (CSD). For supporting CSD's applied research contributing to this book, the authors are grateful to the Ford Foundation, the Charles Stewart Mott Foundation, the Annie E. Casey Foundation, the F. B. Heron Foundation, the Ewing Marion Kauffman Foundation, and the MetLife Foundation.

We thank John Tambornino for conceptualizing the need for a comprehensive assessment and critique of asset-building research and policy. He provided the catalyst for this book. We thank Kathy Courrier of the Urban Institute Press and two anonymous reviewers for helpful comments on earlier drafts of the book, and Scott Forrey and Devlan O'Connor for managing the book publication and copyedits. We also thank the many reviewers who provided comments on the reports and briefs drawn on for this book, including Jeremías Alvarez, Robert Avery, Laura Chadwick, Gordon Fisher, Jim Gatz, Alfred Gottschalck, Susan Hauan, Arthur Kennickell, Alana Landey, Gretchen Lehman, Elizabeth Lower-Basch, Linda Mellgren, Ann McCormick, Zoe Neuberger, Don Oellerich, Canta Pian, Annette Rogers, Joan Turek, Robert Schoeni, Reuben Snipper, Frank Stafford, Leonard Sternbach, C. Eugene Steuerle, Kendall Swenson, Joan Turek, and Michael Wiseman. Any remaining errors are our own.

Elizabeth Bell, Katie Vinopal, William Margrabe, and Daniel Moskowitz of the Urban Institute, and Carrie Freeman, Eunhee Han, Jung Hee Han, Jennifer Kim, and Julia Stevens at the Center for Social Development provided invaluable research assistance.

Introduction

S ocial policies put into place during the 20th century, both in the
United States and abroad, are today in a period of strain, question-
ing, and, sometimes, revision. Although typically discussed in political
terms—conservative or liberal, left or right—the sources of policy strain
are primarily technological and economic. Social policies of the 20th century were designed for an industrial society with low-skilled and relatively
stable labor markets. When a household was without labor income—due
to death, disability, job loss, age, or some other factor—social policy was
designed to provide income to support basic consumption. These policies
were successful in many respects (notwithstanding the fact that America's
social policy was never as comprehensive or generous as most policies in
Western Europe). In the 21st century, however, we live in a world where
technological changes have produced very different labor markets. Greater
skills are needed, jobs are less stable, and income inequality is growing.
It is no longer clear that basic income support is a sufficient social policy
response in these more demanding economic circumstances. As a result,
industrial-era policies are being questioned and new policy directions are
being considered and explored in many countries.

In this environment, an active discussion of asset-based policy arose
in the United States (Oliver and Shapiro 1995; Sherraden 1991) and has
led to a growing body of theory, research, policy innovation, and testing.
In simple terms, asset-based policy suggests that individual, household,

and community well-being (or "welfare") is derived not solely from a certain level of income and consumption, but also from building assets to invest in life goals and to enhance long-term economic stability and social protections. In this book we seek to take the measure of asset-based policy. We gather the existing evidence, assess theory, examine data sources, and point to potential directions for research and policy.

Overall, theory and evidence suggest that asset-based policies may promote development of individuals, families, and perhaps communities and society as a whole. Yet traditional social policies that assist the poor have focused mainly on income and consumption. The United States and many other countries do have large asset-based subsidies, but the poor are frequently left out because (1) the subsidies operate through the tax system (e.g., the mortgage interest deduction, tax breaks for contributions to retirement and education accounts) and the poor have little or no tax liability; and (2) the poor are less likely to own homes, investments, or retirement accounts, where most asset-based policies are targeted. In addition, asset limits in means-tested transfer policies have the potential to discourage saving by the poor. In many respects, the poor do not have access to the same structures and incentives for asset accumulation as those who are not poor. This is unfortunate because saving and asset building for low-income households are activities that may enable a family to eventually move up and out of poverty.

The potential of asset building to promote long-term development of low-income households motivates this book. *Asset Building and Low-Income Families* provides a comprehensive assessment and critique of the knowledge base and policy potential of asset building for the poor. Specifically, the book evaluates what is known regarding the measures, distributions, determinants, and effects of asset holding; charts directions for future research; and sets the stage for future asset policies that may include low-income households.

While the focus of this book is on asset accumulation and asset-based policies for low-income individuals and families, the conceptual frameworks developed are not limited to low-income populations. This broad approach is an effective way to identify critical issues that relate to asset holding for all populations. Where appropriate, however, various chapters point out when the framework specifically applies to low-income, minority, and single-parent households. This distinction is important because these subgroups are particularly vulnerable to low asset accumulation. The definition of *low income* used in this book is necessarily imprecise.

The book reflects a broad research and policy synthesis, and definitions of low income are not uniform across studies, surveys, or public programs. For our purposes, *low income* can be broadly thought of as affecting households in the bottom income quintiles.

Why Assets Are Important

In describing why assets are important, it is useful to begin by distinguishing income from assets. *Incomes* are flows of resources. They are what people receive as a return on their labor or the use of their capital, or as a public program transfer. Most income is spent on current consumption. *Assets* are stocks of resources. They are what people accumulate and hold over time. Assets provide for future consumption and are a source of security against contingencies. As investments, they also generate returns that generally increase aggregate lifetime consumption and improve a family's well-being over an extended time horizon.

The dimensions of poverty and its relative distribution among different social classes are significantly different when approached from an assets perspective as opposed to an income perspective. Those with a low stock of resources to draw on in times of need are asset poor. This *asset poverty* may leave them vulnerable to unexpected economic events and unable to take advantage of the broad opportunities offered by a prosperous society. Many studies have found that the rate of asset poverty exceeds the rate of income poverty (Haveman and Wolff 2005). Many U.S. families have little financial cushion to sustain them in the event of a job loss, illness, or other income shortfall. Also, social and economic development of these families may be limited by a lack of investment in education, homes, businesses, or other assets. To the extent that low resource holdings limit the potential for social and economic development, understanding how low-resource families can build up their asset bases is likely to be an important policy issue.

Income and Assets in Public Policy

Outside of education, traditional social programs that support low-income populations have focused mainly on income and social services that fulfill basic consumption needs, which have been essential to the well-being of families and children. An asset-based approach would complement this traditional approach and shift the focus to long-term development for individuals, families, and communities. This would provide a broader picture of well-being among low-income populations.

Asset-based policy has many potential meanings. These include policies to promote the accumulation and preservation of financial wealth, tangible property, human capital, social capital, political participation and influence, cultural capital, and natural resources (Sherraden 1991). While all of these meanings have value, building financial wealth and tangible nonfinancial assets for the purpose of household social and economic development is the focus of this book.

A Comprehensive Assessment of Asset Building for the Poor

Each chapter of *Asset Building and Low-Income Families* asks specific questions to guide analysis and advance understanding of the nature and dynamics of assets in low-income families. In doing so, the book addresses such questions as the following: How are assets defined, and what implications do these definitions have for asset poverty? What are the asset holdings of low-income families? What determines these asset holdings? Do government programs play a role? What are the effects of asset holdings on social and economic outcomes for families? What are the implications for future research and policy?

Chapter 1 sets the stage with the competing definitions and measures of assets and their implications for asset building and social policy. Three distinct perspectives are considered: the consumption model, social-stratification theory, and an *assets-for-development* perspective. In probing these perspectives, chapter 1 may lay the groundwork for more appropriate measures of assets that can inform future research and policy.

Chapter 2 paints a portrait of the assets and liabilities of low-income families. Assets in themselves may have an effect on social and economic outcomes, but assets alone do not tell the whole financial story. The entire balance sheet must be considered—viewing the different assets a household owns and comparing these against liabilities to arrive at net worth or household wealth. As yet, a comprehensive portrayal of the balance sheets of low-income households does not exist. The portrait approach is a valuable analytical tool because it uses multiple classifiers in tandem—

such as income, education, race, martial status, and housing status—to describe populations of interest. The chapter reveals key differences in the balance sheets of typical low-income and middle-income families.

Determinants of asset holding are examined in chapters 3, 4, and 5. Chapter 3 applies a life-course perspective to understanding why assets are in short supply for many low-income households. Factors such as parental resources, race, earnings, single parenthood, and ill-timed life events play critical roles. Chapter 4 provides an analysis of what determines asset building based on an emerging institutional theory of saving and asset accumulation. In this framework, both individual constructs (such as economic resources and education) and institutional constructs (such as incentives and expectations) affect saving and investment, which in turn lead to asset accumulation. Public policy plays an important role in access to these institutional constructs. Chapter 5 turns to government's role in asset holding. It synthesizes the state of research on the effects of asset tests for means-tested programs and the effect of individual development account (IDA) programs on asset holding.

With knowledge of the types of assets families hold and what determines those holdings, we turn in chapter 6 to effects of assets. It assesses the data, methods, and empirical evidence on effects of asset holding and provides a conceptual framework for relating the theory and evidence. Findings from research are synthesized into five potential areas asset holding can affect: economic well-being, social well-being, civic engagement, child well-being, and health and psychological well-being.

An overview of key findings on measures, distributions, determinants, and effects of asset holding from the first six chapters is presented in chapter 7, pointing to gaps in our knowledge and directions for future research. To help guide future research, the appendix identifies the most informative and reliable data sources for studying assets, presents detailed information about each data source, and suggests options for improving asset data. A separate online appendix at http://www.urban.org/books/assetbuilding/ provides easy reference summaries of over 100 asset research papers grouped by topic.

Chapter 8 presents the closing policy implications of the assets perspective set forth in the book. A new policy discussion has emerged over the past two decades on the role that assets can play in development. The chapter presents characteristics of asset-building policy that may include the poor and offers concrete ideas on how to make asset-based policy more inclusive.

This book is the first comprehensive effort to review and consider what is known in relation to asset-based social policy. We hope the chapters fit together to provide a comprehensive overview, critique, and assessment of theory and evidence on the potential of this policy direction in the years ahead. During a time when existing policies are being scrutinized and may be in transformation, it is especially important to look carefully at potential revisions, alternatives, or complements to traditional income-oriented policies. By examining carefully and asking questions from multiple angles, we may increase the chance of creating better-informed and more effective policy going forward.

REFERENCES

Haveman, Robert, and Edward N. Wolff. 2005. "Who Are the Asset Poor? Levels, Trends, and Composition, 1983–1998." In *Inclusion in the American Dream: Assets, Poverty, and Public Policy,* edited by Michael Sherraden (61–86). New York: Oxford University Press.

Oliver, Melvin L., and Thomas M. Shapiro. 1995. *Black Wealth/White Wealth: A New Perspective on Racial Inequality.* New York: Routledge.

Sherraden, Michael. 1991. *Assets and the Poor: A New American Welfare Policy.* Armonk, NY: M. E. Sharpe.

1

Asset Definitions

Yunju Nam, Jin Huang, and Michael Sherraden

The term *assets* has many possible meanings. This chapter seeks to identify the competing definitions of assets and the assumptions and implications of the definitions of assets and asset poverty. To do so, the chapter considers in detail three major perspectives on assets—the consumption model, social-stratification theory, and an *assets-for-development* perspective—and how each of these perspectives defines and measures assets, along with considerations of these competing viewpoints for research and policy development. Next, definitions and measures of asset poverty in existing studies are reviewed. Then suggestions are offered for developing better measures of assets and asset poverty for future research and policy development.

As a general concept, assets are rights or claims related to property, both tangible and intangible. Such rights or claims are enforced by cultural expectations, formal laws and regulations, or both. Assets can be put to use, that is, can be invested or otherwise made active to generate returns. Broadly conceived, assets can refer to anything that has a potential for positive returns. It may be useful to categorize assets as tangible or intangible. To simplify, the tangible category includes financial wealth and physical property, and the intangible category includes human talents, behaviors, connections, and influence. Sherraden (1991) listed *tangible assets* as including (1) money savings; (2) stocks, bonds, and other financial securities; (3) real property; (4) hard assets other than real estate, such as automobiles, jewelry, art, and collectibles; (5) machines, equipment, tools, and other tangible components of production; (6) durable household goods; (7) natural resources; and (8) copyrights, patents, and other intellectual property. *Intangible assets* include (1) access to credit, (2) human capital, (3) cultural capital, (4) informal social capital, (5) formal social capital or organizational capital, and (6) political capital. This list is not definitive, but illustrates that the term *assets* (along with a related term, *capital*) has been broadly applied.

A broad definition may be useful for some purposes, but it runs the risk of blurring a great many meanings of assets and may not serve very well in thinking about social issues related to government policies. Although this may be an oversimplification, the government has two major options in promoting the economic well-being of its citizens. These are to support income (flows) to meet immediate needs or to support assets (stocks) that can be used by individuals and families for the intended social purposes. Stocks of assets in the context of social policy are usually in the form of financial wealth (e.g., subsidies for retirement accounts or educational savings accounts) or tangible wealth (e.g., subsidies for homeownership). For this reason, this chapter focuses on financial assets and physical property and defines assets somewhat narrowly.

Concepts and Measures of Assets in Existing Research: Three Different Theoretical Perspectives on Assets

There are many options for measuring both assets and net worth. At this point, little is known about which measures of assets and net worth might be best for which purposes. In taking up this question, it seems most fruitful to ask first how assets are conceived from different theoretical perspectives and then to consider implications for measurement. This is a large and previously uncharted task, but it is worth pursuing because it has the potential to lead to measures of assets that are suited to the purposes of particular policies.

Assets as a Storehouse for Future Consumption

With few exceptions (e.g., Shapiro 2001; Sherraden 1991), theory and research on asset accumulation in the United States defines assets as a storehouse for future consumption. In the two major economic theories of asset accumulation—the life-cycle hypothesis (Ando and Modigliani 1963; Banterle 2002; Modigliani 1986; Shefrin and Thaler 1988) and buffer-stock theory (Carroll 1997; Hubbard, Skinner, and Zeldes 1994; Leland 1968)—saving is defined as a way of balancing the fluctuation of household financial resources for consumption throughout a lifetime (also see the discussion in chapter 4 of this book).

Both types of theories of asset accumulation—life cycle and buffer stock—are based on the same assumptions. The first assumption is that people want to maintain the highest living standard possible. Since level of consumption determines living standard, people consume as much as their financial resources permit. The second assumption is that people want to maintain a relatively constant standard of living across time. To achieve these two goals, people make financial decisions so as to maintain a smooth consumption pattern at a maximum level throughout their lifetimes. Accordingly, current consumption level is not determined by current income but rather by permanent income (Friedman 1957). That is to say, forward-looking individuals save when they estimate their current incomes to be higher than their expected permanent incomes, and they spend when they estimate it to be lower (Fisher 1987; Friedman 1957; Leland 1968).

Although the life-cycle hypothesis and the buffer-stock theory share the assumptions described above, they differ in explaining particular motives to save. In the life-cycle hypothesis, variations in (usually earned) income across the life course provide a major motivation to save. From this perspective, saving is caused by the desire to ensure a steady flow of financial resources for stable consumption after retirement. Accordingly, the life-cycle hypothesis predicts the typical saving pattern to be "hump shaped" in accordance with income levels at each life-cycle stage (Ando and Modigliani 1963; Banterle 2002; Modigliani 1986).

While an expected sharp income decline in retirement is a major motive for asset accumulation in the life-cycle hypothesis, unexpected income loss or expense is the major motivation for saving in the buffer-stock model. According to this theory, people save to prepare for economic emergencies, such as unemployment or sudden medical costs. Emphasizing the precautionary saving motive, this model predicts a higher level of saving when future income is uncertain (Carroll 1997; Hubbard et al. 1994; Leland 1968).

In sum, people save as a response to income fluctuations over time in both life-cycle and buffer-stock theories. As such, saving is a choice between present and future consumption, and assets are a storehouse for future consumption. Both consumption models, therefore, focus on the amount of assets available for future consumption (most often measured as net worth) and the level of liquidity in asset holdings, because these measures often determine how much and how quickly financial resources can become available to a household when needed.

Measures of Assets in the Consumption Framework

Since consumption models define assets as a storehouse of future consumption, they are concerned with how much financial value a household can obtain from assets and how easily and quickly assets can be converted into cash for consumption. The most commonly used measure of the total amount of assets is net worth, defined as the sum of values of all assets net of all liabilities (Aizcorbe, Kennickell, and Moore 2003; Gustman and Steinmeier 2002; McNeil and Lamas 1989; Spilerman 2000). Net worth, however, is not identically measured across studies. Most measures of net worth include the following six asset items: (1) net financial assets (values in checking and saving accounts, money market funds, certificates of deposit, bonds, stocks, and investment trusts, all net of unsecured debt); (2) home equity; (3) other real estate equity; (4) net business equity; (5) value of individual retirement assets (e.g., IRA, Keogh, and 401(k) balances); and (6) vehicle equity (Aizcorbe et al. 2003; Burkhauser and Weathers 2001; Gustman and Steinmeier 2002; McNeil and Lamas 1989; Oliver and Shapiro 1990; Spilerman 2000; Venti and Wise 1990).

Some studies also include Social Security wealth and the value of employment-based pensions (Burkhauser and Weathers 2001; Gustman and Steinmeier 2002; Venti and Wise 1990). Social Security wealth is usually defined as the present discounted value of the stream of Social Security benefits owed to individuals, while employer-provided pension wealth is calculated as the present discounted value of future pension benefits (Burkhauser and Weathers 2001; Wolff 2001). Proponents of this measure argue that the inclusion of pension and Social Security wealth provides a better indicator of potential future consumption. Since people are likely to include income from pension plans and Social Security when estimating their consumption levels after retirement, their behaviors, especially financial resource allocation related to retirement, are probably influenced by the amount of retirement wealth (Feldstein 1976; Wolff 2002).

Researchers using consumption models have developed subcategories of assets based on liquidity. Most studies use financial assets, liquid assets, or fungible wealth to measure assets that can be easily converted into cash. Several studies define financial assets as net worth (excluding pension and Social Security wealth) minus home equity, vehicle value, and business wealth (Oliver and Shapiro 1990; Wolff 2002).

Gruber (2001) presents an alternative classification system for assets: gross financial assets, net financial assets, and total net worth. His approach is of interest because he attempts to take into account accessibility to the debt market by separating gross financial assets and net financial assets. Gross and net financial assets measure liquid wealth. Gross financial assets are considered to be the total amount of financial resources accumulated as precautionary savings. Net financial assets are calculated by subtracting unsecured debt (e.g., credit card debt) from gross financial assets. This measure is considered a good indicator of a household's capacity for smoothing consumption through loans. On one hand, the level of debt may reflect a household's access to the credit market and ability for short-term smoothing by means of a consumption loan. On the other hand, it may indicate financial constraints, since a household with sizeable unsecured debt is likely to have difficulties in borrowing more at the time of economic emergency. The third measure, net worth, is considered a summary indicator of total available financial resources to the household, combining liquid and illiquid assets.

As in asset research, consumption models have had strong influence on public policies related to assets. Asset measures in many public assistance programs reflect a consumption perspective in defining assets. Asset tests in Temporary Assistance for Needy Families, Supplemental Security Income, Food Stamps, and other public assistance programs use countable assets in determining the eligibility of program participants and applicants. Countable assets include cash on hand, values in saving and checking accounts, bonds, stocks, and vehicle values that exceed the vehicle asset limit (Corporation for Enterprise Development 2002). Illiquid assets, such as home values, are not included as countable assets. The definition of assets in these asset tests reflects the assumptions of traditional income-support programs, which view public assistance programs as a tool to guarantee a minimum level of consumption and thus consider assets to be for consumption.

Alternative Measures in the Consumption Framework

Another focus of scholarly discussion in the consumption model is how to calculate wealth into a stream of income and create a joint measure of economic well-being. Recognizing that income is not perfectly correlated with wealth (Shapiro 2004; Weisbrod and Hansen 1968; Wolff 1990) and that an income measure alone is therefore not a perfect measure of economic well-being, researchers seek to develop better indicators by taking assets into account. A challenge lies in the fact that assets and income have different forms: assets are a stock of financial resources while income is a flow. Accordingly, it has been the focus of the consumption model to develop appropriate methods of converting assets into income in creating a joint measure of well-being and poverty. The two major approaches are the annuitization approach and the fill-the-gap approach.

Weisbrod and Hansen (1968) developed an early joint index of income and wealth using annuitization. Their joint income-wealth measure of economic positions is the sum of current annual income and annual lifetime annuity value of current net worth.[1] The value of the annual lifetime annuity is the total expected lifetime value of current net worth (current net worth plus its expected lifetime interest) divided by the number of years of remaining life (life expectancy). Accordingly, the shorter one's life expectancy, the greater one's current net worth, and the higher the interest rate, the greater one's annuity value. Based on their index, Weisbrod and Hansen suggest an alternative measure of poverty. They propose to replace "income" with their "joint income-wealth index," while keeping the official poverty threshold intact.

Wolff's (1990) approach is slightly different. He does not assume that individuals use up their wealth by the time of death. Instead, he focuses on financial resources readily available to individuals. First, he uses fungible net worth instead of total net worth in calculating a joint measure of economic well-being, based on the assumption that the former is a better measure of disposable wealth than the latter. Wolff's fungible wealth includes home equity, liquid assets, business equity, and investment real estate, but it excludes consumer durables and household inventories. Second, he converts household fungible net worth into an annuity differently from Weisbrod and Hansen (1968). The annuity converted from the fungible net worth is paid out like a bond coupon at a given interest rate. The amount of annuity would be equal to the product of the capital value of fungible net worth and the interest rate. In this way, fungible wealth remains unchanged. Third, he estimates the net imputed rent of owner-occupied housing. Net imputed rent is the imputed rent value of owner-occupied housing minus the costs of owning a house, such as actual mortgage interest payment, homeowners insurance, and property taxes. Wolff calculates a household's available financial resources as the sum of family income, the annuity related to fungible wealth, and net imputed rent value of owner-occupied housing.

With this financial resources measure, Wolff develops an alternative measure of poverty. A family is considered poor if its financial resources are less than the official poverty threshold defined by the Census Bureau. Using data from the 1983 Survey of Consumer Finances, Wolff calculates that his joint income-wealth measure of poverty reduces the poverty rate. The poverty rate calculated with Wolff's alternative measure is about 10 percent lower than the official poverty rate.

A joint income-wealth measure developed by Short and Ruggles (2004) also takes the annuitization approach. Short and Ruggles's measure is different because it assigns low interest rates to gross financial assets (2 percent) and high rates to debts (10 percent for unsecured debt such as credit card debt, and 6 percent for secured debt such as a mortgage). They slightly modify the "standard lifetime annuity method" for nonfinancial assets, a method developed by Weisbrod and Hansen (1968), by adjusting annuity over the lifetime based on age of the head of household. A household is defined as poor if the sum of annuitized net worth and family income is below the poverty threshold.

The different treatment of financial assets and debt produces contrasting outcomes to Wolff (1990). Short and Ruggles's (2004) estimations, based on the Survey of Income and Program Participation, find a higher poverty rate with the annuitized wealth and income measure than the poverty rate based on the traditional measure that is constructed using only income. When the official poverty threshold is used, the poverty rate in 2001 is 14.0 percent with the income-wealth joint measure, while it is estimated as 11.9 percent with an income-only measure of financial resources.

The fill-the-gap approach does not attempt to convert assets into an annuity. Instead, this approach treats the current value of financial assets the same as income. This approach assumes that a household will use financial assets when current income is not enough to meet consumption needs. The fill-the-gap approach takes only financial assets into account, since illiquid assets are not easily converted to cash and, therefore, are difficult to use for short-term consumption needs. This method does not include debt in calculating poverty rates because a household at the time of financial constraint is assumed not to pay off the principal on its debt. For example, if a family's total income falls $500 short of the poverty level for each of two months, family assets of $1,000 or more would fill the poverty gap entirely. If the family only has $500 in assets, the spell of family poverty would be one month. The poverty rate for the year of 2001 is calculated as 9.5 percent for the fill-the-gap approach, compared to 11.9 percent with the income-only measure (Ruggles and Williams 1989; Short and Ruggles 2004).

Assets as a Vehicle for Social Stratification

In social-stratification theory and research, assets are viewed as a major vehicle for transmitting class status from one generation to the next. Assets, therefore, serve as a critical mechanism maintaining the current socioeconomic structure and inequalities. In this regard, assets are conceptually distinct from income. The roles of assets go far beyond the satisfaction of consumption needs (Caner and Wolff 2004; Conley 1999; Keister 2000; Oliver and Shapiro 1990; Shapiro 2004; Spilerman 2000; also see the discussion of intergenerational transfer of assets in chapter 3).

Criticizing the traditional focus on income, Oliver and Shapiro (1990) emphasize the importance of assets in understanding inequality in the United States.

> Income is a transitory measure; past income does not necessarily indicate what resources are available currently, as it may have been spent as fast as it was received and the goods purchased quickly consumed. Wealth, on the other hand, is a more stable indicator of status or position in society and represents stored-up purchasing power. Furthermore, wealth, unlike income, is accumulated over a lifetime and seldom changes quickly, except through inheritance or severe economic crises. (131)

From this perspective, assets are a better indicator than income for long-term well-being.

In addition, financial assets and physical properties can be passed from one generation to the next. Material assets are viewed as having historical origins and reflect inequality accumulated across generations, as well as socioeconomic disparity generated in contemporary contexts. This characteristic places assets in a unique position in studying racial inequality. The white-black gap in asset accumulation reflects the "historical legacy of low wages, personal and organizational discrimination, and institutionalized racism" (Oliver and Shapiro 1995, 5). To illustrate, the low level of wealth accumulation among blacks results in part from the historical legacy of slavery, Jim Crow laws, segregation, and discrimination in housing and labor markets (Conley 1999; Oliver and Shapiro 1995). While most of these conditions no longer exist, their impact is present in patterns of long-term wealth accumulation.

Furthermore, assets provide owners a wide range of opportunities that go beyond the economic value created by income. Assets offer the opportunity to achieve and maintain a "good life" by providing command over financial resources. That is to say, assets enable owners to make purchases that may help them move up to and maintain middle- (or upper-) class status, such as an education, a business property, or a home. Income is often an insufficient source of financial support for these critical life goals because the costs of higher education, the initial payment for a home purchase (the down payment and closing costs), and the financial risks associated with a start-up business are not modest (Conley 1999; Keister 2000; Oliver and Shapiro 1990; Shapiro 2004).

Assets, especially those from parents, provide critical resources at crucial life-cycle events. As shown in in-depth interviews by Shapiro (2004), intergenerational transfers of assets, both bequests and intra vivos transfers, make meaningful differences in the lives of many young adults and even middle-aged adults. The financial future of a young adult is much brighter if his or her college expenses are fully paid with parents' savings than if he or she graduates with large debts due to educational loans. It is much easier for a young couple to achieve and maintain middle- or upper-class status if parents help them with the down payment on their first home. In this way, financial assets, especially those from parents, lift an individual beyond his or her own achievement. This is in part why Shapiro (2004) argues that assets are "transformative." Inherited financial assets can lift class status to a level that is seldom reached with income alone (Keister 2000; Oliver and Shapiro 1995; Shapiro 2004; Spilerman 2000).

Social-stratification research often uses asset measures similar to the consumption model, such as net worth and financial assets (Conley 1999; Oliver and Shapiro 1995; Shapiro 2004). Social-stratification studies have analyzed indicators of wealth inequality created with net worth and financial assets across racial and income groups. For example, Wolff (2001) creates distribution ratios based on net worth and financial assets to estimate overall inequality in wealth, and Shapiro (2004) compares mean and median values of net worth and financial assets between blacks and whites to estimate racial gaps in wealth holding.

As in the consumption model, social-stratification theory distinguishes net worth from financial assets, but for a slightly different reason. Net worth is a comprehensive measure that includes all assets and debt, while financial assets are an indicator of command over financial resources for one's self and family. The emphasis on control over economic resources is closely connected with critical life events and opportunities. Social-stratification theory pays attention to the timing of possession (or transfer) of financial assets and properties because there are critical lifetime events at which financial assets and properties make huge differences in one's long-term economic well-being. Qualitative interviews described in Oliver and Shapiro (1995) and Shapiro (2004) show that parents' financial investments at milestone life events (e.g., going to college and first-time home purchase) leverage their children's life chances by maintaining or lifting socioeconomic status. For this reason, financial assets are considered a more effective tool in transmitting class status than is net worth because the former are immediately available for investments at each critical life stage or event (Oliver and Shapiro 1995).

Considering the focus on intergenerational transfer of socioeconomic status, it is not surprising that the social-stratification perspective pays special attention to intergenerational transfer of assets. There are two key methodological issues in measuring an intergenerational transfer. The first is to ask what can be categorized as measures of intra vivos transfers. For example, some researchers include parents' payment of college expenditures, while others exclude it. The former argue that children's education is consumption from the parents' perspective, since children in school are still dependent. The latter maintain that what is important is the amount of resources transferred, not the form of the resources, since it does not make sense to exclude parents' financial assistance for a child's education at age 21 while cash transfers at the same age are included (Gale and Scholz 1994; Spilerman 2000; Wilhelm 2001). The second issue is whether financial gains from inheritance could be included as part of transferred money. Although a gift of $10,000 is undoubtedly a transfer, it is ambiguous whether an additional $10,000 of accrued interest or capital gains from the original inherited money is an intergenerational transfer or a new accumulation (Spilerman 2000; Wilhelm 2001). Most researchers take the latter approach by calculating a present value of a past transfer with an assumed rate of return (Wilhelm 2001).

In addition, homeownership receives special treatment in social-stratification theory in comparison with other types of assets. This is due to the wide range of opportunities provided by living in a neighborhood with high-quality public education and city services (Shapiro 2004). In addition, homeownership is of special interest to those interested in white-black wealth gaps, because of the legacy of racial discrimination in housing and mortgage markets that often blocks minority households from the full benefits of homeownership (Conley 1999; Keister 2000; Oliver and Shapiro 1990; Shapiro 2004).

Assets as a Tool for Socioeconomic Development

Another view is that assets may facilitate economic and social development. From this perspective, assets are an instrument in promoting the general capacity of individuals to advance economically, socially, psychologically, and politically, and achieve goals beyond the satisfaction of consumption needs[2] (Sen 1999; Sherraden 1991). This is both a structural and an agent-oriented view. The assets-for-development framework suggests that individuals, including those at the bottom of the socioeconomic ladder, are capable of shaping their own destinies effectively only if they have adequate social and economic opportunities (Sen 1999). Asset building can be an effective tool in reducing poverty and inequality because it increases capacities at individual and household levels (Attanasio and Székely 2001; Paxton 2001; Sen 1999; Shapiro and Wolff 2001; Sherraden 1991) and also at the community level (Weber and Smith 2003).

A key question is how assets build capacities as the development perspective suggests. According to Sherraden (1991), financial assets and physical property may facilitate socioeconomic development through "asset effects," which are capacities, attitudes, and behaviors that assets may generate independently from income. From a neoclassic economics perspective, the two different forms of financial resources—income and assets—do not have different utilities because they are used only for consumption. But from a development perspective, assets generate distinct social, psychological, and economic effects for their owners. In other words, the utilities of financial and tangible resources in the form of assets go beyond deferred consumption. For example, financial assets and physical property may improve household stability, not only in economic terms but also in social and psychological terms; assets may encourage future orientation by connecting people with a viable and hopeful future; financial assets and physical properties may promote development of other types of assets including human capital; assets may allow people to take prudent risks and not make costly financial decisions based on short-term economic pressures; and assets may increase social influence and civic participation (Paxton 2001; Sherraden 1991). All of this may seem reasonable and consistent with mainstream values and social philosophy in America dating back to Thomas Jefferson, but theoretical specifications are still primitive, and careful empirical research is needed to investigate whether assets indeed generate positive asset effects, some of which are not easy to observe and record in research.

Empirically, the assets-for-development framework often relies on measures similar to the consumption model. Net worth and financial assets are frequently used in estimating asset effects. Homeownership also receives special attention because of its psychological meaning and symbolic power. Homeownership represents an "American dream" that is associated with a variety of opportunities and provides a feeling of stability and stakeholding (Lombe 2004; McBride 2003; Sherraden 1991). For example, Yadama and Sherraden (1996) use household savings and home value in studying asset effects on attitudes and behaviors. Zhan and Sherraden (2003) use the total value of savings and homeownership in studying mothers' expectations and children's educational performance.

In addition, the development approach has focused on asset-building interventions and the measured assets accumulated through these interventions. Examples include measures of participation and the amount of savings in individual development account (IDA) programs. However, asset definitions and measures from the development perspective do not fully capture the complexity of the asset-accumulation process and asset effects. More work may be necessary to understand and empirically test this approach if this body of work is to inform an inclusive social policy based on asset accumulation.

Concepts and Measures of Asset Poverty in Existing Research

In contrast to extensive discussions on income-poverty measures in both research and policy development (Citro and Michael 1995; Iceland 2005; Short 2001), less attention has been paid to development of asset-poverty measures. Discussion of poverty measures has focused almost exclusively on income (and less often directly on consumption). Even when assets are mentioned, they are treated as a supplement to income. Discussions of financial assets and physical property typically focus on how to estimate their values to improve income-poverty measures (Citro and Michael 1995; Ruggles and Williams 1989; Short and Ruggles 2004; Weisbrod and Hansen 1968; Wolff 1990). Assets are rarely an independent topic in developing poverty measures. Lack of attention to asset-poverty measures is not surprising because the major goal of public assistance programs has been income maintenance during a time of economic need (Caner and Wolff 2004). Less attention to assets, however, may deter development of public policies that include assets for low-income households.

Asset-Poverty Measures within the Consumption Framework

The first asset-poverty measure was perhaps offered by Oliver and Shapiro (1990). They define a household as asset poor if its financial asset value is zero or negative. Their estimation, based on the 1984 Survey of Income and Program Participation, is that at least one-third of households are asset poor.

Haveman and Wolff (2005) provide a more detailed attempt to develop asset-poverty measures independent from income-poverty measures. They define a household as being asset poor "if the access that family members have to wealth-type resources is insufficient to enable them to meet its basic needs for some limited period of time" (Haveman and Wolff 2005, 64). As such, an "asset-poverty" measure was developed based on the buffer-stock model of saving (Carroll 1997; Hubbard et al. 1994; Leland 1968) and the fill-the-gap approach. Based on this definition, Haveman and Wolff define asset poverty as the lack of wealth to maintain a household for three months, without income, above a poverty threshold proposed by the National Research Council. The choice of three months is based on the assumption that a major event associated with economic hardship is job loss. The expected duration of unemployment is estimated as 2.2 to 4.2 months (Caner and Wolff 2004; Haveman and Wolff 2005).

Caner and Wolff (2004) and Haveman and Wolff (2005) estimate asset-poverty rates with three different measures of wealth: (1) net worth, (2) net worth minus home equity, and (3) liquid wealth. Caner and Wolff's estimates, based on the data from the Panel Study of Income Dynamics, show a huge gap between the first and second measures and a small difference between the second and third measures. The asset-poverty rate in 1999 was 25.9 percent when measured with net worth, 40.1 percent with net worth excluding home equity, and 41.7 percent with liquid wealth (Caner and Wolff 2004). These results reflect the pattern of wealth distribution in the United States. A home is the most commonly held asset in the United States, while illiquid assets other than primary residence (e.g., business assets and rental properties) are owned by only a small percentage of households.

Taking a different approach, Shapiro (2004) argues for the creation of an asset-poverty measure based on net financial (liquid) assets, not net worth. He suggests the use of net financial assets because a household rarely sells its own house or takes out a home equity loan unless it falls into an extremely difficult financial situation. Accordingly, a household forced to do so would be considered asset poor. More discussion and empirical studies will follow before it becomes possible to identify which measures of asset poverty are good indicators and for what purposes.

Comparisons with income poverty, however, illuminate the importance of efforts to develop separate measures of asset poverty. Caner and Wolff (2004) demonstrate that asset-poverty rates did not decline during the economic expansion in the late 1990s when income-poverty rates decreased. The asset-poverty rate was 26.1 percent in 1994 and was almost the same at 25.9 percent in 1999 when measured with net worth. However, the poverty rate was 37.8 percent in 1994 and 41.7 percent in 1999 when measured with liquid assets. Furthermore, asset poverty is thought to be much more persistent than income poverty. More than 60 percent of households that were asset poor in 1984 remained so in 1994, while only 42 percent of income-poor households remained poor over the same period (Caner and Wolff 2004).

Asset-Poverty Measures outside the Consumption Framework

Neither social-stratification research nor the assets-for-development approach has attempted to create a direct measure of asset poverty. Although leading social-stratification scholars have estimated the black-white gap in asset-poverty rates (Oliver and Shapiro 1995; Shapiro 2004), they use Haveman and Wolff's (2005) definition of asset poverty: an amount of assets a family needs to meet its basic needs over a specified period. In considering future research, the development of asset-poverty measures based on social-stratification theory and an assets-for-development framework may be useful because these two perspectives have assumptions and definitions of assets distinct from the consumption model.

Shapiro's (2004) concept of "head-start" assets[3] may be helpful in exploring asset-poverty measures for future research outside a consumption framework, although it is not a measure of asset poverty. Shapiro (2004) defines head-start assets as the amount of assets large enough to help a household achieve or maintain a "middle-class" status. This is in some ways similar to the idea of an asset "threshold" above which development might occur (Sherraden 1991).

Since homeownership in a middle-class neighborhood often helps children obtain a middle-class education and other social and cultural resources needed to maintain a middle-class lifestyle, Shapiro uses financial ability to purchase a home in defining head-start assets. Head-start assets are defined as the amount of financial assets required to buy a typical (median-priced) home in the United States. Accordingly, head-start assets include down payment and closing costs for a median-priced home. Shapiro estimates that a household required between $9,600 and $17,600 in 1999 to buy a median-priced house ($160,100), to cover the down payment (5 to 10 percent of house value), and to meet the closing costs (typically 1 percent). To be sure, this definition and measurement specification is a step forward, but empirical future testing can help ascertain whether head-start assets as operationalized by Shapiro (2004) represent the best measure of this concept and have the impacts he suggests.

Alternative Measures of Assets and Asset Poverty

As indicated above, assets are viewed differently from the three major perspectives. The consumption model defines assets as a storehouse of future consumption (Ando and Modigliani 1963; Carroll 1997; Leland 1968; Modigliani 1986; Shefrin and Thaler 1988). Social stratification focuses on the role of assets in perpetuating social and economic inequality by transferring economic resources from one generation to another (Conley 1999; Oliver and Shapiro 1995; Shapiro 2004). The assets-for-development perspective perceives assets as a tool for socioeconomic development by building capacity (Sen 1999; Sherraden 1991; Siegel and Alwang 1999).

Despite these distinct roles and concepts associated with assets in the three frameworks, definitions and measures of assets are often not distinctive enough to reflect theoretical and conceptual differences. Commonly, the social-stratification and assets-for-development perspectives de facto rely on asset measures based on the consumption model. Therefore, the link between theories and measures is often tenuous, especially regarding the social-stratification and assets-for-development perspectives.

Assets are more complex and multifaceted than the consumption model suggests. Individuals accumulate assets for more than one reason. They save to move up economically (e.g., saving for an education or a small business); they save to improve social standing; they save to smooth consumption in preparation for retirement; and they accumulate assets to improve life chances of offspring (Oliver and Shapiro 1995; Shapiro 2004; Sherraden 1991). That is to say, diverse aspects of assets exist at different time points. The current level of asset possession is important, but the purposes and plans of saving and the process of asset accumulation may also be critical.

Accordingly, current measures that focus on the possession of financial resources (measured as the amount of total possessed assets and the level of liquidity) may not be sufficient in studying the dynamics of asset accumulation—that is, identifying factors that promote and prevent asset accumulation and how assets affect individuals' economic, social, psychological, and political well-being. As Paxton (2001) suggests, indicators that measure various aspects of assets have not yet been developed. Using his framework, we suggest three categories of asset measures: asset-accumulation-process measures, asset-possession measures, and expected assets.[4]

In addition, attention to perspectives of the low-income population may be useful.[5] Existing studies do not take into account different social and economic conditions in measuring financial assets and physical properties but rather assume that individuals share the same concepts and definitions of assets regardless of their age, experience, and economic conditions. Although the use of identical asset measures may facilitate comparisons among different income groups, it may impede in-depth understanding of assets among the low-income population.

Qualitative research suggests that different people at distinct positions define the same property differently. Oliver and Shapiro (1995) write about home equity as follows:

People's age and experience, their feelings about what the future holds, and their stage in the life cycle all contribute to how they feel about their homes and any equity that may have built up over time. Old people may have a great deal of equity in their houses but have no immediate plans to cash it out . . . In any case, the pertinent point is that one cannot presume that home equity is viewed as a financial resource. (60)

Shapiro (2004) also describes class differences in the way people view assets.

Working-class and poor families use wealth for life support, to cushion bad times, and to meet emergencies. Middle-class families, in contrast, use their assets to provide better opportunities that advantage them. In our conversations about the power of assets, working-class and asset-poor families dream that assets will give them freedom from a situation, ease a difficulty, relieve a fear, or overcome a hardship. Middle-class and asset-wealth families see assets as power and freedom to leverage opportunities. (35)

If low-income people view assets differently from middle-class people, as suggested by Shapiro (2004), it is reasonable to think that the former might define assets differently from the latter. However, little is known about poor people's perceptions and definitions of assets. Few surveys have asked the poor in the United States what they count as assets and how much value they assign each of these items.

Alternative Measures of Assets

It is clear that various asset measures may be useful to test different theories on assets and understand the relationship between assets and poverty, because the existing measures have been developed without strong theoretical foundations. In this chapter, we suggest three categories of asset measures for future research: asset-accumulation-process measures, asset-possession measures, and expected assets. In addition, we discuss the ways we incorporate low-income people's own perceptions and definitions of assets into asset measures. However, these are preliminary conceptualizations, and readers are advised to be cautious since measures have not been specified or empirically tested.

Asset-Accumulation-Process Measures

Existing measures of assets focus on a current level of asset possession and do not reflect the process through which assets have been accumulated. When viewed as a tool for development, the process and stage at which one accumulates financial assets, however, may be as important as the total amount of accumulated assets. From this perspective, what matters is the way asset accumulation may empower and inspire individual actors (Paxton 2001; Sherraden 1991).

First, asset-accumulation stage measures could be created that differentiate one stage of asset accumulation from another. Beverly, McBride, and Schreiner (2003) categorize asset accumulation in three stages: reallocation, conversion, and maintenance. At the reallocation stage, people reallocate their resources to make their current resource inflow exceed current consumption. There are two ways of reallocating resources to increase saving: one is to reduce consumption (e.g., by eating out less and shopping more carefully); the other way is to increase income (e.g., by working more hours). At the conversion stage, people convert financial resources into a more difficult-to-spend form (e.g., depositing pocket cash into a saving account). At the maintenance stage, people resist pressure for more consumption to change saving into asset accumulation. That is to say, people are able to avoid withdrawals from their accounts until they reach their saving goals.

The mindset and behavior of people at the reallocation stage may be different from the mindset and behavior of those at the maintenance stage. People at the reallocation stage may try to earmark a certain type of earnings (e.g., earnings from a second job) for saving or seek encouragement to save from friends. People at the conversion stage may deposit a certain percentage of income into a saving account as soon as they receive paychecks and before making other purchases or payments. At the maintenance stage, people may try to think of savings as something "unavailable" or choose financial services that make withdrawals costly (Beverly et al. 2003; Sherraden et al. 2005). It may or may not be a continuous and easy process to move from one stage to the next stage. Furthermore, it is not clear whether there are clear boundaries between stages. More evidence is needed to differentiate one stage from another and to identify indicators of each stage.

Second, measures of saving patterns could also be developed. A person who accumulates financial assets through frequent and steady saving actions may have very different personal characteristics and motivations from a person who does so through one-time saving, even though the amounts of financial assets in their possession are the same. The effects of accumulated financial assets on their owners may differ across types of savers. Schreiner's (2004) measures of saving are a good starting point. After defining saving as the movement of resources through time,

Schreiner suggests development of saving measures for distinct stages of saving: putting in (depositing), keeping in (maintaining a balance), and taking out (withdrawing). He suggests measures of consistency of saving pattern, such as deposit frequency (e.g., the ratio of the number of months with a deposit divided by the number of observed months). Schreiner's measures allow researchers to distinguish a "slow and steady" saver from a "one-time big" saver even when the amounts of savings are the same. Based on Schreiner (2004), Sherraden and her coauthors (2005) develop a measure of saving pattern. They categorize a saving pattern into three categories: "consistent and regular" saving (saving with a certain pattern, e.g., saving every month), "irregular" saving (saving without a clear pattern, e.g., saving money when available), and no saving.

Asset-Possession Measures

Existing research usually uses net worth and financial (liquid) assets in measuring the level of asset possession at a certain point in time. As useful as they are, net worth and financial assets are insufficient to understand asset accumulation and assets' effects among a low-income population. Additional measures of assets are needed.

First, accumulated assets can be categorized into active and passive forms. Actively accumulated assets are those accumulated through one's own efforts and planning, such as saving and deliberate portfolio building through various types of investments. Passively accumulated assets are those that did not depend on self effort, such as inheritance and financial gifts from relatives and friends (Paxton 2001).

Existing empirical studies have produced conflicting results on whether these different types of assets affect individuals. Bynner (2001), using a British dataset, finds that inherited financial assets at age 23 do not have any significant effects on later lives, as measured with labor market experience, marital breakdown, and political interests, while actively accumulated assets are associated with significant differences on these outcomes. In contrast, Shapiro's (2004) in-depth interviews of families with school-aged children show strong effects of intergenerational asset transfers on socioeconomic status. His study contrasts life trajectories and various aspects of lives (e.g., residences and career choices) among families with similar characteristics (e.g., income and education) with the exception of one factor, financial gifts and inheritance from parents or relatives. Different results between these two studies may reflect distinct research methods (quantitative versus qualitative research) and different samples (a random sample of young adults from the United Kingdom versus a nonrandom sample of middle-class adults with school-aged children in the United States). More research is necessary to identify reasons for these differences.

Matched savings in asset-building interventions, such as employment-based saving incentives (e.g., 401(k)s) and poverty-reduction programs (e.g., IDAs), are perhaps in the middle. They can be categorized as actively accumulated assets because they require account holders' deliberate efforts, such as saving and preserving money in the accounts. They can be viewed as passively accumulated assets since they are given to account holders by outside sources. Further empirical investigation will help classify these assets into either category. Institutional theories of saving and asset accumulation may better specify "active" and "passive" into multiple constructs such as access, information, facilitation, and restrictions, and connect these constructs with emerging theory and evidence in behavioral economics (for a detailed discussion see chapter 4).

Second, it may be useful to distinguish assets accumulated for long-term goals from those accumulated for short-term goals. The amount in checking accounts can be categorized as intended for short-term use; savings accounts and CDs as mid-term assets; and IDAs, retirement accounts, Education IRAs, and 30-year bonds as long-term assets.[6] It is challenging to draw a definite boundary between assets accumulated for short-term goals and those for long-term goals, especially when people occasionally change their saving goals and when they sometimes use assets saved for long-term goals to support current consumption in a time of economic hardship. It may be useful to differentiate assets based on restrictions and costs associated with early withdrawals because choices of different types of accounts may reflect saving goals and the level of commitment to the goals. Going forward, the allocation of financial resources into distinct types of accounts may be of interest to researchers and policymakers.

Third, the creation of a typology of assets by their purposes may be informative. As mentioned above, people often accumulate assets for particular reasons, ranging from a precautionary motive to children's achievement. Accordingly, assets may be categorized into precautionary savings (e.g., to prepare for sudden job loss or illness), assets for retirement, and assets for long-term development (e.g., saving for children's education or a small business). It would be ideal, though challenging, to have strategies to distinguish one type of asset from another in this regard. People rarely set up a separate account for every single purpose (more often, for example, saving money in one account for both emergencies and children's educations). People also use money in an account for reasons other than the original saving goals (e.g., using money saved for a house for children's education).

Expected Assets

It could be that some aspects of social and economic development are affected not by what people own today, but by what they anticipate owning across their lives (Sherraden 1991). This concept might be called "expected assets." People accumulate assets with certain goals in mind. Therefore, the expected form and amounts of accumulated assets may be as or more important than the actual amount of assets at present. Mark Schreiner has written thusly on this topic.

> What we want to look at is something that captures the fact that it is not only assets right now that matter (affect opportunities, outlooks, etc.) but rather expected assets (resources) over the remainder of the lifetime. For example, a child who knows she will come into ownership of an inheritance at age 18 is likely to act differently at ages before 18, compared with someone without that expectation.[7]

How might expected assets be measured? Schreiner goes on to offer one possibility.

> I think this idea could be measured in principle as the expected number of dollar-years of resources that the person expects to control from now until expected death. So if I expect to die in two years and expect to have $100 of assets in year 1 and $200 in assets in year 2, I would have expected lifetime assets (resources) of 300 dollar-years.

Taking another and perhaps simpler tack, expected assets could be measured by expected types of asset holding (e.g., the expectation of homeownership or IRA ownership) or expected key investments of assets (e.g., the expectation of college education or international travel).

At this stage "expected assets" is little more than a concept, not yet well developed in theory or measurement, but it may turn out to be an important concept. For example, there is evidence from in-depth interviews with IDA participants that the IDA program creates the expectation of future asset ownership (especially in the case of homeownership), and these expectations appear to affect IDA saving behavior and future outlook (Sherraden et al. 2005).

Asset Measures from the Perspective of Low-Income People

As described earlier, it is likely that low-income people's definitions and concepts of assets differ from those of middle-class people, which are frequently used in existing studies. However, little is known about poor people's perceptions and definitions of assets simply because existing studies rarely asked the poor what they count as assets and how much value they assign each of these items.

One important area for future inquiry is the treatment of consumer durables in measuring assets. Fewer low-income households possess items considered as financial wealth and properties (e.g., a house, savings in bank accounts, and stocks), and therefore durable household goods may compose the bulk of asset holdings among poor households (Spilerman 2000). Interviews with low-income individuals find that cars, washers and dryers, and furniture are often listed as significant assets among low-income populations (Sherraden et al. 2005). Household appliances such as televisions and air conditioners are sometimes used as a source of cash at the time of an economic emergency (Caskey 1994). Edin's (2001) study shows that the value of vehicles and small tools is high among low-income people with entrepreneurial skills because these assets are often used as income-generating tools. For example, a low-income father started a junk business after buying a truck and another low-income father worked as an informal messenger thanks to his bicycle (Edin 2001).

A study of a no-interest loan program for low-income households in Australia also shows that durable goods can have social and emotional value as well as financial value among low-income households. Some respondents and their children were socially isolated because they did not have proper furniture and were, therefore, too embarrassed to invite friends to their houses (Ayres-Wearne and Palafox 2005). In these examples, the economic, social, and psychological value of the asset could be far greater than its purchase price.

Despite their importance in low-income people's lives, the value of consumer durables, except automobiles, is rarely included in calculating net worth in existing studies. Some researchers intentionally exclude consumer durables from wealth measures on the grounds that they cannot be sold easily and, therefore, cannot be readily converted into cash (Spilerman 2000; Wolff 2002). Other researchers are not able to include consumer durables simply because of the lack of information. Most existing surveys do not collect full information on consumer durables, except vehicle assets.

The first step in developing better measures of assets among low-income people would be to ask them directly about their perceptions and definitions of assets. Some researchers have noted the importance of the inclusion of voices and opinions of low-income people in the study of poverty (Lister 2004; Lister and Beresford 2000).

Alternative Measures of Asset Poverty

To the best of our knowledge, there exist no operational definitions and measures of asset poverty, either from an assets-for-development perspective or from a social-stratification perspective. Most existing asset-poverty measures are based on the consumption model as described in the previous section. This section begins to explore measures of asset poverty in frameworks other than the consumption model. The following are examples that may have conceptual and empirical potential: (1) asset thresholds in household development, (2) assets that change cognition and behavior, and (3) assets that make the next generation better off. These are not the only possible approaches to measures of asset poverty based on the assets-for-development or social-stratification frameworks, but these may serve as a starting point for this discussion and stimulate further thinking and empirical work in the future.

Asset Thresholds in Household Development

From an assets-for-development perspective, "asset poverty" can be considered as the lack of assets that prohibits a family from "taking off" from poverty (or the lack of assets that traps a family in current economic conditions). An "asset-poverty" threshold might be defined as the minimum level of financial assets at which a "virtuous circle" of asset accumulation and positive effects begins, which can eventually lead a family to a higher level of economic functioning and status.

Identifying asset thresholds may be complex. Previous studies suggest that there are asset thresholds; effects of assets on various outcomes may be lumpy or notched instead of linear (Sherraden 1991). One empirical study based on British data (the National Child Development Study) points to key asset thresholds (Bynner 2001). In this study, the asset level at age 23 is estimated to be positively associated with various measures of economic and psychological well-being at age 32, including employment and mental health outcomes. An increase in asset amount above a certain point, however, does not make any difference in outcomes. For most outcomes, possession of assets above £200 (comparable to about $360 at this writing) is not associated with improved outcomes.

It may not be easy to specify an asset threshold where households are able to take off from poverty. Threshold values may vary by life stage and by situation (Paxton 2001). A key threshold might be an amount of financial assets large enough to manage a checking account efficiently (i.e., the level at which the owner can use bank services and accumulate credit without paying excessive bank service charges and without worrying about bounced checks). In another situation, the key threshold might be the amount of financial assets needed to finish college for a young adult. In yet another situation, it might be the amount needed to start a small business for an underemployed single mother with entrepreneurial skills and ambition.

It is uncertain whether there can be an overall threshold measure for the whole population. One option for such a measure is homeownership. Based on previous empirical work, it is likely that homeownership has multiple positive effects for household development and is, therefore, a good candidate for a "head-start" or threshold approach to asset building for development (Shapiro 2004). From this perspective, asset poverty could be measured as the minimum amount of financial assets necessary to achieve this goal. For this measure, Shapiro's head-start asset measure might be modified into the bottom-quartile house price instead of the median house price. The choice of bottom-quartile house price is at this stage arbitrary, aiming at the idea of a "starter" home. Empirical evidence would be important to establish a more objective threshold level for this measure, and this would vary across housing markets in different parts of the country.

Asset Threshold at Which Owners' Cognition and Behavior May Be Changed

Depending on particular circumstances, it is possible that poverty and development are influenced not only by current economic circumstances, but also by attitudes and behaviors. Sherraden (1991) suggests that asset holding may change cognitive schema, leading to more positive outlook and behavior. In qualitative research on IDAs (Sherraden et al. 2005), one of the strongest findings is that having an IDA changes the way people think, especially in terms of sense of control and goal formation. IDA participants are quite articulate about IDAs being different from traditional welfare programs because IDAs are about development, not merely survival. Goal orientation, in turn, appears to be associated with behaviors that can lead to goal attainment. If this in fact occurs, it is relevant to ask what type and level of assets might have this effect.

In IDA research, it appears that just being in the IDA program leads to changes in outlook. This suggests that process measures of asset building (see above) may be as or more important than amounts of accumulation or having accounts with a long-term goal (nonzero values) in changing cognition and behavior. These are, however, preliminary findings and more empirical work would be illuminating. It is possible that asset thresholds would result in a "virtuous circle" of asset accumulation and positive attitudinal and behavioral effects.

Asset Thresholds for the Development of the Next Generation

Development occurs across generations. In thinking about assets and development, a key guidepost would be to ask whether or not the next generation is better off (Oliver and Shapiro 1995). One suggestion is to ask how much and what kind of assets low-income children need to develop and reach their potential. There is evidence that, controlling for other factors, homeownership is associated with positive effects on children (for details, please refer to chapter 6 in this book). Overall, research results are suggestive. There is much more to learn about what types and what amounts of assets can lead to improved children's outcomes, especially for children in low-income households. As indicated above, some promising lines of inquiry may be assets for college education, assets for residence in a neighborhood with good public schools, and assets for key developmental experiences.

Conclusion

This chapter has assessed the state of theory, definitions, and measurement of assets and asset poverty in the context of social science research and policy. Notwithstanding the emergence of asset building in policy and academic discussions and identification of a need for measures of asset poverty as early as 1991, little has been accomplished to date on concepts, definitions, and measures.

The consumption model has dominated concepts of "welfare," or well-being, in social policy. Consumption is the guiding idea behind income-support policies—which, in a fiscal sense, make up a very large fraction of "government" spending in advanced economies. To date, when assets are considered at all in measures of well-being, they are usually translated into a flow of resources and incorporated into a measure of income. Thus, most measures of assets are in the tradition of the consumption model.

However, several academic and policy discussions of assets have pushed the idea of well-being much further. This chapter takes up two examples: social stratification and assets for development. In social-stratification theory, assets play a key role in inequality, and inequality by itself—apart from level of consumption—has social meaning and consequences. In an assets-for-development framework, attention is paid not to consumption alone, but to building capacities. Asset-based policy can be viewed as one expression of a capacity-building orientation. Because social-stratification and assets-for-development theories *conceptualize assets as more than their consumption potential,* alternative definitions and measures of assets and asset poverty will be necessary if these theories are eventually to guide knowledge building that can inform social policy.

In stratification theory, intergenerational transfers and threshold (or "head-start") assets that can enable a family to achieve and maintain a certain status, such as homeownership or college education, may be useful in empirical models. In the assets-for-development framework, attention could be devoted to forms and amounts of assets that might lead to "virtuous cycles" of asset building and positive economic, social, and civic participation outcomes. From a more psychological perspective, the assets-for-development framework could focus on forms and amounts of assets that change cognitive structures and behaviors related to future options.

In considering alternative measures of assets that can build knowledge in the social-stratification and assets-for-development perspectives, it may be necessary to focus not only on the amount of assets but also to pay particular attention to (1) asset-accumulation-process measures, (2) asset-possession measures, (3) expected assets, (4) asset measures from the perspective of low-income people, and (5) asset-poverty measures based on an assets-for-development framework and the social-stratification perspective.

Going forward, there is substantial work to do in specifying and testing measures of assets and asset poverty that can enrich understanding and also serve as tools in shaping social policy. Thoughtful and detailed empirical work will be invaluable. Better definitions and measures of asset holding can increase knowledge and inform policies of asset building that may prove to be more effective in reaching the entire population.

NOTES

1. Weisbrod and Hansen (1968) do not define net worth in their theory section. They calculate net worth for their empirical section based on the Survey of Financial Characteristics of Consumers (SFCC). Net worth is defined as all assets minus all debts included in the SFCC, except life insurance investments, equities in annuities, and equities in retirement plans. Therefore, their measure of net worth is the sum of values for home, automobile, business, liquid assets, investment assets, and other assets, subtracting mortgages for own home and investment properties, personal debt, and debt on life insurance policies.

2. The focus on building capacities or capabilities is, at this writing, a common and overarching conceptualization, especially in discussions of economic development in "developing" countries and increasingly in discussions of well-being in more economically advanced nations. Indeed, this discourse has for the first time linked scholarship on "economic development" in poor nations with scholarship on "welfare" or "well-being" vis-à-vis the social policies of richer nations. This in itself is a promising development, but it is only a preliminary discussion.
On the positive side, the term *capacities* or *capabilities* is a useful guiding and organizing device, pointing to much more than consumption as a definition of well-being. Sen (1999) defines capabilities as an individual's ability to achieve or obtain what he or she has reason to value. Another way to define this would be conditions that permit the achievement of potential. On the negative side, these are quite grand ideas with only vague specifications at this stage. Sen goes to some length to say that desired capabilities cannot be listed for everyone but rather are to be defined by each individual. Another view which may be more comfortable for social science planners and analysts would be that certain capabilities or capacities are fundamental (e.g., basic security, nutrition, intellectual development, and civic participation). All of this has a long way to go in both theoretical specification and testing.

3. Shapiro (2004) defines head-start assets based on "transformative" assets. He defines transformative assets as "inherited wealth lifting a family beyond their own achievement" (10). Although clearly important as a general concept, it is difficult to quantify transformative assets because this concept is likely to be relative and depend on a family's starting point. For example, the amount of financial resources needed to move a family from low- to middle-class status may differ from that needed for upward mobility from middle- to upper-middle class.

4. Paxton (2001) develops three categories of financial asset measures in order to study "asset effects." He suggests measures of "asset experience" that consist of "asset accumulation," "asset possession," and "asset spending." Since one of the goals of this report is to develop asset measures that can be used in studying "the determinants of

financial asset accumulation" and "the effects of financial assets," the authors of this report have modified Paxton's categorization. Sherraden (1991) suggests that the concept of "permanent assets" might be useful in the same sense as permanent income (i.e., asset holdings anticipated across the life course). This chapter, upon the suggestion of Mark Schreiner at the Center for Social Development, uses the term *expected assets*.

5. The use of asset measures that are developed based on low-income people's perspectives may have its own disadvantages. First, these asset measures may not reflect middle- and upper-income people's perspectives accurately. Some items considered as valuable assets by low-income people (e.g., a bicycle) may be trivial for middle- and upper-income people. The latter might forget to report these items when answering survey questions, which could produce nonrandom measurement errors by income group. Second, it may be costly to include a wide range of asset items in survey questionnaires in terms of time and money. However, it is imperative to understand low-income people's own definitions of assets. Future research may be able to develop asset measures that reflect different perspectives by economic level.

6. Researchers could also obtain information on short-term versus long-term asset accounts by asking questions directly to respondents in surveys.

7. Mark Schreiner, Center for Social Development, internal e-mail memo on expected assets, July 6, 2005.

REFERENCES

Aizcorbe, Ana M., Arthur B. Kennickell, and Kevin B. Moore. 2003. "Recent Changes in U.S. Family Finances: Evidence from the 1998 and 2001 Survey of Consumer Finances." *Federal Reserve Bulletin* 89(1): 1–32.

Ando, Albert, and Franco Modigliani. 1963. "The 'Life Cycle' Hypothesis of Saving: Aggregate Implications and Tests." *American Economic Review* 53(1): 55–84.

Attanasio, Orazio, and Miguel Székely. 2001. "Going Beyond Income: Redefining Poverty in Latin America." In *A Portrait of the Poor: An Assets-Based Approach*, edited by Orazio Attanasio and Miguel Székely (1–44). Baltimore: Johns Hopkins University Press.

Ayres-Wearne, Valerie, and Janet Palafox. 2005. *NILS: Small Loans, Big Changes*. Collingwood, Australia: Good Shepherd Youth and Family Service.

Banterle, Clara Busana. 2002. "Incentive to Contributing to Supplementary Pension Funds: Going beyond Tax Incentives." *Geneva Papers on Risk and Insurance* 27(4): 555–70.

Beverly, Sondra G., Amanda Moore McBride, and Mark Schreiner. 2003. "A Framework of Asset-Accumulation Stages and Strategies." *Journal of Family and Economic Issues* 24(2): 143–56.

Burkhauser, Richard V., and Robert R. Weathers II. 2001. "Access to Wealth among Older Workers in the 1990s and How It Is Distributed: Data from the Health and Retirement Study." In *Assets for the Poor: The Benefits of Spreading Asset Ownership*, edited by Thomas M. Shapiro and Edward N. Wolff (74–131). New York: Russell Sage Foundation.

Bynner, John. 2001. "The Effect of Assets on Life Changes." In *The Asset-Effect*, edited by John Bynner and Will Paxton (17–37). London: Institute for Public Policy Research.

Caner, Asena, and Edward. N. Wolff. 2004. "Asset Poverty in the United States, 1984–99: Evidence from the Panel Study of Income Dynamics." *Review of Income and Wealth* 50(4): 493–518.

Carroll, Christopher D. 1997. "Buffer-Stock Saving and the Life Cycle/Permanent Income Hypothesis." *Quarterly Journal of Economics* 12(1): 1–55.

Caskey, John P. 1994. *Fringe Banking: Check-Cashing Outlets, Pawnshops, and the Poor.* New York: Russell Sage Foundation.

Citro, Constance F., and Robert T. Michael, eds. 1995. *Measuring Poverty: A New Approach.* Washington, DC: National Academies Press.

Conley, Dalton. 1999. *Being Black, Living in the Red: Race, Wealth, and Social Policy in America.* Berkeley: University of California Press.

Corporation for Enterprise Development. 2002. *The 2002 Federal IDA Briefing Book: How IDAs Affect Eligibility for Federal Programs.* Washington, DC: Corporation for Enterprise Development.

Edin, Kathryn J. 2001. "More than Money: The Role of Assets in the Survival Strategies and Material Well-Being of the Poor." In *Assets for the Poor: The Benefits of Spreading Asset Ownership*, edited by Thomas M. Shapiro and Edward N. Wolff (206–31). New York: Russell Sage Foundation.

Feldstein, Martin S. 1976. "Social Security and the Distribution of Wealth." *Journal of the American Statistical Association* 71(356): 800–807.

Fisher, Malcolm R. 1987. "Life-Cycle Hypothesis." In *The New Palgrave: A Dictionary of Economics*, edited by John Eatwell, Murray Millgate, and Peter Newman (177–79). London and Basingstoke: Macmillan.

Friedman, Milton. 1957. *A Theory of the Consumption Function.* Princeton, NJ: Princeton University Press.

Gale, William G., and John Karl Scholz. 1994. "Intergenerational Transfers and the Accumulation of Wealth." *Journal of Economic Perspectives* 8(4): 145–60.

Gruber, Jonathan. 2001. "The Wealth of the Unemployed." *Industrial and Labor Relations Review* 55(1): 79–94.

Gustman, Alan L., and Thomas L. Steinmeier. 2002. "Retirement and Wealth." *Social Security Bulletin* 64(2): 66–91.

Haveman, Robert, and Edward N. Wolff. 2005. "Who Are the Asset Poor? Levels, Trends, and Composition, 1983–1998." In *Inclusion in the American Dream: Assets, Poverty, and Public Policy*, edited by Michael Sherraden (61–86). New York: Oxford University Press.

Hubbard, R. Glenn, Jonathan Skinner, and Stephen P. Zeldes. 1994. "Expanding the Life-Cycle Model: Precautionary Saving and Public Policy." *American Economic Review* 84(2): 174–79.

Iceland, John. 2005. *Experimental Poverty Measures: Summary of a Workshop.* Washington, DC: National Academies Press.

Keister, Lisa A. 2000. *Wealth in America: Trends in Wealth Inequality.* New York: Cambridge University Press.

Leland, Hayne E. 1968. "Saving and Uncertainty: The Precautionary Demand for Saving." *Quarterly Journal of Economics* 82(3): 465–73.

Lister, Ruth. 2004. *Poverty*. Cambridge, UK: Polity Press.

Lister, Ruth, and Peter Beresford. 2000. "Where are 'the Poor' in the Future of Poverty Research?" In *Researching Poverty*, edited by Jonathan Bradshaw and Joy Sainsbury (284–304). Aldershot, UK: Ashgate.

Lombe, Margaret. 2004. "Impacts of Asset Ownership on Social Inclusion." Ph.D. diss., Washington University, St. Louis, MO.

McBride, Amanda Moore. 2003. "Asset-Ownership among Low-Income and Low-Wealth Individuals: Opportunity, Stakeholding, and Civic Engagement." Ph.D. diss., Washington University, St. Louis, MO.

McNeil, John M., and Enrique J. Lamas. 1989. "Year-Apart Estimates of Household Net Worth from the Survey of Income and Program Participation." In *The Measurement of Saving, Investment, and Wealth*, edited by Robert E. Lipsey and Helen Stone Tice (431–71). Chicago: University of Chicago Press.

Modigliani, Franco. 1986. "Life Cycle, Individual Thrift, and the Wealth of Nations." *American Economic Review* 76(3): 297–313.

Oliver, Melvin L., and Thomas M. Shapiro. 1990. "Wealth of a Nation: A Reassessment of Asset Inequality in America Shows at Least One Third of Households Are Asset Poor." *American Journal of Economics and Sociology* 49(2): 129–51.

———. 1995. *Black Wealth/White Wealth: A New Perspective on Racial Inequality*. New York: Routledge.

Paxton, Will. 2001. "The Asset-Effect: An Overview." In *The Asset-Effect*, edited by John Bynner and Will Paxton (1–17). London: Institute for Public Policy Research.

Ruggles, Patricia, and Roberton Williams. 1989. "Longitudinal Measures of Poverty: Accounting for Income and Assets over Time." *Review of Income and Wealth* 35(3): 225–43.

Schreiner, Mark. 2004. "Measuring Saving." Center for Social Development Working Paper 04–08. St. Louis, MO: Washington University in St. Louis.

Sen, Amartya. 1999. *Development as Freedom*. New York: Knopf.

Shapiro, Thomas M. 2001. "The Importance of Assets." In *Assets for the Poor: The Benefits of Spreading Asset Ownership*, edited by Thomas M. Shapiro and Edward N. Wolff (11–33). New York: Russell Sage Foundation.

———. 2004. *The Hidden Cost of Being African American: How Wealth Perpetuates Inequality*. New York: Oxford University Press.

Shapiro, Thomas M., and Edward N. Wolff, eds. 2001. *Assets for the Poor: The Benefits of Spreading Asset Ownership*. New York: Russell Sage Foundation.

Shefrin, Hersh M., and Richard H. Thaler. 1988. "The Behavioral Life-Cycle Hypothesis." *Economic Inquiry* 26(4): 609–43.

Sherraden, Margaret, Amanda Moore McBride, Elizabeth Johnson, Stacie Hanson, Fred M. Ssewamala, and Trina R. Shanks. 2005. *Saving in Low-Income Households: Evidence from Interviews with Participants in the American Dream Demonstration*. St. Louis, MO: Washington University in St. Louis, Center for Social Development.

Sherraden, Michael. 1991. *Assets and the Poor: A New American Welfare Policy*. Armonk, NY: M. E. Sharpe.

Short, Kathleen. 2001. *Experimental Poverty Measures: 1999.* U.S. Census Bureau Current Population Report 60–216. Washington, DC: U.S. Government Printing Office.

Short, Kathleen, and Patricia Ruggles. 2004. "Experimental Measures of Poverty and Net Worth: 1996." Paper presented at Eastern Economic Association meeting, Washington, DC, Feb. 19–22.

Siegel, Paul B., and Jeffery Alwang. 1999. *An Asset-Based Approach to Social Risk Management: A Conceptual Framework.* World Bank Social Protection Discussion Paper 9926. Washington, DC: World Bank.

Spilerman, Seymour. 2000. "Wealth and Stratification Processes." *Annual Review of Sociology* 26(1): 497–524.

Venti, Steven F., and David A. Wise. 1990. "Have IRAs Increased U.S. Saving? Evidence from Consumer Expenditure Surveys." *Quarterly Journal of Economics* 105(3): 661–98.

Weber, Rachel N., and Janet L. Smith. 2003. "Assets and Neighborhoods: The Role of Individual Assets in Neighborhood Revitalization." *Housing Policy Debate* 14(1&2): 169–202.

Weisbrod, Burton A., and W. Lee Hansen. 1968. "An Income-Net Worth Approach to Measuring Economic Welfare." *American Economic Review* 58(5): 1315–29.

Wilhelm, Mark O. 2001. "The Role of Intergenerational Transfers in Spreading Asset Ownership." In *Assets for the Poor: The Benefits of Spreading Asset Ownership,* edited by Thomas M. Shapiro and Edward N. Wolff (132–64). New York: Russell Sage Foundation.

Wolff, Edward N. 1990. "Wealth Holdings and Poverty Status in the United States." *Review of Income and Wealth* 36(2): 143–65.

———. 2001. "Recent Trends in Wealth Ownership, from 1983 to 1998." In *Assets for the Poor: The Benefits of Spreading Asset Ownership,* edited by Thomas M. Shapiro and Edward N. Wolff (34–73). New York: Russell Sage Foundation.

———. 2002. *Top Heavy: A Study of Increasing Inequality of Wealth in America.* New York: New Press.

Yadama, Gautam, and Michael Sherraden. 1996. "Effects of Assets on Attitudes and Behaviors: Advance Test of a Social Policy Proposal." *Social Work Research* 20(1): 3–11.

Zhan, Min, and Michael Sherraden. 2003. "Assets, Expectations, and Educational Achievement." *Social Service Review* 77(2): 191–211.

2

Asset Holdings
and Liabilities

Adam Carasso and Signe-Mary McKernan

B uilding up assets and avoiding excessive debt can help families
insure against unforeseen disruptions, increase economic independence, and improve socioeconomic status. Assets are especially important
for low-income families because holding them can limit the likelihood
of material hardships. However, a comprehensive portrait of the balance
sheets of low-income households does not exist. This chapter begins to
paint a portrait of the assets of low-income households by synthesizing
current research to answer the central question, *what are the significant
assets and liabilities of low-income families?* The chapter describes what is
known and not known about the types and amount of assets held by
these families and sets the stage for future research and policy discussion.

Data Sources and Methods Used

We reviewed the findings of some 20 studies to synthesize available information on the assets and liabilities of low-income households. These
studies and their key findings are summarized in an online appendix at
http://www.urban.org/books/assetbuilding/.

Most of the wealth data in this chapter come from tables produced by
Bucks, Kennickell, and Moore (2006) using the 1995–2004 Survey of Consumer Finances (SCF), Lerman (2005) using the 2001 Survey of Income

and Program Participation (SIPP), and Lupton and Smith (1999) using the 1992 Health and Retirement Study.

All of these findings come from high-quality surveys, but it is still important to bear in mind some of the data limitations such as (1) imputations for missing asset and liability data, (2) survey response rates of between 50 and 98 percent, and (3) the fact that some assets are very difficult to measure and, consequently, are not included in many surveys. For example, regarding this last point, Social Security benefits and defined benefit pensions may be particularly important assets for low-income families, yet national surveys generally do not capture them. Vehicles are often counted, but other consumer durables such as appliances are missed (the SIPP is an exception). As this chapter depends in large part on national household surveys to paint portraits of assets and liabilities, little can be said about Social Security benefits, defined benefit pensions, and holdings of durable goods other than vehicles. These and additional asset data limitations are discussed in detail in this book's appendix. Social Security and defined benefit pensions are also discussed in the Net Worth section of this chapter.

In describing findings, the term "household" or "family" is used as appropriate for the particular survey and research cited—the "unit of analysis" tends to differ slightly from survey to survey, but the findings can be easily generalized. That is, a low-income "family" in the SCF would be a low-income household in the SIPP, and vice versa. For most surveys, a cohabiting partner who shares income and assets will be included in the unit of analysis.

Our analysis focuses on the income, assets, debts, or net worth held by those families that are at the median or 50th percentile—that is, 50 percent of families would have more and 50 percent would have less. Since most income and net worth in society is held by the wealthiest groups, focusing on families at the mean, or "average," would paint a skewed picture. Notably, the median (and where applicable, mean) asset and debt values we report in the figures that follow apply only to families that actually *hold* the particular asset or debt. We also present data on the likelihood of holding the item. This conditional median or mean provides a sense of the "typical" holding. To allow comparisons over time and across datasets from different time periods, all values are converted to 2004 dollars using the Consumer Price Index for All Urban Consumers.

To paint a portrait of the assets and liabilities of low-income households and compare how assets and liabilities are distributed among them, we provide comparisons by income, education, age, race or ethnicity, and family structure. While current income is often used to determine who is low income, this study also uses education because it helps differentiate the long-term poor, who have low-paying jobs, from the short-term poor, who may be pursuing education. It is also important to differentiate households by age: for example, it would be unreasonable to expect meaningful accumulations of assets like home equity or pension wealth among younger families just starting out. For these families, *holding* an asset—that is, purchasing an asset like a home or contributing to an asset like a pension—may be more crucial than the current value of that asset.

Empirical Evidence on the Assets and Liabilities of Low-Income Households

Assets alone may have an effect on outcomes, but assets alone do not tell the whole financial story. It is important to look at the entire balance sheet: viewing the different assets a household owns and comparing their values against the household's liabilities to arrive at net worth or household wealth. The subprime mortgage crisis highlights the key role of the level and form of liabilities for the economic well-being of families.

Asset Holdings

In this section, we examine asset holdings, looking at total assets, financial assets, nonfinancial tangible assets, and then liquidity. First, the distribution of the given type of assets in the general population is described, then findings by income, educational attainment, age, race or ethnicity, and family structure are presented.

Total Asset Holdings

Total assets include all financial assets (such as bank accounts, stocks, bonds, and pensions) and nonfinancial tangible assets (such as homes and real estate, businesses, and vehicles). Asset values reflect the values reported at the time of the interview and so, in theory, include the net accumulation of all capital gains and losses.

A look at total asset holdings by income reveals large disparities. Bottom–income quintile families hold median total assets of $17,000, almost 5 times less than second-quintile families ($78,300), 9 times less than third-quintile families ($154,400), 17 times less than fourth-quintile families ($289,400), and 48 times less than fifth-quintile families ($808,100).

Classifying families by education status, one of the best proxies for long-term economic status, reveals that families headed by someone who did not complete high school have only $49,900 in median asset holdings, compared with families headed by a college graduate, which have asset holdings of $357,000, or seven times as much (figure 2.1).

Classifying families by age reveals the important life-cycle patterns of asset accumulation. Those below age 35 have median asset holdings of just

Figure 2.1. Median Total Asset Holdings by Family Characteristic, 2004 (thousands of 2004 dollars)

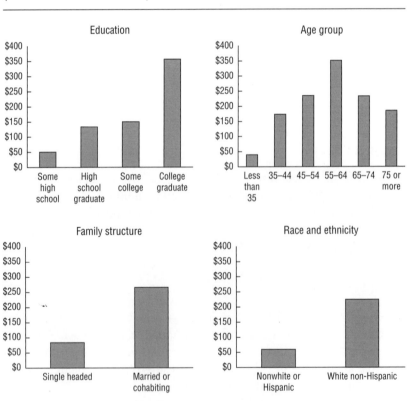

Source: The Urban Institute. Data from Bucks et al. (2006) and Urban Institute tabulations using the 2004 Survey of Consumer Finances.
Note: See online appendix table 2.A.5 for details at http://www.urban.org/books/assetbuilding/.

$39,200, compared with peak median asset holdings of $351,200 at ages 55–64, or nine times as much (figure 2.1). Ideally, one would account for these age differences when looking at the role of income, housing status, family structure, or any other classifier on assets. Without accounting for these age patterns, the numbers can be misleading because age partly explains differences in asset holdings between low-income and higher-income families (if younger families are more likely to be low income) and between homeowners and renters (if older families are more likely to own).

Classifying families by race or ethnicity begins to reveal the large asset divide discussed in detail in Oliver and Shapiro (1997). The median asset holdings of nonwhite and Hispanic families were just $59,600 in 2004, while the median for white non-Hispanic families was more than three times as much at $224,500 (figure 2.1).

Family structure also has a strong correlation with total family asset holdings. The median asset holdings for single-headed families was just $83,400 while for married or cohabiting families the median was $265,800, again about three times as much (figure 2.1).

Portrait of a low-asset family. A typical low-asset family would be headed by a single adult under 35 years of age, nonwhite or Hispanic, and lacking a high school diploma.

Financial Asset Holdings

Families often distinguish between financial decisions about small, day-to-day purchases and major ones (Sherraden et al. 2005). Here we first describe the financial asset holdings that are more likely to reflect day-to-day financial decisions. In the next section we describe the nonfinancial tangible assets that likely reflect major decisions.

Financial assets include transaction accounts (checking and saving accounts), certificates of deposit, financial securities and options, mutual funds, pooled investment funds, retirement accounts, cash value life insurance, personal annuities and trusts, royalties, leases, futures contracts, proceeds from lawsuits and estates, and loans made to others. Nonfinancial, tangible asset holdings, like homes, vehicles, and businesses, are discussed separately below.

Eighty percent of families in the bottom income quintile hold some type of financial asset. Seventy-six percent of bottom-quintile families have transaction (checking or savings) accounts (figure 2.2), although the median balance is $600. Roughly 5 percent of bottom-quintile families

Figure 2.2. Families Holding Financial Assets and Median Value of Financial Assets, by Family Characteristic, 2004

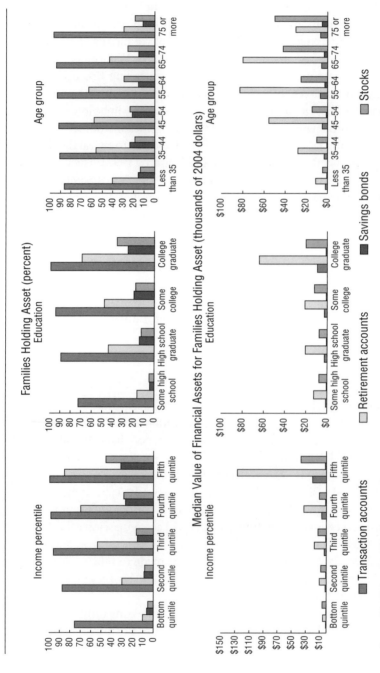

Source: The Urban Institute. Data from Bucks et al. (2006) and Urban Institute tabulations using the 2004 Survey of Consumer Finances.

Notes: Median asset values are calculated only for families holding assets. Breakout of income quintiles: Q1: <$18,000; Q2: $18,000–$31,999; Q3: $32,000–$51,999; Q4: $52,000–$85,999; Q5: >$85,999. See online appendix table 2.A.1 for details at http://www.urban.org/books/assetbuilding/.

have any holdings of stocks, bonds, certificates of deposit, or pooled investment funds, and just 10 percent have retirement accounts.

Transaction accounts, such as checking and savings accounts, are widely held across families at all incomes (70 percent or greater, regardless of the classifier used, figures 2.2 and 2.3). The likelihood of holding other financial assets, like stocks or retirement accounts (i.e., participating in an employer-sponsored pension plan or an individual retirement

Figure 2.3. Families Holding Financial Assets and Median Value of Financial Assets, by Family Characteristic, 2004

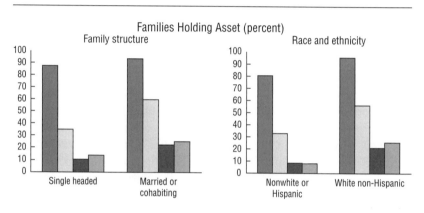

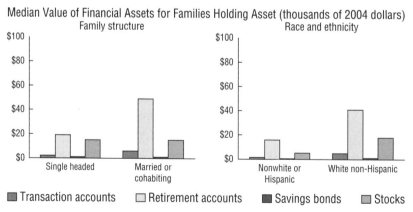

Source: The Urban Institute. Data from Bucks et al. (2006) and Urban Institute tabulations using the 2004 Survey of Consumer Finances.

Note: Median asset values are calculated only for families holding assets. See online appendix table 2.A.1 for details at http://www.urban.org/books/assetbuilding/.

account), is less overall and falls to very low rates for families in the bottom income quintile (10 percent) or with less than a high school diploma (16 percent). Families headed by someone who is single, nonwhite, or Hispanic have roughly a 35 percent chance each of participating in a retirement account. While a smaller proportion of families hold stocks and retirement accounts than hold transaction accounts, the median value held in stocks and retirement accounts is much higher for those that hold them.

Overall, median financial asset values (for families holding financial assets) differ substantially by income group (online appendix table 2.A.1). For families holding any financial asset, bottom-quintile families hold $1,300, while third-quintile families hold $15,500. Fifth-quintile families, meanwhile, hold $236,700.

Age differences may partially explain the large differences in financial account holdings by income. These charts of financial asset holdings indicate a high correlation between age and those families falling in the bottom income quintile. It is not surprising that young families, who are often low-income families, have not accrued much in retirement wealth. The concern is the low participation rate. While the top panel of figure 2.2 shows that, by age alone, the percentage of families holding a retirement account rises significantly from 40 percent for those under 35 to over 55 percent in the 35 to 44 age bracket, the participation rate never approaches anywhere near 60 percent for families with heads that either lack a high school diploma, or in figure 2.3, are single or nonwhite.

Portrait of a low-asset family. With regard to financial assets, a low-asset family is likely to have a checking or savings account, but the median holding in such an account is around $600. The family is unlikely to have a retirement account, such as an employer-sponsored pension plan or an individual retirement account (IRA), or to hold any securities.

Nonfinancial, Tangible Asset Holdings

These assets include vehicles, equity in residential and nonresidential property, and equity in privately held businesses, artwork, jewelry, precious metals and stones, antiques, and collectibles.

Vehicles are the most commonly held nonfinancial asset (figures 2.4 and 2.5). Only 65 percent of families in the bottom income quintile own one, compared with 95 percent of families in the fifth income quintile and 86 percent of families overall. The low car ownership among the poorest families stands out given that 85 percent of families in the second quintile own a vehicle. Differences in car-ownership rates are also large when we look by education: 70 percent of families with less than a high school education own a vehicle compared with 91 percent of college graduates. Those who are single or nonwhite have markedly lower vehicle-ownership rates than those who are married or cohabiting, or white.

Not surprisingly, the homeownership rate for bottom–income quintile families is less than the national homeownership rate (68.3 percent in 2003).[1] While 40 percent of bottom-quintile families owned a home, their ownership rate was low compared with a 57 percent homeownership rate among second-quintile families and a 93 percent rate among fifth-quintile families. However, if we use less education as a proxy for low income, about 56 percent of families headed by someone without a high school diploma own a home. These relationships between homeownership and income and education interact with age patterns of homeownership. Only 42 percent of families headed by persons under age 35 own homes, compared with 79 percent of families headed by persons ages 55–64. Do less-educated families not own a home because they are younger? Not entirely. The net worth findings discussed below suggest a positive relationship between educational attainment and net worth, even after taking age into account.

Homeownership rates for nonwhites or Hispanics are below average. Only about 51 percent of families headed by nonwhites or Hispanics own a home, compared with 76 percent of white non-Hispanics. Several factors other than race and Hispanic origin may explain this differential, such as income, prior net worth, education, and single parenthood.

Similar to financial assets, nonfinancial asset holdings vary widely across income groups. The median value of nonfinancial assets for families holding any such asset was just $22,400 for bottom-quintile families, compared with $131,200 for third-quintile families and $466,500 for fifth-quintile families (online appendix table 2.A.2). The distribution of specific nonfinancial assets like homes and business equity follows a similar trend, with fifth-quintile families reporting median values many, many times greater than first- and second-quintile families.

Some debate whether vehicles constitute an asset because vehicles depreciate in value and families that lease rather than own vehicles may not be at a disadvantage. Median values of vehicles, although dwarfed by home and business median values, rise with family income and rise slightly with the age and education of the family head, and are higher value for married or cohabiting couples and whites or non-Hispanics (figures 2.4 and 2.5). Only by income group are there substantial increases in median values.

While median home values increase with age of the family head (from $135,000 for families headed by persons under 35 to $200,000 for families headed by persons 55–64), the larger contrasts are by education of the family head ($75,000 for those with no diploma compared with $240,000 for college graduates) and income ($70,000 for the bottom quintile compared with $337,500 for the fifth quintile, in figure 2.4 and online appendix table 2.A.2). Marital status and race also show marked differences: $120,000 median home value for a family that is single headed compared with $185,000 for a married or cohabiting family; and $130,000 for a family headed by someone nonwhite or Hispanic versus $165,000 for white non-Hispanic.

Due to low holding rates across the population—and low sample sizes in the SCF—observed patterns in the distribution of median business equity by classifier can sometimes yield a fluke of small numbers, and so should be regarded with caution. In the 2004 SCF, only 3.7 percent of families in the bottom income quintile had any business equity (median value of $30,000), while a striking 25.4 percent of families in the fifth quintile owned a business (median value of $225,000). Unfortunately, the SCF survey sample size for holders of business equity is too small to allow us to present meaningful equity values by education, race, or age.

Portrait of a low-asset family. Overall, a portrait of a low-asset family with respect to nonfinancial assets probably shows a family that owns a car but not a home or business, or collectibles like artwork or jewelry. Edin (2001) provides an explanation for these low asset holdings through her qualitative research. She finds that families must have some faith in their income trajectories to make the hard consumption choices necessary to invest in assets. Because the incomes of low-income families fluctuate widely, their lack of faith is well founded. This family is likely headed by a person who is single, nonwhite or Hispanic, younger, and less educated.

Debt Holdings

What happens when income and assets are not sufficient to cover costs? Low-income families use several strategies to deal with their financial difficulties, including increasing frugality, reducing and postponing spending,

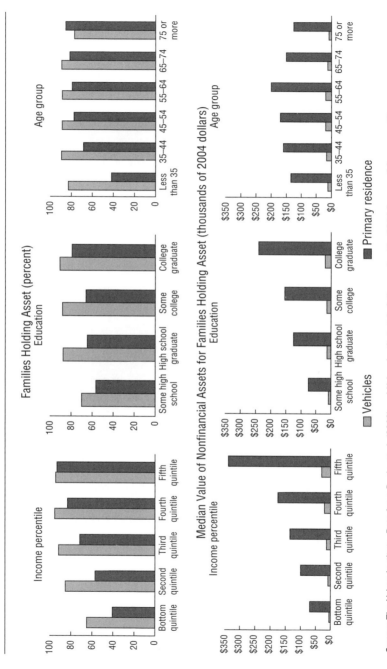

Figure 2.4. Families Holding Select Nonfinancial Assets and Median Value of Nonfinancial Assets, by Family Characteristic, 2004

Source: The Urban Institute. Data from Bucks et al. (2006) and Urban Institute tabulations using the 2004 Survey of Consumer Finances.

Notes: Median asset values are calculated only for families holding assets. Breakout of income quintiles: Q1: <$18,000; Q2: $18,000–$31,999; Q3: $32,000–$51,999; Q4: $52,000–$85,999; Q5: >$85,999. See online appendix table 2.A.2 for details at http://www.urban.org/books/assetbuilding/.

Figure 2.5. Families Holding Select Nonfinancial Assets and Median Value of Nonfinancial Assets, by Family Characteristic, 2004

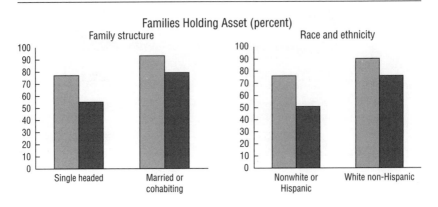

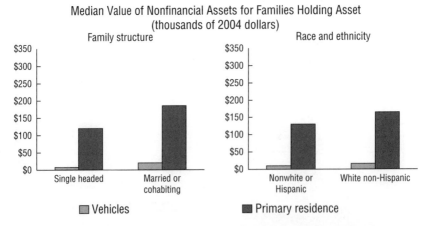

Source: The Urban Institute. Data from Bucks et al. (2006) and Urban Institute tabulations using the 2004 Survey of Consumer Finances.

Note: Median asset values are calculated only for families holding assets. See online appendix table 2.A.2 for details at http://www.urban.org/books/assetbuilding/.

negotiating bill payment schedules, increasing hours of work, utilizing savings and tax returns, and borrowing money (Sherraden et al. 2005). In this section, we discuss low-income families' borrowing behavior.

Understanding the patterns of asset holdings among low-income families and relating them to their patterns of debt holding is key to developing sound asset policies. An important consideration is the holding of both secure debt, that is, debt linked to an asset such as a home, and unsecured debt, such as credit card balances or installment loans.[2] If a family buys a house, the house is considered an asset but the mortgage they must pay is a debt. The debt is secured for the lender if the house has a value equal to or greater than the debt. As a result, mortgage interest rates are lower when compared to unsecured debts. However, when home values dip below the value of their underlying mortgages or families experience prolonged income shocks, the security of this debt comes into question, as the current housing meltdown has painfully illustrated.

Families usually incur unsecured debts when their current consumption exceeds current available income. Although most families accumulate debt slowly over time from financial stress, sometimes a crisis, often medical, creates a large amount of debt rapidly (Sherraden et al. 2005).

Debts that families hold include home-secured debt (mortgages), secured debt on other residential property, installment loans, credit card balances, lines of credit (other than home equity), and other borrowing that includes loans against insurance policies, loans against pension accounts, borrowing against margin accounts, and a residual category for all loans not explicitly referenced elsewhere.

Debts, like assets, display a life-cycle pattern, tending to first rise and then decline with age; the cycle may be driven by the acquisition of a home mortgage and its gradual amortization (figure 2.6). Figures 2.6 and 2.7 describe the distribution of debt by select type of debt. The likelihood of holding any debt—as well as the median debt holding—actually is *higher* for families with more income, headed by persons who are married or cohabiting, better educated, or in the 35–54 age ranges. While families that are in the lower-income quintiles, headed by persons who are single or without a college degree, are less likely to have debt, they are more likely to have unsecured debts (such as installment loans and credit card debts) than secured debt like home mortgages. The differences observed by race and ethnicity are in the same direction but attenuated. (See online appendix table 2.A.3 for the data that underlie the figures on debts and debt holdings.)

For those who hold debt, home-secured debt dominates median debt values across all classifiers (income, education, age, race or ethnicity, and family structure) except, as would be expected, for housing status. Since by definition, renters do not have home-secured debt, there is a substantial difference in the amount of debt holding between renters and owners. Renters hold a median total debt value of just $7,800, while homeowners hold a median debt of $95,800. Levels of debt holdings rise steadily with

Figure 2.6. Families Holding Debts and Median Value of Debts, by Family Characteristic, 2004

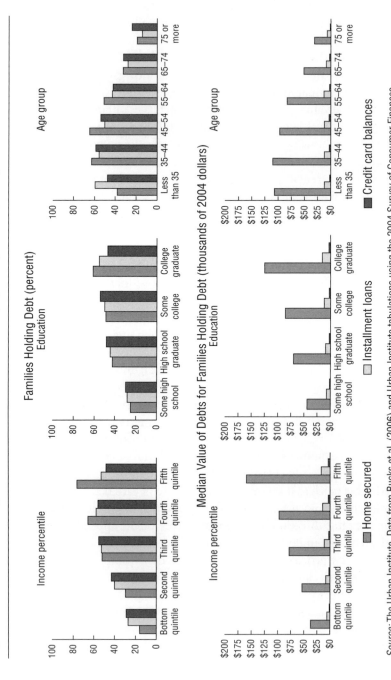

Source: The Urban Institute. Data from Bucks et al. (2006) and Urban Institute tabulations using the 2004 Survey of Consumer Finances.

Notes: Median debt values are calculated only for families holding debts. Breakout of income quintiles: Q1: <$18,000; Q2: $18,000–$31,999; Q3: $32,000–$51,999; Q4: $52,000–$85,999; Q5: >$85,999. See online appendix table 2.A.3 for details at http://www.urban.org/books/assetbuilding/.

Figure 2.7. Families Holding Debts and Median Value of Debts, by Family Characteristic, 2004

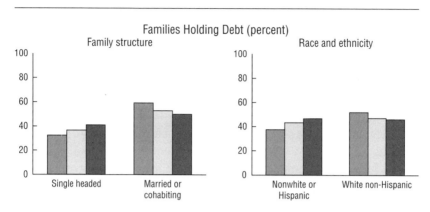

Families Holding Debt (percent)

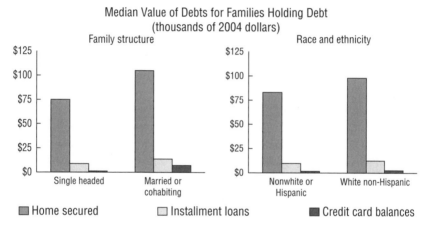

Median Value of Debts for Families Holding Debt (thousands of 2004 dollars)

Home secured   Installment loans   Credit card balances

Source: The Urban Institute. Data from Bucks et al. (2006) and Urban Institute tabulations using the 2004 Survey of Consumer Finances.

Note: Median debt values are calculated only for families holding debts. See online appendix table 2.A.3 for details at http://www.urban.org/books/assetbuilding/.

education ($12,000 for families headed by persons without a high school diploma, in stark contrast to $107,200 for families headed by college graduates) and by income ($7,000 for the bottom quintile, $44,700 for the third quintile, and $172,500 for the top quintile), and are much lower for single-headed families ($24,000) than for married or cohabiting families ($86,000) (online appendix table 2.A.3).

The data also show that the median level of credit card or installment loan debt is not necessarily higher (and is often lower) for typically lower-income families (e.g., singles, renters, headed by nonwhite or Hispanic people, less educated, younger) than for other groups—but lower-income families are more likely to hold these forms of debt rather than secured debt. The more specific question then, for low-income families, is how debt levels compare with income on hand to service this debt, discussed in the section on debt burdens below.

How do family assets compare with family debts at the median? Generally, debts are less than assets but rise with asset levels. Owning or not owning a home likely drives these results—the asset value of a home and the debt value of the accompanying mortgage are the largest sources of assets and debts for most families surveyed. At the median, families that do not own a home have little in the way of assets ($12,200) or debts ($7,800).

Net Worth

Net worth, or *wealth,* refers to the difference between asset and debt holdings. The bottom quintile, at a median value of $7,500, has about one-fifth the wealth of the second quintile, one-eighth of the wealth in the third quintile, and one-seventeenth of the fourth quintile. The distribution of net worth by income is more skewed than the distribution of assets, presumably because families in the highest income quintile are more likely to hold financial wealth, like stocks, that does not carry corresponding liabilities.

Because debts often are proportional to assets, the graphs of net worth by classifier resemble the graphs of assets by classifier, except the contrasts are even starker (see figures 2.1 and 2.8 and online appendix table 2.A.6). First, age is clearly associated with net worth accumulation, as the median jumps from $14,000 for the families headed by persons under 35 to $69,000 for 35–44 year olds, before peaking at $249,000 for 55–64 year olds. A similar relationship is seen for education of the family head, although, as with assets, families headed by persons who do not graduate from high school accumulate far less net worth ($21,000) than other groups, particularly those who graduate from college ($226,000). Nonwhite or Hispanic families have median net worth of just $25,000 compared with $141,000 for whites or non-Hispanics—nearly six times more. Similarly, single-headed families have just $40,000 of net worth compared with $155,000 for married or cohabiting couples.

Figure 2.8. Median Net Worth by Family Characteristic, 2004 (thousands of 2004 dollars)

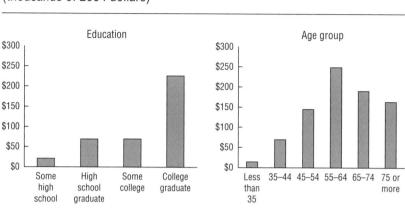

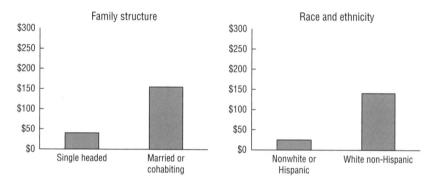

Source: The Urban Institute. Data from Bucks et al. (2006) and Urban Institute tabulations using the 2004 Survey of Consumer Finances.
Note: See online appendix table 2.A.6 for details at http://www.urban.org/books/assetbuilding/.

Accounting for age highlights the strong relationship between education and net worth. As Lerman's (2005) figure based on SIPP data illustrates, net worth for all education categories is similar at ages 25–29 (figure 2.9). However, already by age 30–34, net worth for college graduates is rising at a fast clip while net worth for those less educated remains little changed. By ages 45–49, median net worth for high school dropouts is just around $11,000. It is only when households headed by persons without a high school diploma reach their late 50s or early 60s that they begin to accumulate net worth. By ages 60–64, the median of these less-educated households has accumulated about $75,000 in net worth—an amount the median college graduate–headed family had accumulated before age 35.

Figure 2.9. Median Net Worth of Age Groups by Family Characteristic, 2001 (thousands of 2004 dollars)

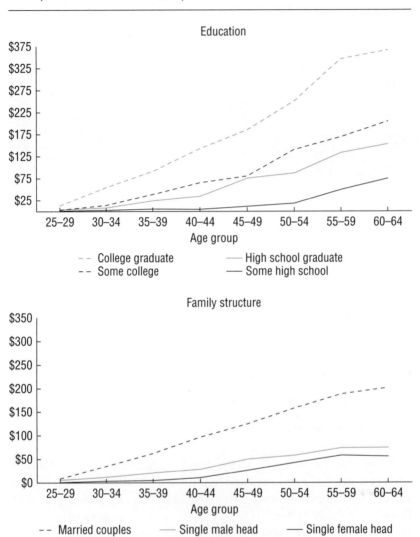

Source: Lerman (2005), tabulations from wave 3 of the 2001 SIPP panel.

Notes: Figures are adjusted to 2004 dollars. In the bottom chart, marriage is defined as married at the time of wave 3 of the survey.

Accounting for age also highlights the relationship between marital status and net worth (figure 2.9). As in the case of the education findings, net worth accumulates more quickly with age for married couples than for single-headed households. By ages 60–64, households headed by single men and by single women had accumulated $55,600 and $74,500 in net worth at the median, respectively, while married-couple households had amassed $201,000.[3]

A subgroup of concern is households with *negative* net worth (debts exceeding assets). Based on the 2001 SIPP and using means rather than medians, Lerman (2005) finds that nearly 20 percent of households age 25–44 have negative net worth, and that this varies little by education. Among households age 45–64, 8.5 percent have negative net worth, with slightly higher rates for those without a high school diploma and slightly lower for college graduates. While older households were about half as likely to have negative net worth, their average deficit was larger than for the younger households. There is no clear trend in negative net worth by education for either age group, other than generally higher levels of assets and debts for the older group. Lerman also notes that renters were twice as likely to have negative net worth as homeowners, but that the levels of assets and debts involved for renters were lower than those for homeowners. It would be important to explore more fully what family characteristics seem to be associated with negative net worth.

Trends in Net Worth and Income

Overall, families' mean net worth saw real growth of 72 percent over the 1992–2004 time period, while median net worth grew 32 percent. Figure 2.10 shows trends in median real net worth by education and race or ethnicity. The trends are not as promising for less-educated families. Families headed by persons without a high school diploma saw their net worth decline 16 percent, from $24,600 to $20,600. By contrast, college graduates saw a 74 percent increase at the median (from $129,800 to $226,100). The median net worth of nonwhite or Hispanic families rose 57 percent (from $15,800 to $24,800), while for white families it grew 53 percent (from $91,900 to $140,700). Online appendix table 2.A.6 provides additional trends in median and mean net worth by family characteristic.

Growth in median income over the same period is as high for low-income groups as for the other groups in proportional terms, but their low initial income levels imply much lower absolute gains. Figure 2.11 shows the percentage change in median income and net worth by income

Figure 2.10. Total Median Net Worth by Family Characteristic, 1992–2004 (thousands of 2004 dollars)

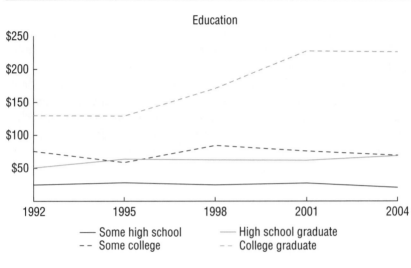

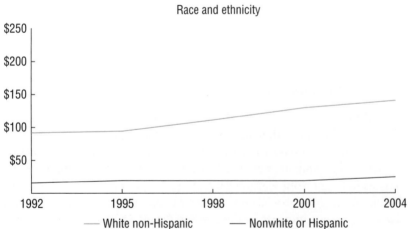

Source: The Urban Institute. Data from Bucks et al. (2006) using the 2004 Survey of Consumer Finances.

quintile for 1992–2004. Median income in all quintiles grew in the SCF at roughly the same rate—around 23–28 percentage points, depending on the quintile, over 1992–2004. (The same pattern is seen for mean income—again, growth in each quintile is between 21 and 25 percent except for the fifth quintile, which grew 44 percent over the period.)

Figure 2.11. Change in Real Median Income and Net Worth, 1992–2004 (percent)

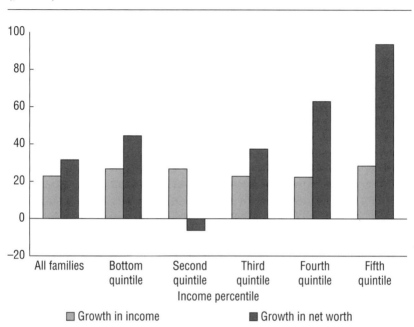

Source: The Urban Institute. Data from Bucks et al. (2006) using the 2004 Survey of Consumer Finances.
Note: See online appendix table 2.A.6 for details at http://www.urban.org/books/assetbuilding/.

The Census Bureau's historical income tables (U.S. Census Bureau 2007) show a comparable change in household median income from 1992 to 2003 of 18 percent. While income growth is similar in percentage terms, a family that earns $20,000 per year and sees its income rise by 20 percent gains only $4,000, while a family that earns $100,000 per year and sees it income rise by 20 percent gains $20,000. A greater portion of the income growth for the family making $100,000 can be saved and used to purchase additional assets. The additional income for the family making $20,000 is more likely to go for current consumption and debt service.

The second bar in figure 2.11 shows growth in net worth. While the robust growth (44 percent) in median net worth for families in the bottom quintile is encouraging, this growth rate must be placed against the backdrop of absolute gains (in online appendix table 2.A.6), which shows median net worth for this group rising only from $5,200 to $7,500.

How did different groups fare in terms of the amount of income they were able to save? The SCF quantifies stocks of savings (assets and debts) but does not address the flows from annual income into saving, beyond querying families whether they saved or not. The SCF does not ask how much was saved, which would allow calculation of a savings rate. Reported saving is computed as the percentage of families that report spending less than their income over the year preceding the SCF survey. These results are presented in figure 2.12.

Looking at all families, the majority saved in each survey year over the last decade, although the percentage of savers remained relatively flat at around 56 percent. The proportion of families in the bottom quintile that reported saving trended up very slightly over the 1992–2004 period (from 30 to 34 percent), while a somewhat declining fraction of families in the second and third quintiles saved. The fraction of families in the fourth and fifth quintiles that reported saving remained constant over time (about 70 percent and 78 percent, respectively). The percentage of

Figure 2.12. Families That Report Saving by Income, 1992 and 2004 (percent)

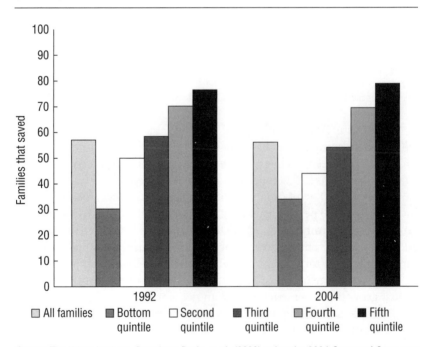

Source: The Urban Institute. Data from Bucks et al. (2006) using the 2004 Survey of Consumer Finances.

families at the highest incomes that report saving are about double the percentage of families at the lowest income.

While overall net worth increased and the percentage of families that save remained relatively constant from 1992 to 2004, some evidence shows that the amount saved is falling in the United States (Marquis 2002). A falling saving rate is not inconsistent with overall net worth increasing, especially when stock values and home prices are rising. In fact, the impact of these asset price increases on consumption, called the "wealth effect," helps explain falling personal savings (Marquis 2002).

The Role of Social Security and Medicare in Net Worth

Estimates based on the Survey of Consumer Finances, as presented above, do not include Social Security or Medicare benefits. Social Security and Medicare benefits are difficult to measure and are not always considered assets in the same sense as private pension benefits or other investments. Social scientists debate whether Social Security and Medicare benefits constitute actual wealth. Recipients do not have property rights over their benefits; Congress and the president can amend benefit levels and eligibility at any time. Individuals cannot borrow against or bequeath these benefits. Moreover, in the case of Medicare, the level of benefits received is dependent on the frequency and intensity of the medical services used. Workers who pay into Social Security and become disabled receive disability benefits, and survivors of working parents who paid into Social Security receive survivors' benefits until age 18.[4]

Social Security and Medicare benefits alter the net worth picture substantially, if considered wealth. Together, they are the major source of wealth for most low- and middle-income families and over 90 percent of wealth for low-income families (Kennickell and Sundén 1997; Lerman 2005; Steuerle and Carasso 2004). Social Security alone accounts for over 70 percent of wealth for low-income families (Mermin 2008). The bottom line is that, while very difficult to value—especially for younger households—Social Security and Medicare benefits, when considered wealth, contribute a substantial amount to household balance sheets in retirement.

Debt Burdens

Measures of debt burden indicate families' required debt service payments in relation to the total income and assets families have on hand to service these debts. Defining the debt burden as the annual ratio of esti-mated debt service payments to total family income, we see that median debt burdens are relatively constant across families classified by income and age—in the 15–21 percent range for all family income groups and all families headed by a person under age 75. While debt burdens for families at very low or high net worth or older ages (75 or older) are gen-erally less than for other groups (about 13 percent), the presumed sig-nificance of homeownership in understanding debt burden is evident in the comparison between renters, who have a median debt burden of 8 percent of their total income, and homeowners, who have a median of 22 percent (more than twice as much).

Two measures of financial distress are high debt burdens (debt-to-income ratios greater than 40 percent) and payments past due 60 days or more. Unlike median family debt burdens, the percentage of families with high debt burdens varies substantially across income groups. About 27 percent of debtor families in the bottom income quintile have high debt burdens, compared with 14 percent in the third quintile and 2 per-cent in the fifth quintile. Similarly, the percentage of families with payments past due 60 days or more falls as family income increases. These findings suggest that though debt burdens are similar for the typical median fam-ily of each income group, moving away from the typical median family uncovers that families in the lower-income groups have greater financial distress than families in the higher-income groups.

Bankruptcy

Building on the prior discussions of debt burdens and negative net worth, we now look at the potential for bankruptcy as a consequence of accu-mulating liabilities that outstrip income from employment and assets. One can think of bankruptcy as not necessarily an issue for households with very negative net worth, but rather for households that lack the income (or assets) to service their debts. Most households file for bank-ruptcy to save their homes or to allay creditors. Filing for bankruptcy, though, has a negative effect on future asset building as it affects the type of credit that is available (likely preventing families from obtaining a home mortgage) and the price of credit.

While data from the American Bankruptcy Institute indicate that the number of bankruptcy filings per one million individuals between 1990 and 2005 grew 139 percent (from 2,879 to 6,892), several caveats are worth noting. First, the bankruptcy laws were significantly revamped in 2005, putting additional constraints on families' ability to file for bankruptcy, and so causing filing rates to tumble in 2006 and 2007. So current filing rates are likely much less illuminating of the dire financial straits some families are in. Second, many low-income families do not have the financial mechanisms at their disposal to get too deeply into debt. Third, at low incomes, debt of $3,000, $5,000, or $10,000 can seem insurmountable yet often does not compare with the sums at stake in most bankruptcy settlements. Fourth, many lower-income households simply stop making debt payments—perhaps as a result of frequent moves such that bills no longer reach them or because of a conscious decision to stop paying—and their creditors write off the debts, as the sums involved are not worth the time and cost for some (but not all) creditors to pursue collection further.

According to Domowitz and Sartain (1999); Stavins (2000); and Fay, Hurst, and White (2002), credit card debt is more closely correlated with rates of delinquency and bankruptcy than is total debt. In fact, levels of total debt (including home mortgage) are *negatively* correlated with bankruptcy. Fay and his coauthors (2002) conclude that far fewer households file for bankruptcy than the number that would actually benefit from filing. Gross and Souleles (2002) note that unemployment and lack of health insurance, while significant, only explain a small part of the decision to file.

This review of the literature suggests that many factors aside from the level of debt predict whether a household files for bankruptcy. Among them are state and federal laws, the concentration of law practices handling bankruptcy filings in a given region, the unemployment rate, liquidity of other household assets, interest rates and a household's current debt service demands, and the like. What is also not clear is whether those who file for bankruptcy are worse off economically than those who do not. More research in these areas is needed.

Data Conclusions

By synthesizing data on the balance sheets of low-income households from current literature and available public-use datasets, this chapter begins to paint portraits of the assets and liabilities of low-income, less-educated, minority, and single-headed families. Below, we summarize our findings into *portraits* for each family type.

The Assets of Low-Income Families. The typical bottom-quintile family may own a car (65 percent of families) valued at $4,500 and hold a checking or savings account (76 percent of families) valued at $600. The bottom-quintile families that own a home (40 percent) valued at $70,000 raise total median assets for all bottom-quintile families to $17,000, a figure still nine times less than what third-quintile families own. Most bottom-quintile families do not own a home (60 percent), have no retirement accounts (90 percent), and have no business equity (96 percent). Social Security comprises roughly 70 percent of expected wealth for low-income families.

The Liabilities of Low-Income Families. The typical bottom-quintile family (53 percent) may hold debt valued at $7,000, a level six times less than the debt that most (84 percent) third-quintile families hold. Bottom-quintile family debt is most likely to be credit card debt (29 percent of families) valued at $1,000, installment loans (27 percent of families) valued at $5,600, and home-secured debt (16 percent of families) valued at $37,000. Debt burdens for bottom-quintile families that carry debt can be high: 27 percent of bottom-quintile families have debt-to-income ratios greater than 40 percent. The combination of assets and liabilities for bottom-quintile families results in median net worth valued at $7,500, only about one-tenth of the net worth of third-quintile families.

The Assets of Less-Educated Families. The typical family headed by someone who did not graduate high school owns a home (56 percent) valued at $75,000 and a car (70 percent) worth $7,400, and holds a checking or savings account (72 percent) worth $1,100. In total, a typical less-educated family may own assets worth $49,900 or a little less than one-seventh of the assets owned by the typical family headed by a college graduate. Most families with less than a high school education do not own any retirement accounts (84 percent) or any business equity (96 percent). While less-educated families may not appear well off, the majority own a home (although home purchases may be completed later in life relative to higher-income groups).

The Liabilities of Less-Educated Families. The typical family headed by a person with less than a high school diploma holds debt (53 percent) valued at $12,000 or about one-ninth the debt of a family headed by a college graduate. The reason for the disparity is that while 56 percent of families without a high school diploma own a home, only 25 percent owe mortgage debt (valued at $44,000) compared with 61 percent of college-graduate families (valued at $125,000). Families headed by a person without a high school diploma are slightly more likely to carry installment debt (28 percent) valued at $7,000 and credit card balances (30 percent) valued at $1,200 than mortgage debt. The combination of assets and liabilities for families headed by a person without a high school diploma results in median net worth valued at $21,000, just one-tenth the net worth of families headed by a person with a college degree. The net worth gap by education group starts out small at younger ages and then widens sharply with age. However, unlike bottom-quintile families, the majority of less-educated families are homeowners, which makes them relatively better off from an asset standpoint.

The Assets of Single-Headed Families. The typical single-headed family may own a home (55 percent) worth $120,000 and a car (77 percent) valued at $7,600, and hold a checking or savings account (88 percent) valued at $2,000. In total, a typical single-headed family may own assets worth $83,400, or less than one-third of the assets owned by the typical married or cohabiting family. Most single-headed families do not own any retirement accounts (65 percent), financial assets beyond their checking or savings accounts, or business equity (94 percent). Again, as with families headed by persons without a high school diploma, single-headed families may not be as badly off as bottom-quintile families from an asset standpoint, as a slim majority are homeowners.

The Liabilities of Single-Headed Families. The typical single-headed family holds debt (67 percent) valued at $24,000, a little more than a quarter of the debt that most (82 percent) married or cohabiting families hold. The reason for the disparity is that, similar to less-educated families, only 32 percent of single-headed families owe mortgage debt (valued at $75,000) compared with 59 percent of married or cohabiting families (valued at $105,000). The typical debts owed by a single-headed family, therefore, are most likely to be credit card debt (41 percent) valued at $1,000 or installment loan debt (37 percent) valued at $8,600. The combination of assets and liabilities for single families results in median net worth valued at $40,000 or about one-fourth the net worth of married or cohabiting families. The net worth gap by marital status starts out small at younger ages and then widens sharply with age.

The Assets of Nonwhite or Hispanic Families. The typical family headed by someone who is nonwhite or Hispanic owns a vehicle (76 percent) worth $9,800 and a checking or savings account (81 percent) worth

$1,500. This nonwhite- or Hispanic-headed family may own a home (51 percent) worth $130,000 or a retirement account (33 percent) worth $16,000. In total, a typical family headed by a nonwhite- or Hispanic-headed family holds assets worth $60,000 or a little more than a quarter of the assets held by a white non-Hispanic headed family. While only 49 percent of nonwhite- or Hispanic-headed families do not own a home, 67 percent have no retirement account and 94 percent have no business equity.

The Liabilities of Nonwhite or Hispanic Families. The typical non-white- or Hispanic-headed family holds debt (73 percent) valued at $30,500, less than half of the debt that most (78 percent) white non-Hispanic families hold. The reason the gap is not larger is because enough nonwhite- or Hispanic-headed families pay mortgages (37 percent) worth $83,000 in comparison with white non-Hispanic families (52 percent) with mortgages worth $98,000. Nonwhite- or Hispanic-headed family debt is somewhat more likely to be credit card debt (47 percent) valued at $1,600 or installment loan debt (43 percent) valued at $9,600 than mortgage debt. The combination of assets and liabilities for nonwhite- or Hispanic-headed families results in median net worth valued at $25,000, less than one-sixth the net worth of families headed by white non-Hispanics.

The Assets of Renter Families. Based on our findings, the typical renter family owns a car (73 percent) valued at $7,200 and holds a checking or savings account (81 percent) valued at $1,100. Renter families that own a retirement account (26 percent) valued at $11,000 raise total median assets for all renter families to $12,200. Still, this amount is less than one twenty-fourth of the median assets held by homeowner families. Renter families do not own homes (almost by definition). They are unlikely to hold retirement accounts (74 percent) or other financial assets other than a transaction account (about 43 percent) and have no business equity (96 percent).

The Liabilities of Renter Families. The typical renter family holds debt (63 percent) valued at $7,800, about one-twelfth the debt that most (82 percent) homeowner families hold. This is almost entirely because these families do not own homes and so do not pay mortgages. Renter family debt is therefore most likely to be installment loan debt (45 percent) valued at $8,700 or credit card debt (also 40 percent) valued at $1,500. Debt burdens for renter families that carry debt are typically very low: only 4 percent of renter families have debt ratios greater than 40 percent compared with 15 percent of homeowners. Still, 19 percent of renters are delinquent on their debts compared with just 6 percent of homeowners. The combination of assets and liabilities for renter families results in median net worth valued at $4,000, just one forty-sixth the net worth of homeowner families. Our findings indicate that homeownership status makes the largest difference in net worth among all of the classifiers considered.

Portrait of a Low Net Worth Family. A descriptive portrait of a low–net worth family is of a family in the bottom income quintile, headed by someone under 35 years of age, lacking a high school diploma, nonwhite or Hispanic, and single families that do not own a home are much more likely to have low net worth than families that do own a home.

Policy Implications

Asset building through homeownership and other means is a potential path for some low-income families. While low-income families hold low amounts of assets absolutely and relative to middle-income families, 76 percent hold transaction accounts, 65 percent own cars, and 40 percent own homes. Policymakers and researchers might think that only income-support policies are relevant to low-income families and that asset-based policies are relevant only further up the income distribution. The finding that a substantial number of low-income families have accumulated assets suggests that asset-based policies should be targeted to low-income as well as moderate- and high-income families.

The 40 percent homeownership rate among low-income families suggests that many low-income families could benefit from the same types of homeownership incentives available to middle- and upper-income families. Under current policy, low-income housing subsidies provide a financial disincentive for many low-income families to own a home because moving from renting to homeownership might cause them to lose their rental housing subsidies (Olsen 2007). In addition, most subsidies for homeownership go to higher-income families in the form of tax savings; most low-income families cannot take advantage of these subsidies because they owe little or no income tax (Carasso et al. 2005).

Homeownership may not be advantageous for some low-income families, as the subprime crisis has made clear. However, extending homeownership subsidies to low-income families and reducing their *disincentives* to own are likely to result in (1) raising the share of low-income families owning their homes beyond the current 40 percent level, and (2) improving the balance sheets of current low-income homeowners.[5] Future research can help identify the numbers and types of additional low-income families that may be suited to owning a home. Findings from the current subprime mortgage fallout should inform this research.

Given the evidence about the balance sheets of low-income households, the key to raising asset levels is to encourage low-income families to hold major assets like vehicles, bank accounts, pensions, and homes—particularly early in the life cycle. Vehicles and bank accounts are important starter assets that can increase earnings (vehicle) and savings (vehicle and bank accounts). Pensions and homes are the most critical assets. In fact, Social Security, private retirement, and housing comprise nearly all wealth for these households at their peak (Mermin 2008). The natural question is what holding rate goals are reasonable for policymakers to strive for. An ambitious goal may be for policymakers to strive to replicate the balance-sheet outcomes of second-quintile families for those in the bottom income quintile.

A menu of specific policy prescriptions that can better extend the ladder of assets to the bottom quintile could include the following:

- *supporting vehicle ownership* with federal subsidies to help low-income families purchase and maintain a car for work.
- *incentivizing savings accounts,* such as universal children's accounts issued to all newborns with a one-time federal subsidy and income-related federal matches, which cannot be liquidated before age 18.
- *increasing pension participation* through automatic pension enrollment with opt-out and employer credits for facilitating automatic IRAs, as well as potentially for 401(k)s and 403(b)s.
- *increasing health insurance coverage,* notably, universal health insurance. (While not an asset in itself, it could lead to fewer bankruptcies and help free up money in low-income families that now goes to paying for high-cost health insurance in the individual group market. Instead, newly insured families could use the money they save to build up private assets.)
- *incentivizing homeownership* through a number of policy options, such as allowing all housing subsidies to go toward renting or owning; gradually replacing the current mortgage interest and real estate tax deductions with flat, capped, refundable homeownership credits;

and providing individual development accounts or direct federal subsidies for home down payments and closing costs. (Much tighter controls on mortgage underwriting and mortgage products for low-income families, which will likely evolve in the wake of the current housing crisis, are also clearly in order.)

We do not endorse any of these policy options but rather forward a menu that can point lawmakers in the right direction. Because of the significant gap in asset values and holding rates between the bottom and second quintiles, policy planners ought to pursue a broad array of policy options while adopting a long time horizon for the necessary gains to be made.

Suggestions for Future Research

The chapter synthesizes findings from major research reports and available public-use datasets to paint portraits of the balance sheets of low-income families. Based on the findings and assessment of the literature, the following directions for future research would help fill the gaps in knowledge and understanding of the relationships between income, assets, and debts.

Paint Better Portraits of Low-Income Families

Portraits of asset and debt holdings are far from complete. Further research is needed before we can fully understand the balance sheets of low-income families and how best to use them to improve well-being. Portraying the assets of low-income families by age group, as Lerman (2005) starts to do, would better account for the role that the life cycle plays in asset accumulation. Creating more detailed portraits of families of interest for policy purposes, such as welfare participants and nonparticipants, could reveal ways that welfare policies and programs affect asset building. Assessing the role that different assets and liabilities play in overall asset accumulation could help answer questions such as, are families better off owning a home or a savings account, having secured versus unsecured debt, or holding consumption versus investment debt? Research on these subjects can inform and influence public policy.

Painting a more detailed portrait of the role that bankruptcy plays in the asset accumulation of low-income families is also important. The current research (known to the authors) provides little information on the relationship between bankruptcy and future asset accumulation.

Important to the portraits of low-income families are family holdings of consumer durables such as furniture, appliances, and equipment—as they may be important time-saving and income-generating assets for low-income families.

Future portraits of low-income families can assess the role that region and rural status play on asset accumulation and the types of assets families accumulate. Furthermore, these portraits could also consider the assets and liabilities of families below the median. How different is the portrait for families at the 10th, 20th, 30th, and 40th percentiles of the income distribution from the portrait of families at the median? Alternatively, deciles rather than quintiles could be used to expand the reach of medians.

In addition to considering asset-holding rates and values, computations of *expected* levels of assets and liabilities, using asset- and liability-holding rates and median and mean levels of such assets or liabilities, could prove useful. These expected levels may better illustrate the dual disadvantage faced by many low-income families: not only do they tend to hold lower levels of assets and liabilities than higher-income families, they are also much less likely to hold these assets or liabilities.

Future research could also examine the role that Social Security, Medicare, and defined benefit plans play in asset accumulation for low-income families and how best to value these important programs alongside more traditional concepts of assets such as homes and bank accounts.

Future Research Using Portraits of Low-Income Families

Families in the United States accumulate assets primarily through owning homes, pensions, and cars. The lack of homeownership and pension ownership among low-income families, along with the relatively low car ownership rate, goes a long way toward explaining the low asset holdings of low-income families in this country. It is important to understand the benefits of owning homes, pensions, and cars more fully. Important for undertaking policy initiatives in this area is an understanding of the incentives and disincentives low-income families face in trying to acquire these assets.

The portraits presented in this chapter uncover some important differences in outcomes for families that hold secured versus unsecured debt. Future research has the potential to assess the role that different types of assets and debts play in overall asset accumulation, upward mobility, and the well being of low- and moderate-income families. It may be that some types of debts place families in a position to accumulate wealth while other debts effectively limit or drain wealth.

From a policy perspective, research to evaluate policies that could better replicate the wealth outcomes of moderate-income families for low-income families would be useful. The data often reveal striking differences in asset and liability outcomes for families in the second quintile compared with the bottom quintile.

NOTES

1. The year to which most responses to the SCF 2004 survey pertain.

2. Installment borrowing refers to consumer loans that have fixed payments over a fixed term. Common examples of installment borrowing are automobile loans, student loans, and loans for furniture, appliances, and other consumer durables.

3. Note that marital status can change over time and that this graph shows a snapshot at a point in time. One might get a different picture if the graph showed those never married versus those always married.

4. Furthermore, Social Security disability and survivors' benefits are financed by worker payroll contributions, require two years of contributions for workers or their survivors to be eligible, are an entitlement, and are paid out based on a formula related to average earnings. To consider Temporary Assistance to Needy Families, Food Stamps, Medicaid and similar "welfare" benefits as wealth is less sound because these benefits are not financed out of payroll taxes, have constrained eligibility, and vary widely by state and family type.

5. That is, a housing policy that does not subsidize higher-income households to own while subsidizing lower-income households to rent.

REFERENCES

Bucks, Brian K., Arthur B. Kennickell, and Kevin B. Moore. 2006. "Recent Changes in U.S. Family Finances: Evidence from the 2001 and 2004 Survey of Consumer Finances." *Federal Reserve Bulletin* 92(1): 1–38.

Carasso, Adam, Elizabeth Bell, Edgar O. Olsen, and C. Eugene Steuerle. 2005. "Improving Homeownership among Poor and Moderate-Income Households." Washington, DC: The Urban Institute. Opportunity and Ownership Project Brief 2. http://www.urban.org/url.cfm?ID=311184. (Accessed July 9, 2008.)

Domowitz, Ian, and Robert L. Sartain. 1999. "Determinants of the Consumer Bankruptcy Decision." *Journal of Finance* 54(1): 403–20.

Edin, Kathryn J. 2001. "More than Money: The Role of Assets in the Survival Strategies and Material Well-Being of the Poor." In *Assets for the Poor: The Benefits of Spreading Asset Ownership,* edited by Thomas M. Shaprio and Edward N. Wolff (206–31). New York: Russell Sage Foundation.

Fay, Scott, Erik Hurst, and Michelle J. White. 2002. "The Household Bankruptcy Decision." *American Economic Review* 92(3): 706–18.

Gross, David B., and Nicholas S. Souleles. 2002. "An Empirical Analysis of Personal Bankruptcy and Delinquency." *Review of Financial Studies* 15(1): 319–47.

Kennickell, Arthur B., and Annika E. Sundén. 1997. "Pensions, Social Security, and the Distribution of Wealth." Washington, DC: Board of Governors of the Federal Reserve System. October.

Lerman, Robert I. 2005. "Are Low-Income Households Accumulating Assets and Avoiding Unhealthy Debt? A Review of the Evidence." Washington, DC: The Urban Institute. Opportunity and Ownership Project Brief 1. http://www.urban.org/url.cfm?ID= 311185. (Accessed July 9, 2008.)

Lupton, Joseph, and James P. Smith. 1999. "Marriage, Assets, and Savings." Labor and Population Program Working Paper 99–12. Santa Monica, CA: RAND.

Marquis, Milt. 2002. "What's Behind the Low U.S. Personal Saving Rate?" FRBSF Economic Letter 2002–09. San Francisco: Federal Reserve Bank of San Francisco.

Mermin, Gordon. 2008. "Wealth Accumulation over the Life Cycle." Presentation at the Opportunity and Ownership over the Life Cycle Conference. Washington, DC: The Urban Institute.

Oliver, Melvin L., and Thomas M. Shapiro. 1997. *Black Wealth/White Wealth: A New Perspective on Racial Inequality.* New York: Routledge.

Olsen, Edgar O. 2007. "Promoting Homeownership among Low-Income Households." Washington, DC: The Urban Institute. Opportunity and Ownership Project Report 2. http://www.urban.org/url.cfm?ID=411523. (Accessed July 9, 2008.)

Sherraden, Margaret, Amanda Moore McBride, Elizabeth Johnson, Stacie Hanson, Fred M. Ssewamala, and Trina R. Shanks. 2005. *Saving in Low-Income Households: Evidence from Interviews with Participants in the American Dream Demonstration.* St. Louis, MO: Washington University in St. Louis, Center for Social Development.

Stavins, Joanna. 2000. "Credit Card Borrowing, Delinquency, and Personal Bankruptcy." *New England Economic Review* July/August: 15–30.

Steuerle, C. Eugene, and Adam Carasso. 2004. "The *USA Today* Lifetime Social Security and Medicare Benefits Calculator: Assumptions and Methods." Washington, DC: The Urban Institute. http://www.urban.org/url.cfm?ID=900746. (Accessed July 9, 2008.)

U.S. Census Bureau. 2007. Historical Income Tables, Table H-6, "All Races by Median and Mean Income, 1975–2006." http://www.census.gov/hhes/www/income/histinc/ h06ar.html. (Accessed March 2006.)

3

Asset Building across the Life Course

Mark R. Rank

The area of asset building lends itself quite naturally to a life-course framework. By its very nature, asset accumulation unfolds over a period of years and decades within an individual's life, while the effects of such accumulation are best understood within the context of the entire life course. Assets can be particularly important to lower-income households in that they may temper some of the negative effects of poverty, as well as provide protection against future economic shocks.

In this chapter, a life-course perspective is applied to understanding several aspects of asset building. We begin by discussing the background of the life-course perspective and its applicability to asset building.

The level of assets held by low-income households is then examined. For many lower-income households, assets are in short supply, particularly financial assets such as savings or stocks. In fact, between one-quarter and one-third of all Americans have failed to accumulate any financial assets whatsoever. The major asset that is held by lower-income households is a home. Yet the value of these homes and the amount of equity accrued is often quite modest.

In understanding this lack of assets across the life course, several factors are discussed that are of particular importance in explaining such scarcity. These include a lack of parental resources resulting in little inter-generational transmission of assets, being nonwhite and its effects over time, low levels of earned income throughout one's prime earning years, experiencing single parenthood or other family disruptions, and being at certain stages of the life course coupled with experiencing ill-timed life events.

Finally, to illustrate how these factors potentially interact to produce minimal asset accumulation among lower-income households, a brief case example is given. This example points to the importance of these factors within the context of time, aging, development, and sequencing, all of which are critical in the building of assets across the life course.

Background of the Life-Course Perspective

The concept of the life course has had a long and distinguished history in the social and applied sciences (Dewilde 2003; Elder 1994; Moen, Elder, and Luscher 1995; Riley 1999; Settersten and Mayer 1997). It has provided a useful framework for thinking about how individual lives unfold and how particular events and transitions affect these trajectories (Elder 1995; Voyer 2004). The term itself refers to "social processes extending over the individual life span or over significant portions of it, especially [with regard to] the family cycle, educational and training histories, and employment and occupational careers" (Mayer and Tuma 1990, 3). In addition, as Settersten and Mayer (1997) have argued, "While these dimensions describe the primary activities across life, a more complete picture of the life course must also include more marginal periods and events—such as brief periods of training, second or part-time jobs, or periods of unemployment or sickness" (252).

Interestingly, several of the earliest social scientific studies examining these more marginal periods incorporated a life-course perspective. Rowntree's (1902) description of 11,560 working-class families in the English city of York was pioneering in developing this approach. Rowntree estimated the likelihood of falling into poverty at various stages of the life course (based upon household economic conditions in 1899). His research indicated that working-class families were more likely to experience poverty at certain stages in the family life cycle when they were economically vulnerable (e.g., the period of starting a new family or during retirement). Similarly, Hunter (1904), in his book *Poverty*, attempted to place impoverishment within the context of the life course. Like Rowntree, Hunter viewed poverty as a critical life event tending to occur for working-class families at several points during their life courses.

During the 1950s and 1960s, the concept of the family life cycle became a central organizing concept. Families were viewed as progressing through distinct stages, which included getting married, having children, the empty nest, and so on (Duvall 1957; Glick 1947; Hill 1964). To understand family dynamics, it was felt important to understand these stages as well as the transitions from one family life-cycle stage to another.

However, by the early 1970s, the idea of the family life cycle came under growing criticism. As Dewilde (2003) notes, the family life-cycle approach was attacked on both theoretical and methodological grounds. It assumed a normative nature in terms of the stages that families were viewed as progressing through. This has become less tenable over time, with many types and variations of family progression possible. Second, the emphasis on the family life cycle ignores many other events and trajectories that individuals pass through during their lives. Third, there is considerable methodological difficulty in delineating the different stages of the family life cycle.

As a result of these and other criticisms, researchers have increasingly emphasized the broader concept of the life course in understanding various aspects of individual development and aging.

> The life-course perspective, which was developed in the 1970s in response to criticism of the traditional family-cycle approach, would appear to provide a solid basis in this respect. First, it should be noted that, as a concept, the life course is more flexible and more complex than either the life cycle or the family cycle. Moreover, differentiation and heterogeneity are usually regarded as given in the life-course perspective. Indeed, the study of events, transitions and trajectories is inherent in an approach based on a multidimensional life-course concept. (Dewilde 2003, 115)

The life-course approach has emphasized the importance of several key concepts for understanding individual development, including the importance of historical time, cohorts, transitions, trajectories, life events, and turning points (Hutchison 2005). Key themes that have characterized life-course research over the past 30 years have included the interplay of human lives and historical time, the timing and sequencing of lives, the linking of human lives with each other, the importance of human agency in making choices, the diversity in life-course trajectories, and the factors that lead to developmental risk or protection across the life course (Elder 1994; Hutchison 2005).

Applying a Life-Course Perspective to Asset Building

As stated above, the area of asset building lends itself quite naturally to a life-course framework. By its very nature, asset accumulation unfolds over a period of years and decades within an individual's lifetime, and the effects of such accumulation can best be understood within the context of the entire life course. Whether the asset is a college degree, home-ownership, or retirement savings, the process of asset building is readily understood within the wider framework of the life course (see Voyer [2004] for an extended example of this process).

In addition, understanding the dynamics of asset building is important to further our understanding of the life course. Assets provide individuals and households a greater means to fully reach their potential during their lives. As Sherraden (1991) argues, "simply put, when people are accumulating assets, they behave differently, and the world responds to them differently as well" (295). This includes a variety of positive effects, including greater labor force attachment, political and civic interest, marital stability, better health, and so on (Bynner 2001).

In short, asset building allows individuals and families to more fully develop their human capacity and potential. This is particularly important for low-income households and individuals. As many social scientists have noted, one of the defining characteristics of poverty and economic deprivation is the undermining of human potential (Rank 2004; Sen 1992). The role of assets may be critical in allowing low-income households to avoid some of the more detrimental effects of poverty.

This leads to a second important function of asset building within the context of the life course. Assets allow individuals and households to accrue some amount of security to be used during times of economic downturn. Economists refer to this as the ability of assets to protect consumption against unexpected shocks (Cagetti 2003). Recent research suggests that this function may be increasingly important in today's society. For example, the work of Rank and Hirschl (1999a) demonstrates that the lifetime risk of experiencing poverty at some point during adulthood is very high. Between the ages of 20 and 75, 58 percent of Americans will experience at least one year below the official poverty level, while 75 percent will encounter at least one year below 150 percent of the poverty level. The life-course risk of poverty is particularly high during early adulthood (Rank and Hirschl 2001). Furthermore, two-thirds of Americans will rely on a means-tested safety net program between the ages of 20 and

65 (Rank and Hirschl 2002), and 40 percent of Americans will use such a program in five or more separate years. Additional work (Sandoval, Hirschl, and Rank 2004) indicates that the life-course risk of poverty has been on the increase during the past 30 years, particularly during the 1990s, mirroring the increase in job and work insecurity (Fligstein and Shin 2004).

Similar findings have been observed cross-culturally as well. For example, Leisering and Leibfried (1999) write the following with regard to their life-course analysis of poverty in Germany.

> Poverty is no longer (if ever it was) a fixed condition or a personal or group characteristic, but rather it is an experience or stage in the life course. It is not necessarily associated with a marginal position in society but reaches well into the middle class. Poverty is specifically located in time and individual biographies, and, by implication, has come to transcend traditional social boundaries of class. (239)

Hacker's (2004, 2006) work has also documented the increasing prevalence of income volatility, particularly downward mobility. Using the Panel Study of Income Dynamics (PSID), Hacker (2006) demonstrates that income instability in the mid-1990s was nearly five times higher than in the early 1970s. He notes that such patterns of rising income instability and insecurity mirror an overall trend in the United States: "As both employment-based social benefits and government programs have eroded, social risks have shifted from collective intermediaries— government, employers, large insurance pools—onto individuals and families" (2004, 252).

All of this work indicates that more Americans, particularly those in the bottom half of the income distribution, are vulnerable to periods of economic deprivation at points along the life course. The presence of assets can partially alleviate the shocks of such deprivation, along with the capacity-building function mentioned earlier. Yet how widespread are such assets for lower-income households?

The Lack of Assets among Low-Income Households across the Life Course

Empirical research indicates that a significant percentage of the population is lacking in assets, particularly financial assets such as savings or stocks. Oliver and Shapiro (1990) find that one-third of American households have no financial assets at all, while Wolff (1998) shows that families in the middle income quintile have financial assets that would maintain their standard of living without income for 1.2 months, while those in the bottom quintile would not be able to replace their income for any period of time. Carney and Gale (2001) report that 20 percent of all households have no basic transaction accounts (i.e., a savings or checking account) and that more than half of all households have less than $5,000 in financial assets. Those in the bottom 25 percent of the income distribution have virtually no financial assets whatsoever.

In analyzing the level of financial assets for workers experiencing a spell of unemployment, Gruber (2001) finds that for median workers, financial asset holdings are sufficient to replace 5.4 weeks of earnings. This represented approximately three-quarters of their lost income from a spell of unemployment. However, for nearly one-third of workers, not even 10 percent of lost income could be replaced through their financial asset holdings.

One measure recently developed to assess the lack of adequate assets across the American life course has been that of asset poverty. Although first suggested by Oliver and Shapiro (1990, 1995), Haveman and Wolff (2000) operationalized the concept: "a household or person [is] 'asset poor' if the access that they have to wealth-type resources is insufficient to enable them to meet their basic needs for some limited period of time" (4). They then constructed several different measures of asset poverty based upon this overall definition. For example, "wealth-type resources" might be defined in terms of a household's overall net worth, "basic needs" could be defined as being above the official poverty level, while "limited period of time" might consist of three months. Consequently, a household that does not have sufficient net worth to sustain themselves above the poverty level for three months would be considered asset poor.

Using these and similar measures, Haveman and Wolff (2000) were able to estimate the cross-sectional rates of asset poverty for the years 1983, 1989, 1992, 1995, and 1998 using the Survey of Consumer Finances. Their findings revealed that the incidence of asset poverty was quite high among households, typically between 25 and 45 percent.

More recently, Caner and Wolff (2004) focus on the years of 1984, 1989, 1994, and 1999 within the PSID. Consistent with Haveman and Wolff's (2000) research, they find that overall rates of asset poverty during these years varied between 26 and 42 percent. Measures of asset poverty that relied on net worth were on the lower side of this range, while measures using only liquid wealth were higher. They also find that asset poverty was greatest during young adulthood and then decreased as individuals reached their forties, fifties, and sixties. For example, in 1999, asset poverty (as measured through net worth) was 80 percent for those under age 25, 44 percent for those 25 to 34, 23 percent for those 35 to 49, 9 percent for those 50 to 61, 11 percent for those 62 to 69, and 11 percent for those 70 and over. Race, education, and owning a home were important factors affecting the likelihood of asset poverty, as well as changes in family structure.

The major asset owned by Americans (including low-income households) is owner-occupied housing—44 percent of all wealth in the United States is based in home equity (U.S. Census Bureau 2001). Across the life course, most Americans will purchase homes and subsequently build some amount of equity in their homes. This is quite consistent with the strong emphasis in American society on the importance of homeownership as a vital component of the American dream (Cullen 2003). An analysis by Hirschl and Rank (2006) shows that by the age of 35, 74 percent of Americans have purchased homes, and by age 50, 88 percent. Even for those with less-favorable human capital characteristics, the percentages are high (e.g., 63 percent of those with less than 12 years of education have purchased homes by age 35, and 78 percent have done so by age 50).

Yet for low-income households, the home value and amount of equity accrued over the course of their lives are substantially less than their middle- and upper-income counterparts. In a study of 5,000 renters in the PSID, Reid (2004) finds that the financial returns to home-ownership are small for low-income minorities, low-income whites, and middle-income minorities, even when homes are owned for 10 or more years. For example, she estimates that the average value of housing for low-income minority homeowners increased from $50,000 to only $65,000 over a 10-year period. Furthermore, the loss of one's home is a very real threat.

> My analysis shows that homeownership is an incredibly fluid category, with many families moving in and out of homeownership several times over the course of their lives . . . Four years after buying a house, less than half of low-income minority households in the sample remain homeowners. Low-income white households fare better, but still only 60 percent remain homeowners after four years. (Reid 2004, 20)

In sum, previous empirical work indicates that a lack of assets across the life course is typical for low-income households. We now turn to several reasons that partially explain this shortage of assets.

Factors Affecting Asset Building across the Life Course

In seeking to understand the life-course patterns of asset building and, in particular, why low-income households lack assets, several key factors are discussed in this section. These include social class, race, income, family structure, and the timing of life events.

Social Class and the Intergenerational Transmission of Assets

Analyses of the American system of stratification have shown that, while some amount of social mobility does occur, social class as a whole tends to perpetuate itself (Beeghley 2008; Fischer et al. 1996). Those with working- or lower-class parents are likely to remain working or lower class themselves. Similarly, those whose parents are affluent are likely to remain affluent. The primary reason for this is that parents' class differences result in significant differences in the resources and opportunities available to their children. These differences in turn affect children's future life chances and outcomes, including their accumulation of assets.

Research over the past 15 years has revealed a sizable correlation between fathers' and sons' incomes, averaging around 0.4 (Aughinbaugh 2000; Beller and Hout 2006; Corcoran et al. 1992; Mulligan 1997; Solon 1992; Zimmerman 1992). For fathers with incomes in the bottom 5 percent of the income distribution, 42 percent of their sons will be in the bottom quintile of the income distribution when they grow up, while only 5 percent will reach the top quintile. On the other hand, if a father has income in the top 5 percent of the income distribution, 42 percent of his sons will earn incomes in the top quintile of the income distribution, while only 5 percent will fall into the bottom quintile (Solon 1992). Recent studies find even higher correlations. For example, using Social Security records for fathers' and sons' earnings, Mazumder (2001) reports an intergenerational correlation of 0.6 (in addition, see Bowles, Gintis, and Groves 2005).

A similar pattern of intergenerational stability emerges for wealth. Gale and Scholz (1994) estimate that intended family transfers and bequests account for 51 percent of current wealth in the United States, while an additional 12 percent of wealth is acquired through the payment of college expenses by parents. Consequently, nearly two-thirds of the net worth that individuals acquire comes through family transfers. An even higher estimate comes from Kotlikoff and Summers (1981) who argue that, as of 1974, more than 80 percent of the net worth in this country was the result of intergenerational transfers. Parents with considerable wealth are therefore able to successfully pass on these assets and advantages to their children. As a result, it is estimated that "children of the very rich have roughly 40 times better odds of being very rich than do the children of the poor" (Gokhale and Kotlikoff 2002, 268).

One important mechanism through which wealthier families are able to utilize their assets intergenerationally is through the educational process. Wealthy families are able to acquire high-quality primary and secondary educations for their children. This is accomplished either by purchasing a home in an affluent school district or by sending their children to private schools. Shapiro's (2004) in-depth interviews conducted with parents in Boston, St. Louis, and Los Angeles make this point abundantly clear. As Shapiro and Johnson note, "By accessing quality school systems parents ensure specific kinds of schooling for their children and in this way help to pass their own social position along to the next generation" (2000, 2). This process has been shown to be robust with quantitative data as well. Hochschild and Scovronick summarize this body of research with the following: "Inequalities in family wealth are a major cause of inequalities in schooling, and inequalities of schooling do much to reinforce inequalities of wealth among families in the next generation" (2003, 23).

And of course, this process continues with higher education (Haveman and Smeeding 2006). As McMurrer and Sawhill (1998) observe, "Family background has a significant and increasing effect on who goes to college, where, and for how long. With the rewards for going to college greater than ever and family background now a stronger influence over who reaps those rewards, the United States is at risk of becoming more class stratified in coming decades" (69).

Low-income parents who are lacking in assets are largely unable to maximize the educational opportunities for their children, which in turn hinders their children's ability to build assets during their own adulthoods. Other mechanisms for transferring wealth include inter vivos transfers and inheritances, each of which serves to reinforce social class disparities in asset accumulation across the life course (see also chapter 2).

In sum, as Keister (2000) notes, "The transfer of wealth from one generation to the next may be the single most important determinant of who owns what, how they got it, and what effects it has on both individual- and system-level outcomes" (252).

Race

Partially as a result of these intergenerational patterns in the transmission of wealth, racial minorities have been at a distinct disadvantage in their ability to build assets across the life course. A large body of work (Conley 1999; Feagin 2000; Oliver and Shapiro 1995; Shapiro 2004) indicates that race, and particularly being African American, plays an important role in constraining the ability of individuals to accumulate significant assets during their lifetimes. As is well known, the black-white wealth gap is significantly larger than the income gap. While the typical black household earns roughly 60 cents for every dollar earned by its white counterpart, it holds only 10 cents worth of wealth for every dollar of wealth held by a white household (Shapiro 2004).

Part of this racial effect is related to the first factor discussed—the intergenerational transmission of wealth. Black families have much less wealth to transfer from one generation to the next, resulting in continued patterns of inequality. As Shapiro (2004) writes, "The enormous racial wealth gap perpetuates race inequality in the United States. Racial inequality appears intransigent because the way families use wealth transmits advantages from generation to generation" (183). Shapiro (2004) finds that the most important factors explaining differences in net worth between white and black families are differences in inheritance, family income, and homeownership. Likewise, Conley (1999) also demonstrates the importance of intergenerational differences in the transmission of wealth to explain the current black-white gap in asset holding.

Continuing patterns of racial discrimination also serve to reinforce the racial life-course disparities in assets and wealth. For example, patterns of racial residential segregation mean that black children are more likely than white children from similar social class backgrounds to attend schools that are severely segregated and lacking in resources (Massey and Denton 1993; Orfield and Yun 1999). These patterns also apply to Latino children, albeit to a lesser extent (Orfield and Lee 2004). As a result, minority children are less able to compete in the labor market, which in turn affects their ability to build assets.

Likewise, racial minorities continue to be discriminated against in the housing market. Research has indicated that black and Hispanic renters are more likely to be excluded from housing made available to white renters; furthermore, black and Hispanic homebuyers learn about fewer available homes than white homebuyers and are more likely to be turned down for home loans than their white counterparts (Yinger 1995, 2001).

For example, one influential study found that blacks and Hispanics applying for mortgage loans in Boston were 82 percent more likely to be turned down than whites, even after controlling for credit qualifications and type of loan (Munnell et al. 1996). A reanalysis by Ross and Yinger (2002) produced similar patterns.

The result of such housing-market discrimination is higher rent burdens, poorer-quality housing, and increased residential segregation for African Americans and Hispanic Americans. This, in turn, reduces the ability of racial minorities to build significant wealth.

Income

A third important factor in the building of assets across adulthood is having an adequate and stable source of income. As Edin (2001) and others have demonstrated, the accumulation of assets over the life course largely depends on having an income surplus, along with the belief and faith that one's income will remain relatively stable from one month to the next. Given the nature of poverty and low-wage jobs, both of these requirements are often in short supply. Or as Warren and Britton (2003) note, "It is likely that people with low, insecure incomes—resulting from unemployment, intermittent or low-paid employment, or both—are less able to accumulate various types of economic capital over the course of their lives. Conversely, people with secure employment and higher incomes have more opportunities to acquire different kinds of assets" (103).

The role of income in building assets and wealth across time has been empirically demonstrated in a number of studies (Keister 2000; Ziliak 2003). Using a simulation model, Keister (2000) finds a strong positive association between income and wealth mobility (as measured by increase in deciles of net worth) during the 1980s and early 1990s. For example, she finds for "those making more than $100,000, the increase in the odds of upward mobility was a remarkable 7.535 times greater than for those in the omitted income category (those earning less than $10,000). These increases in odds are even more incredible given that they are estimated with many other demographic influences on wealth ownership and mobility controlled" (226–27).

Having a strong and reliable source of income is clearly fundamental to an individual's and a family's ability to build assets over time. Although it is true that even those in poverty have the ability to save (Schreiner and Sherraden 2007; Schreiner, Clancy, and Sherraden 2002), a critical factor in the building of assets is nevertheless the amount and stability of income over time.

It should be noted that a substantial body of research has demonstrated over the past 40 years that income is highly dependent on human capital, including education, work experience, skills, and so on. Consequently, these human-capital factors can be seen as playing an indirect role in asset building over the life course through their direct effects on income. However, there is also evidence to suggest that education in particular exerts an independent effect on asset building above and beyond its effects through increased income. For example, Keister (2000) shows a sizeable effect of education on upward wealth mobility, controlling for income and other demographic factors. This effect may be the result of several different mechanisms, including a greater propensity to save and defer consumption among those with higher levels of education.

Family Structure

A fourth factor particularly important in the life-course patterns of asset building is family structure. Research shows that family structure and changes in family structure strongly affect the accumulation of wealth. In particular, single-mother families are at a disadvantage compared to married-couple families. In the Caner and Wolff (2004) study mentioned earlier, marriage is found to be an important avenue for escaping from asset poverty, while single parenthood is a route into asset poverty. Reid (2004) finds that "experiencing a divorce is one of the most important factors in the transition from owning to renting, regardless of race or income. For low- and middle-income households, a divorce increases the likelihood of leaving homeownership by 9.8 and 10.6 times respectively" (21). Lupton and Smith (1999), using both the Health and Retirement Survey and the PSID, find a large and significant effect of marriage on the accumulation of financial assets and net worth across the life course. And finally, in an analysis of the National Longitudinal Survey of Youth (NLSY), Zagorsky (2005) reports that married respondents experienced a net worth increase of 77 percent over single respondents during the time of the study. Those who experienced a divorce suffered a significant drop in their overall net worth.

An additional family structure factor of importance across the life course is size of family of origin. Keister (2003) utilizes the NLSY to show that number of siblings has a large negative effect on children's overall levels of net worth as adults. Keister argues that this is the result of a dilution of resources available to each child in the family of origin. She asserts that children in large families tend to receive lower-quality educational experiences and less education. According to Keister, a having large number of children reduces "parental savings, inter vivos transfers, and the wealth that is available to bequeath at the end of the parents' lives. Decreased educational attainment and intergenerational resource transfers, in turn, alter financial behavior and saving trajectories. As a result, those from larger families accumulate smaller portfolios throughout their lives" (539).

Finally, the factor of parental age has been shown to be important with respect to building children's assets. Using the National Education Longitudinal Study of 1988, Powell, Steelman, and Carini (2006) find that the older parents were when they had their children, the more likely they were to have built greater economic resources for their offspring. As the authors note, "The older the mother, the more likely and the earlier parents started to save for college, the more they actually saved for college, the more likely the child attended a private high school, and the more likely the child used a computer in the home for educational purposes" (1374). Consequently, this study provides empirical support for the negative effects of parenthood at early ages on asset building for the next generation.

Stages of the Life Cycle and Timing of Life Events

Two final factors of importance in understanding asset building from a life-course perspective are the stages of the life cycle and the timing of particular life events in relation to these stages. As noted earlier, life-cycle stages are often defined in terms of family compositional changes combined with a rough estimate of the chronological age of an individual (e.g., childhood, young adulthood, starting a family, empty nesthood, retirement).

As mentioned at the beginning of this chapter, Rowntree's (1902) pioneering study of poverty explicitly focused on the risk of economic deprivation vis-à-vis the family life cycle. Rowntree (1902) found that certain stages of the life cycle were associated with a greater risk of economic hardship:

> The life of a labourer is marked by five alternating periods of want and comparative plenty. During early childhood, unless his father is a skilled worker, he probably

will be in poverty; this will last until he, or some of his brothers or sisters, begin to
earn money . . . Then follows the period during which he is earning money and living under his parents' roof . . . This period of comparative prosperity may continue
after marriage until he has two or three children, when poverty will again overtake
him . . . While the children are earning, and before they leave the home to marry,
the man enjoys another period of prosperity—possibly, however, only to sink back
again into poverty when his children have married and left him, and he himself is
too old to work, for his income has never permitted his saving enough for him and
his wife to live upon from for more than a very short period. (169–72)

Economists have also turned to the life cycle in some of their early
work—for example, Modigliani and Brumberg's (1954) utilization of the
life cycle to understand savings and wealth behavior. Recent work has
continued to show the importance of the life cycle in understanding patterns of income and wealth accumulation (Gourinchas and Parker 2002;
Keister 2000; Kennickell and Starr-McCluer 1997; Rigg and Sefton
2004). Individuals at earlier stages of the adult life cycle (e.g., those in
their twenties and thirties who are starting a family) tend to have relatively few assets; those in their prime earning years of the forties and
fifties tend to see their assets grow; while the retirement years display a
leveling off and slight decline in the value of assets.

The concept of Social Security and various retirement plans and pensions has been based upon the life-course awareness of the need for assets
and savings during the later stages of life. As individuals reach retirement, streams of income are needed to maintain a reasonable quality of
life. For most individuals, these streams of income are typically found
within the Social Security system as well as private retirement or pension
plans. Yet even with the widespread presence of these policies, Rank and
Hirschl (1999b) have shown that between the ages of 60 and 90, 40 percent of Americans will experience at least one year below the poverty
level. In the future, as more Americans can expect to live longer lives,
considerably more research should be focused on this important stage of
the life course and the presence of sustainable assets.

In addition, particular events at certain stages of the life cycle can have
large effects on the ability of individuals to accumulate assets in later
adulthood. For example, a teenager who has a child out of wedlock will
likely experience a cascading negative effect on her ability to build assets
later in life. She may have to drop out of school, which in turn will create more difficulties in finding high-wage employment, which in turn
will significantly hinder her ability to save a portion of her income, and
so on. Likewise, the timing of other unanticipated events (unemploy-

ment, health problems, divorce) at particular points in the life course can have profound effects on later patterns of asset building (e.g., see Voyer 2004). Conversely, the presence of assets may reduce the likelihood and the severity of such events, resulting in a virtuous cycle that then leads to greater asset accumulation as individuals age.

An Example of the Utility of the Life Course

The life-course framework provides an extremely helpful tool in understanding the process of asset building in general and asset building among low-income households in particular. As mentioned earlier, the process of asset building is one that takes place over the course of an individual's lifetime. Examining asset building from a life-course framework would appear to be a natural fit. The life course introduces the factors of time, aging, development, and sequencing, all of which are important in asset accumulation.

Building upon these factors, one can begin to illustrate why many low-income households are lacking in assets. Although there are a multitude of life-course patterns and trajectories, a common pattern might be the following. The process begins in childhood, when low-income parents are particularly lacking in resources and are, therefore, unable to maximize their children's early developmental and educational experiences. In addition, if there are several children in the household, parental resources (both time and money) are stretched even further. Although the parents may own their home, it is probably located in a resource-poor and low-achieving school district. As a result, their children may not be able to acquire all of the necessary skills, abilities, and credentials to effectively compete in the labor market.

The children are also at greater risk of an early detrimental life-course event, such as an out-of-wedlock birth, health problems, or incarceration (as a result of lower family income, instability of the neighborhood, or race). These events then dramatically impact one's ability to invest and build human capital. For example, earning a college degree becomes nearly impossible. Even going to a two-year community or technical college is difficult. As a result, such adults frequently become locked into the secondary labor market for much of their adulthood. Their incomes are low, their job stability is precarious, and the jobs themselves are typically lacking in key benefits such as health insurance.

These factors then make it much more difficult for these young and middle-aged adults to save and build assets, and in fact, they are frequently in debt. In addition, not having any assets to draw upon during periods of unemployment and economic hardship makes such periods even more tumultuous. Without good incomes, without jobs that provide stability and benefits, and without parental economic help, they are simply unable to accrue much in the way of assets and wealth. If, in addition to this, a divorce or out-of-wedlock birth occurs, asset building becomes even more difficult. As these individuals reach their late fifties and early sixties, they approach retirement with only a small amount accrued in the Social Security system and, perhaps, an equally small amount of home equity. With little in the way of assets or retirement funds and with only a modest Social Security check, they are likely to be on the verge of poverty throughout their elderly years (see Rank and Hirschl 1999b).

This example illustrates from a life-course perspective why a lack of assets among low-income households is common. It is a process that unfolds across time and is largely dependent upon prior events and processes. Yet the individual life course also has the potential to bend in different directions than the one given here. For example, the United Kingdom's new Children's Trust Fund may make going to college a more realistic option for young adults like those in our example and, hence, may alter labor force trajectories and subsequent asset-building abilities. A life-course perspective is thus both fluid and dynamic.

Conclusion

As this chapter has attempted to demonstrate, future asset-building research can greatly benefit from employing a life-course framework. Yet it is important to note that longitudinal work on the patterns and processes of asset building across the life course is still at a very early stage in its development. One of the reasons for this is that long-running longitudinal asset data have not been available until recently. For example, the Panel Study of Income Dynamics, the longest ongoing economic and demographic longitudinal dataset in the United States, has been gathering information on the same households since 1968. Yet, as its name implies, the primary focus of data collection has been on income rather than asset dynamics. It was not until 1984 that the PSID included a set of questions asking about household assets (since then, this module of questions has been included in the PSID waves of 1989, 1994, 1999, 2001, 2003, and 2005).

Another valuable dataset for potential life-course asset work is the National Longitudinal Survey of Youth, which includes a national sample of American youth age 14 to 21 followed annually from 1979 onward. Researchers in the future need to take full advantage of the longitudinal nature of these and other datasets to model the process of asset building across the life course (see the appendix for an extended discussion of appropriate data sources for asset research).

As argued throughout this chapter, a life-course perspective provides a valuable framework for understanding the process of asset building as it unfolds across a lifetime. It is particularly helpful in understanding the difficulties facing low-income households with respect to asset accumulation. Empirical research has demonstrated that there is a virtual absence of assets among low-income households. In understanding this lack of assets across the life course, several factors are critical. These include a shortage of parental resources resulting in little intergenerational transmission of assets, being nonwhite and its cumulative effects over time, low levels of earned income throughout one's prime earning years, single parenthood or family disruptions, and being at certain stages of the life cycle coupled with experiencing ill-timed life events. Taken as a whole, these factors are best understood within the context of time, aging, development, and sequencing, all of which represent the essence of the life-course perspective.

REFERENCES

Aughinbaugh, Alison. 2000. "Reapplication and Extension: Intergenerational Mobility in the United States." *Labour Economics* 7(6): 785–96.

Beeghley, Leonard. 2008. *The Structure of Social Stratification in the United States.* Boston: Allyn and Bacon.

Beller, Emily, and Michael Hout. 2006. "Intergenerational Social Mobility: The United States in Comparative Perspective." *Future of Children* 16(2): 19–36.

Bowles, Samuel, Herbert Gintis, and Melissa Osborne Groves. 2005. *Unequal Chances: Family Background and Economic Success.* Princeton, NJ: Princeton University Press.

Bynner, John. 2001. "The Effect of Assets on Life Chances." In *The Asset-Effect,* edited by John Bynner and Will Paxton (17–37). London: Institute for Public Policy Research.

Cagetti, Marco. 2003. "Wealth Accumulation over the Life Cycle and Precautionary Savings." *Journal of Business and Economic Statistics* 21(3): 339–53.

Caner, Asena, and Edward N. Wolff. 2004. "Asset Poverty in the United States, 1984–99: Evidence from the Panel Study of Income Dynamics." *Review of Income and Wealth* 50(4): 493–518.

Carney, Stacie, and William G. Gale. 2001. "Asset Accumulation among Low-Income Households." In *Assets for the Poor: The Benefits of Spreading Asset Ownership*, edited by Thomas M. Shapiro and Edward N. Wolff (165–205). The Ford Foundation Series on Asset Building. New York: Russell Sage Foundation.

Conley, Dalton. 1999. *Being Black, Living in the Red: Race, Wealth, and Social Policy in America*. Berkeley: University of California Press.

Corcoran, Mary E., Roger Gordon, Deborah Larn, and Gary Solon. 1992. "The Association between Men's Economic Status and Their Family and Community Origins." *Journal of Human Resources* 27(4): 575–601.

Cullen, Jim. 2003. *The American Dream: A Short History of an Idea that Shaped a Nation*. New York: Oxford University Press.

Dewilde, Caroline. 2003. "A Life-Course Perspective on Social Exclusion and Poverty." *British Journal of Sociology* 54(1): 109–28.

Duvall, Evelyn M. 1957. *Family Development*. Philadelphia: J. B. Lippincott.

Edin, Kathryn J. 2001. "More than Money: The Role of Assets in the Survival Strategies and Material Well-Being of the Poor." In *Assets for the Poor: The Benefits of Spreading Asset Ownership*, edited by Thomas M. Shapiro and Edward N. Wolff (206–31). New York: Russell Sage Foundation.

Elder, Glen H., Jr. 1994. "Time, Human Agency, and Social Change: Perspectives on the Life Course." *Social Psychology Quarterly* 57(1): 4–15.

———. 1995. "The Life Course Paradigm: Social Change and Individual Development." In *Examining Lives in Context: Perspectives on the Ecology of Human Development*, edited by Phyllis Moen, Glenn H. Elder Jr., and Kurt Luscher (101–90). New York: American Psychological Association.

Feagin, Joe R. 2000. *Racist America: Roots, Current Realities, and Future Reparations*. New York: Routledge.

Fischer, Claude S., Michael Hour, Martin Sanchez Jankowski, Samuel R. Lucas, Ann Swidler, and Kim Voss. 1996. *Inequality by Design: Cracking the Bell Curve Myth*. Princeton, NJ: Princeton University Press.

Fligstein, Neil, and Taek-Jin Shin. 2004. "The Shareholder Value Society: A Review of the Changes in Working Conditions and Inequality in the United States, 1976 to 2000." In *Social Inequality*, edited by Kathryn M. Neckman (401–32). New York: Russell Sage Foundation.

Gale, William G., and John Karl Scholz. 1994. "Intergenerational Transfers and the Accumulation of Wealth." *Journal of Economic Perspectives* 8(4): 145–60.

Glick, Paul C. 1947. "The Family Cycle." *American Sociological Review* 12(2): 164–74.

Gokhale, Jagadeesh, and Laurence J. Kotlikoff. 2002. "Simulating the Transmission of Wealth Inequality." *American Economic Review* 92(2): 265–69.

Gourinchas, Pierre-Olivier, and Jonathan A. Parker. 2002. "Consumption over the Life Cycle." *Econometrica* 70(1): 47–89.

Gruber, Jonathan. 2001. "The Wealth of the Unemployed." *Industrial and Labor Relations Review* 55(1): 79–94.

Hacker, Jacob S. 2004. "Privatizing Risk without Privatizing the Welfare State: The Hidden Politics of Social Policy Retrenchment in the Unites States." *American Political Science Review* 98(2): 243–60.

———. 2006. *The Great Risk Shift: The Assault on American Jobs, Families, Health Care, and Retirement—and How You Can Fight Back.* New York: Oxford University Press.

Haveman, Robert, and Timothy Smeeding. 2006. "The Role of Higher Education in Social Mobility." *Future of Children* 16(2): 125–150.

Haveman, Robert, and Edward N. Wolff. 2000. "Who Are the Asset Poor? Levels, Trends and Composition, 1983–1998." Center for Social Development Working Paper 00-12. St. Louis, MO: Washington University in St. Louis.

Hill, Reuben L. 1964. "Methodological Issues in Family Development Research." *Family Process* 35(1): 186–206.

Hirschl, Thomas A., and Mark R. Rank. 2006. "Homeownership across the American Life Course: Estimating the Racial Divide." Center for Social Development Working Paper 06–12. St. Louis, MO: Washington University in St. Louis.

Hochschild, Jennifer, and Nathan Scovronick. 2003. *The American Dream and the Public Schools.* New York: Oxford University Press.

Hunter, Robert. 1904. *Poverty: Social Conscience in the Progressive Era.* New York: Macmillan.

Hutchison, Elizabeth D. 2005. "The Life Course Perspective: A Promising Approach for Bridging the Micro and Macro Worlds for Social Workers." *Families in Society* 86(1): 143–52.

Keister, Lisa A. 2000. *Wealth in America: Trends in Wealth Inequality.* New York: Cambridge University Press.

———. 2003. "Sharing the Wealth: The Effect of Siblings on Adults' Wealth Ownership." *Demography* 40(3): 521–42.

Kennickell, Arthur B., and Martha Starr-McCluer. 1997. "Household Saving and Portfolio Change: Evidence from the 1983–89 SCF Panel." *Review of Income and Wealth* 43(4): 381–99.

Kotlikoff, Laurence J., and Lawrence H. Summers. 1981. "The Role of Intergenerational Transfers in Aggregate Capital Accumulation." *Journal of Political Economy* 89(4): 706–32.

Leisering, Lutz, and Stephan Leibfried. 1999. *Time and Poverty in Western Welfare States: United Germany in Perspective.* Cambridge, UK: Cambridge University Press.

Lupton, Joseph, and James P. Smith. 1999. "Marriage, Assets, and Savings." Labor and Population Program Working Paper 99–12. Santa Monica, CA: RAND.

Massey, Douglas S., and Susan Denton. 1993. *American Apartheid: Segregation and the Making of the Underclass.* Cambridge, MA: Harvard University Press.

Mayer, Karl Ulrich, and Nancy Brandon Tuma. 1990. "Life Course Research and Event History Analysis: An Overview." In *Event History Analysis in Life Course Research,* edited by Karl U. Mayer and Nancy Brandon Tuma (3–20). Madison: University of Wisconsin Press.

Mazumder, Bhashkar. 2001. "Earnings Mobility in the U.S.: A New Look at Intergenerational Inequality." Federal Reserve Board of Chicago Working Paper PW2001–18. Chicago: Federal Reserve Board of Chicago.

McMurrer, Daniel P., and Isabel V. Sawhill. 1998. *Getting Ahead: Economic and Social Mobility in America.* Washington, DC: Urban Institute Press.

Modigliani, Franco, and Richard Brumberg. 1954. "Utility Analysis and the Consumption Function: An Interpretation of Cross-Section Data." In *Post-Keynesian Economics,* edited by Kenneth K. Kurihara (388–436). New Brunswick, NJ: Rutgers University Press.

Moen, Phyllis, Glenn H. Elder Jr., and Kurt Luscher. 1995. *Examining Lives in Context: Perspectives on the Ecology of Human Development.* Washington, DC: American Psychological Association.

Mulligan, Casey B. 1997. *Parental Priorities and Economic Inequality.* Chicago: University of Chicago Press.

Munnell, Alicia H., Lynn E. Browne, James McEneaney, and Geoffrey M. B. Tootell. 1996. "Mortgage Lending in Boston: Interpreting the HMDA Data." *American Economic Review* 86(1): 25–53.

Oliver, Melvin L., and Thomas M. Shapiro. 1990. "Wealth of a Nation: A Reassessment of Asset Inequality in America Shows at Least One Third of Households Are Asset Poor." *American Journal of Economics and Sociology* 49(2): 129–51.

———. 1995. *Black Wealth/White Wealth: A New Perspective on Racial Inequality.* New York: Routledge.

Orfield, Gary, and Chungmei Lee. 2004. "Brown at 50: King's Dream or Plessy's Nightmare?" Cambridge, MA: The Civil Rights Project, Harvard University.

Orfield, Gary, and John T. Yun. 1999. "Resegregation in American Schools." Cambridge, MA: The Civil Rights Project, Harvard University.

Powell, Brian, Lala Carr Steelman, and Robert M. Carini. 2006. "Advancing Age, Advantaged Youth: Parental Age and the Transmission of Resources to Children." *Social Forces* 84(3): 1359–90.

Rank, Mark R. 2004. *One Nation, Underprivileged: Why American Poverty Affects Us All.* New York: Oxford University Press.

Rank, Mark R., and Thomas A. Hirschl. 1999a. "The Likelihood of Poverty across the American Adult Lifespan." *Social Work* 44(3): 201–16.

———. 1999b. "Estimating the Proportion of Americans Ever Experiencing Poverty during Their Elderly Years." *Journal of Gerontology: Social Sciences* 54B(4): S184–S193.

———. 2001. "The Occurrence of Poverty across the Life Cycle: Evidence from the PSID." *Journal of Policy Analysis and Management* 20(4): 727–55.

———. 2002. "Welfare Use as a Life Course Event: Toward a New Understanding of the U.S. Safety Net." *Social Work* 47(3): 237–48.

Reid, Carolina Katz. 2004. "Achieving the American Dream? A Longitudinal Analysis of the Homeownership Experiences of Low-Income Households." Center for Studies in Demography and Ecology Working Paper 04-04. Seattle: University of Washington.

Rigg, John, and Tom Sefton. 2004. "Income Dynamics and the Life Cycle." Center for Analysis of Social Exclusion Working Paper 81. London: London School of Economics.

Riley, Matilda White. 1999. "Sociological Research on Age: Legacy and Challenge." *Aging and Society* 19(1): 123–32.

Ross, Stephen, and John Yinger. 2002. *The Color of Credit: Mortgage Discrimination, Research Methodology, and Fair-Lending Enforcement.* Cambridge, MA: MIT Press.

Rowntree, B. Seebohm. 1902. *Poverty: A Study of Town Life.* London: Thomas Nelson and Sons.

Sandoval, Daniel A., Thomas A. Hirschl, and Mark R. Rank. 2004. "The Increase of Poverty Risk and Income Insecurity in the U.S. since the 1970's." Presented at the American Sociological Association Annual Meeting, San Francisco, California, August 14–17.

Schreiner, Mark, and Michael Sherraden. 2007. *Can the Poor Save? Saving and Asset Building in Individual Development Accounts.* New Brunswick, NJ: Transaction Publishers.

Schreiner, Mark, Margaret Clancy, and Michael Sherraden. 2002. "Saving Performance in the American Dream Demonstration: A National Demonstration of Individual Development Accounts." Center for Social Development Report. St. Louis, MO: Washington University in St. Louis.

Sen, Amartya Kumar. 1992. *Inequality Reexamined.* New York: Russell Sage Foundation.

Settersten, Richard A., Jr., and Karl Ulrich Mayer. 1997. "The Measurement of Age, Age Structuring, and the Life Course." *Annual Review of Sociology* 23: 233–61.

Shapiro, Thomas M. 2004. *The Hidden Cost of Being African American: How Wealth Perpetuates Inequality.* New York: Oxford University Press.

Shapiro, Thomas M., and Heather Beth Johnson. 2000. "Assets, Race, and Educational Choices." Center for Social Development Working Paper 00-7. St. Louis, MO: Washington University in St. Louis.

Sherraden, Michael. 1991. *Assets and the Poor: A New American Welfare Policy.* Armonk, NY: M. E. Sharpe.

Solon, Gary. 1992. "Intergenerational Income Mobility in the United States." *American Economic Review* 82(3): 393–408.

U.S. Census Bureau. 2001. *Did You Know? Homes Account for 44 Percent of All Wealth.* Current Population Reports Series P70-75. Washington, DC: U.S. Government Printing Office.

Voyer, Jean-Pierre. 2004. *A Life-Course Approach to Social Policy Analysis: A Proposed Framework.* Policy Research Initiative Discussion Paper. Ottawa: Human Resources and Social Development Canada

Warren, Tracey, and Nadia Joanne Britton. 2003. "Ethnic Diversity in Economic Well Being: The Combined Significance of Income, Wealth and Asset Levels." *Journal of Ethnic and Migration Studies* 29(1): 103–19.

Wolff, Edward N. 1998. "Recent Trends in Size Distribution of Household Wealth." *Journal of Economic Perspectives* 12(3): 131–50.

Yinger, John. 1995. *Closed Door, Opportunities Lost: The Continuing Costs of Housing Discrimination.* New York: Russell Sage Foundation.

———. 2001. "Housing Discrimination and Residential Segregation as Causes of Poverty." In *Understanding Poverty,* edited by Sheldon H. Danziger and Robert H. Haveman (358–91). New York: Russell Sage Foundation.

Zagorsky, Jay L. 2005. "Marriage and Divorce's Impact on Wealth." *Journal of Sociology* 41(4): 406–24.

Ziliak, James P. 2003. "Income Transfers and Assets of the Poor." *Review of Economics and Statistics* 85(1): 63–76.

Zimmerman, David J. 1992. "Regression toward Mediocrity in Economic Review." *American Economic Review* 82(3): 409–29.

4

Determinants of Asset Holdings

Sondra Beverly, Michael Sherraden, Reid Cramer,
Trina R. Williams Shanks, Yunju Nam, and Min Zhan

Although research on the determinants of saving and asset accumulation is extensive, it remains inadequate for public policy purposes. Most existing theories of saving point to individual characteristics to explain levels of wealth. For example, they note that marital status (Yamokoski and Keister 2006), family size (Keister 2004), and religious affiliation (Keister 2003) influence asset accumulation or point to differences in educational attainment as a primary explanatory factor. Few studies provide sufficient evidence for clear policy recommendations, especially for increasing wealth among the poor. This chapter examines the fundamental question: what factors determine saving and asset accumulation?

The goal is to develop a framework that explains saving and asset accumulation in ways that can inform policy decisions. Thus, the emphasis is both narrow and broad. It is narrow because of the focus on decisions and outcomes related to *assets,* not decisions and outcomes related to consumption, income, participation in means-tested programs, and liabilities. A broader conceptualization of the economic life of low-income households might also be useful but is beyond the scope of this chapter. At the same time, the emphasis is broad because the chapter seeks to develop a framework that explains saving and asset accumulation *across the entire population,* while accounting for low levels of saving and wealth in the low-income population. The goal is not to develop a theory that applies only to the poor, because this theory would not support broad knowledge development and would not connect with larger bodies of work on saving and asset accumulation.

The emphasis on assets does not imply that income- and consumption-oriented strategies are undesirable. Economic constraints are very real and therefore, the optimal decision for some very low income households may be *not* to save because saving would require harmful reductions in consumption. Thus, programs and policies that increase incomes and provide important supports, especially health insurance, are critical for the economic well-being of families. Both income generation and asset building, however, are essential in the economic lives of everyone, rich and poor alike. We focus on assets because policymakers (and others) have generally undervalued the role of assets in the economic well-being of low-income families (Sherraden 1991), and because much more could be done to support the asset-building efforts of low-income families through public policy.

The framework developed here pays particular attention to the role of institutions in saving and asset accumulation. The term *institutions* in this chapter refers to purposefully created policies, programs, products, and services that shape opportunities, constraints, and consequences. In the social sciences, the term is often used much more broadly, but the focus here is narrowly on *conditions that are put in place on purpose,* as in a public policy. Institutions affect world views—and thus actions—because they shape constraints and consequences and expose people to knowledge of opportunities and choices (Schreiner and Sherraden 2007).

From an institutional perspective, saving and asset accumulation are in large part the result of structured mechanisms involving "explicit connections, rules, incentives, and subsidies" (Sherraden 1991, 116). For the nonpoor, these mechanisms include deductions for home mortgage interest and property taxes, exclusions for employment-sponsored pension contributions and earnings, tax deferments for individual retirement accounts (IRAs) and Keogh plans, and employer contributions and tax deferments for employee pension plans. Low- and moderate-income households with little existing savings do not have the same access to or receive the same incentives from institutions that promote and subsidize asset accumulation (Howard 1997; Seidman 2001; Sherraden 1991). For example, the poor are less likely to own homes, and when they do own homes, they receive little or no subsidy because they have low or zero marginal tax rates and the tax benefits are not refundable.

This chapter is organized as follows: We summarize existing theories of saving and asset accumulation and discuss strengths and limitations with an emphasis on ability to explain asset building in low-income households. We then present the conceptual framework and review empirical evidence that supports or challenges the proposed framework. When applicable, this section considers how the hypothesized relationships might differ substantially for low-income, minority, and single-mother households. The chapter concludes with a summary of strengths and weakness of existing empirical evidence and possible directions for future research.

Theories of the Determinants of Asset Building

In this section, we summarize and assess existing concepts and theoretical models of the determinants of saving and asset accumulation. These "theories," which are at various stages of development, may be classified into three categories: (1) neoclassical economic, (2) psychological and sociological, and (3) behavioral economic. Boxes 4.1, 4.2, and 4.3 summarize these perspectives. A fourth theoretical category emphasizes institutional determinants of saving and asset accumulation (see figure 4.1). Because this is the approach we adopt and develop here, we describe this emerging theory when we present our own conceptual model.

Neoclassical Economic Theory

Neoclassical economic theory assumes that individuals are rational beings who respond in predictable ways to changes in incentives. From this perspective, there are two broad determinants of individual behavior: opportunities (or constraints) and individual preferences (Pollak 1998). Preferences are generally assumed to be stable and exogenous (i.e., unaffected by opportunities and constraints). Many economic models also assume that individuals have perfect knowledge and access to perfect markets. Individual utility (i.e., happiness or satisfaction) is usually assumed to be a function of consumption, and economic models often treat savings as a residual—those resources that remain after consumption decisions are made.

The starting point for neoclassical economic research on saving and asset accumulation has been the life-cycle hypothesis (LCH) (Ando and Modigliani 1963; Modigliani and Ando 1957; Modigliani and Brumberg

1954) and the permanent income hypothesis (PIH) (Friedman 1957). Both of these theories assume that individuals and households are concerned about long-term consumption opportunities and therefore explain saving and consumption in terms of expected future income. These models assume that saving is a way to smooth consumption in the face of income fluctuations. Since consumption is determined by anticipated lifetime resources (rather than only current resources), saving over short periods of time (e.g., a year) is expected to reflect departures of current income from average lifetime resources. In other words, according to these theories, when current income falls below average expected lifetime income, individuals and households may borrow to finance consumption. When current income exceeds average expected lifetime resources, individuals and households save (or repay debt).

As its name suggests, the *life-cycle* hypothesis posits that consumption and saving reflect an individual's stage in the life cycle, which is generally proxied by age. Since retirement, for most people, is the most substantial and enduring income fluctuation, this model emphasizes saving for retirement as a primary motivation for deferred consumption. Young households are expected to have negative saving since they typically have relatively low earnings and incur debt for education, home purchases, and other expenses. In the middle period of the life cycle, saving is expected to be positive because individuals pay their debts and begin to save for retirement. Upon retirement, households are expected to dissave (i.e., spend money previously saved). Thus, differences in consumption and saving among households are believed to be partly the product of age differences, and the pattern of saving and dissaving creates an inverted U-shaped pattern across age categories or over time (Ando and Modigliani 1963; Modigliani and Ando 1957; Modigliani and Brumberg 1954).

In recent years, economists have extended the LCH and PIH. *Buffer-stock* models (e.g., Carroll 1997; Carroll and Samwick 1997; Deaton 1991; Samwick 2006) emphasize a precautionary motive for saving, particularly for younger households and for households facing greater income uncertainty. These households are expected to accumulate small stocks of assets (buffer stocks) to smooth consumption in the face of short-term income fluctuations and liquidity constraints. The pattern of asset accumulation predicted by buffer-stock models is very different from the inverted U-shape predicted by the LCH; wealth is expected to remain fairly constant (assuming households have accumulated and can maintain their optimal buffer stocks) until about age 50 when households begin saving for retirement (Carroll and Samwick 1997). Other models, sometimes called *augmented* life-cycle models, have attempted to incorporate the effects of income-maintenance policy on precautionary saving motives (Hubbard, Skinner, and Zeldes 1994, 1995).

Psychological and Sociological Theory

Psychological and sociological theories of saving consider additional determinants of saving and asset accumulation, including personality characteristics, motives, aspirations, expectations, peer and family influences, and the historical influence of wealth as a source of ongoing stratification (Conley 1999; Oliver and Shapiro 1995; Shapiro 2004, 2006; Spilerman 2000). Some of the propositions emphasize the effects of relatively stable personality characteristics on asset building. Other psychological and sociological propositions assume that saving-related preferences and aspirations are not fixed and, in fact, seek to explain how motives, aspirations, and expectations are shaped.

The propositions that emphasize relatively stable personality characteristics typically come from psychology. For example, psychologists have examined the effects of thrift, conscientiousness, emotional stability, autonomy, extraversion, agreeableness, inflexibility, and toughmindedness on saving (e.g., Nyhus and Webley 2001; Wärneryd 1996). The propositions that seek to explain how motives, aspirations, expectations, and even preferences are shaped come from both sociology and psychology. Some scholars have emphasized social norms, suggesting that the norm of "conspicuous consumption" leads people to overspend (and thus to undersave). Some researchers consider the effects of families and peers. Stack (1974) suggests that demands from social network members for money or other material assistance can sabotage efforts to save. And, the literature on financial socialization (e.g., Chiteji and Stafford 1999; Cohen 1994) suggests that social network members can strongly influence an individual's consumption patterns, saving-related beliefs, and aspirations and expectations for saving. For example, a child who knows that her family spends carefully and saves regularly, overhears and perhaps participates in conversations about stock performance, and is encouraged to have her own savings account is expected to be more financially sophisticated and more inclined to save as an adult than an individual raised in a family that does not save and does not make use of a variety of financial products.

Box 4.1. Summary of Neoclassical Economic Theory Related to Saving and Asset Accumulation

Common Assumptions
- Preferences for saving and spending are stable.
- Individuals are forward-thinking; they consider lifetime economic resources and needs when making consumption decisions.
- Individuals have rational expectations regarding lifetime economic resources and needs.
- Individuals want to avoid large fluctuations in consumption; saving, dissaving, and borrowing allow individuals to "smooth" consumption.
- Individuals have perfect information about saving options.
- Individuals have access to perfect credit, saving, and insurance markets.

Key Constructs
- Income
- Consumption
- Age / stage in life cycle
- Incentives / disincentives
- Expectations
- Motives for saving
- Preferences

Explanations for Low Saving and Asset Accumulation
- Households with low incomes have limited resources left over after subsistence requirements are met.
- Young households have negative saving rates because current income is lower than expected lifetime income.
- Asset limits of means-tested transfer programs discourage saving by increasing the cost of asset accumulation.
- Public transfer programs, insurance, and access to credit may discourage saving and asset accumulation by reducing the need for assets.
- Incentives for saving may not increase net saving for two reasons: (1) individuals may finance deposits by withdrawing money from existing assets, and (2) saving incentives decrease the amount of saving needed to finance a given level of future consumption.
- Limited saving and asset accumulation is rational for individuals who do not expect to live long and who do not seek to leave a bequest.
- Some individuals strongly discount future consumption, relative to current consumption.

Other researchers have emphasized the effects of individual experiences. For example, Duesenberry (1949) wrote about personal norms, suggesting that individuals may strive to maintain past consumption levels even when income falls. Economic psychologists (e.g., Furnham 1985; Katona 1975) have proposed that past savings experiences (good and bad) shape individuals' beliefs about their abilities to save in the future. And although not directly linked to savings, some researchers have found evidence of "goal contagion," in that some people pursue the same goals for which they perceive others around them to strive (Aarts, Gollwitzer, and Hassin 2004).

Institutional discrimination and historical inequalities have been precursors to racial differences in wealth (Oliver and Shapiro 1995; Shapiro 2004, 2006). And more generally, differences in household wealth may be a better indicator of a child's life chances, including adult wealth, than other sources of class stratification (Conley 1999; Spilerman 2000). The implication is that these findings represent more than just simply socialization and individual experiences, but rather that inequalities in wealth are self-perpetuating, whether through continuing discrimination or through distinct reference groups and identity formation.

Behavioral Economic Theory

The emerging behavioral theory of saving attempts to explain how people actually behave with regard to financial matters. Unlike neoclassical economic theory, these models do not assume that people are rational and all-knowing. As the title of an article by Thaler (2000) suggests, behavioral theory attempts to explain (and make assumptions that are consistent with) the behavior of *Homo sapiens,* not *Homo economicus.* Behavioral theorists also assume that financial planning has significant nonfinancial costs.

Behavioral theorists have identified a number of common human characteristics that shape financial behavior, including lack of self-control (people tend to place too much weight on current consumption relative to future consumption), limited cognitive abilities (people do not always learn from their mistakes and tend to become overwhelmed by too many choices), inertia (people tend to continue doing what they are currently doing), situation barriers (having to take a bus to the bank, irregular work hours), construal (people respond not to objective experience but to their own construal of that experience), loss aversion (people tend to

---

Box 4.2. Summary of Psychological and Sociological Theory Related to Saving and Asset Accumulation

Key Assumptions
- Economic behavior (e.g., an individual's response to a saving opportunity) is shaped by psychological variables such as personality characteristics, motives, aspirations, and expectations.
- Economic decisions may be influenced by social network members.
- Historical discrimination and barriers to wealth that accumulate over time may sediment and perpetuate economic inequalities.

Key Constructs
- Personality characteristics
- Social and cultural norms related to saving and consumption
- Personal norms related to saving and consumption
- Saving motives and goals
- Expectations of success
- Social network supports and demands
- Discrimination and class stratification

Explanations for Low Saving and Asset Accumulation
- Personality characteristics may cause individuals to choose immediate gratification over future gratification.
- Social norms (e.g., conspicuous consumption) may encourage spending.
- Individuals may strive to maintain past consumption levels even when income falls.
- Individuals may not have salient saving motives.
- Individuals may not attempt to save or accumulate assets because they expect to fail.
- Social networks may discourage saving and asset accumulation by making demands on financial resources.
- Households and communities with little or no wealth historically may find it particularly difficult to initiate savings strategies.

---

feel losses more sharply than gains), the tendency to interpret default options as advice,[1] and the tendency to use mental accounting techniques.[2] Often, according to behavioral theory, these tendencies lead individuals to behave in ways that are inconsistent with their own priorities or inconsistent with maximizing long-term consumption. Also, limited intellectual capabilities and inertia lead people to postpone making financial decisions (Bertrand, Mullainathan, and Shafir 2004, 2006; Thaler 2000; Thaler et al. 1997; Tversky and Kahneman 1991).

If people are aware of these tendencies, they may try to compensate for them. For example, people may attempt to control their spending by imposing "precommitment constraints," such as arranging for direct deposit to saving and investment vehicles. Even if people are naïve about their limitations, saving and investment programs may facilitate saving by deliberately attempting to compensate for these common human characteristics. In fact, behavioral theorists have begun to propose some programmatic reforms and innovations such as simplified investment options and automatic enrollment in 401(k) plans.[3] These program reforms, as we suggest below, are institutional arrangements that will require an institutional theory for knowledge building that can inform policy and program design.

Strengths and Weaknesses of the Existing Theoretical Work

In their current stages of development, none of the existing theories provides a suitable explanation for saving and asset accumulation in low-income households. Neoclassical economic models tend to be specified clearly and tested rigorously, and there is an extensive body of scholarly work. But these models tend to make unrealistic assumptions, such as the assumptions that individuals have near-perfect knowledge and are forward thinking and rational. In reality, the decisions required to optimize consumption (and other financial goals) over the life course are extraordinarily complex (Bernheim and Scholz 1993), and empirical studies suggest that the majority of Americans lack the financial sophistication and information to make even basic economic calculations (Bernheim 1994; Lusardi and Mitchell 2007b). Neoclassical models also assume that saving-related preferences are fixed. The lack of discussion about origins of preferences suggests that preferences are the product of stable personality characteristics. Thus, neoclassical economic models may implicitly "blame" individuals for low rates of saving and asset accumulation, and they may offer no policy pathway for improvement.

Psychological propositions that emphasize personality characteristics also seem to blame individuals and have little to offer in the way of policy implications. Some of the propositions offered by psychologists and sociologists attend to the origins of preferences and aspirations and so are less likely to imply that individuals are solely responsible for limited asset accumulation. Relatively few of these propositions have been tested, however, and still offer little policy guidance.

Box 4.3. Summary of Behavioral Economic Theory Related to Saving and Asset Accumulation

Key Assumptions
- Individuals have imperfect knowledge about financial matters.
- Financial planning has mental costs.
- Individuals tend to be impatient, placing too much weight on present experiences.
- Individuals tend to take the easiest course of action (e.g., prefer the status quo).
- Individuals tend to become overwhelmed by too many choices.
- Wealth is not completely fungible; individuals tend to use mental accounting techniques.
- Individuals feel losses stronger than gains so what they initially have serves as an important reference.

Key Constructs
- Financial knowledge
- Self-control
- Precommitment constraints
- Mental and physical accounting
- Inertia
- Rules of thumb
- Loss aversion

Explanations for Low Saving and Asset Accumulation
- Individuals postpone financial decisions due to lack of knowledge or perceived incompetence.
- Even when they want to save, individuals have trouble resisting spending temptations.
- Individuals are naïve about their own shortsightedness and so do not impose precommitment constraints.
- How individuals perceive saving and investment choices and the way messages are framed or communicated is important (i.e., losing money now vs. gaining money and options later).

Behavioral theory is an important advance. This theory is rooted in neoclassical economic theory and tends to have the theoretical rigor of neoclassical models, but it makes more realistic assumptions about individuals (see box 4.3). These assumptions might be thought of as incorporating psychological variables. Thus, behavioral theory complements and advances psychological as well as economic theories of saving.

The number of empirical studies examining behavioral propositions is growing rapidly. Although these studies largely examine the behavior of middle- and upper-income individuals who are eligible for retirement plans, most of these studies provide support for behavioral theory. And more recent studies are beginning to include low-income households (e.g., Bertrand et al. 2004, 2006). In our opinion, behavioral theory describes most individuals quite accurately. Behavioral theory too often has stopped there, however—with an emphasis on individual deficiencies. Theory could move beyond this focus on individuals to emphasize institutions that can encourage saving and asset accumulation by accounting for, and perhaps even taking advantage of, individual tendencies. The behavioral literature seems to be moving in this direction, and we anticipate a merging of behavioral and institutional theory in the future.

Conceptual Framework for the Determinants of Asset Building

In this section, we begin to develop a conceptual framework to explain saving and asset accumulation in a way that can inform public policy. We begin by presenting the concepts that underlie this framework and proposing a hypothesis related to that concept. We then examine the empirical evidence related to each hypothesis. Concepts considered here include saving and investment action, individual constructs affecting asset accumulation, institutional constructs affecting asset accumulation, and interhousehold sources of asset accumulation through inter vivos transfers and inheritances.

Effects of Saving and Investment Action on Asset Accumulation

We propose that saving action and investment action affect asset accumulation. *Saving action* refers to decisions and behaviors that influence the amount of money or other resources held aside as savings (i.e., not consumed). Saving action includes deposit frequency and deposit amounts. It also includes variables related to dissaving, such as withdrawal frequency and withdrawal amounts, because asset accumulation occurs only when individuals protect their savings (Beverly, McBride,

Figure 4.1. Determinants of Saving and Investment Action and Asset Accumulation

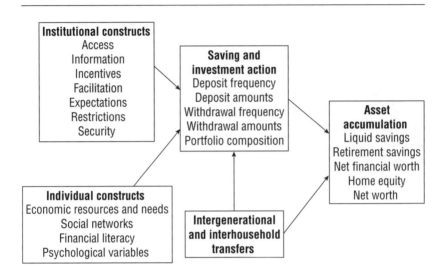

and Schreiner 2003). *Investment action* refers to decisions and behaviors that influence where savings are kept, that is, portfolio composition.

We have in mind simple measures of *asset accumulation,* such as net worth, net financial worth, and levels of liquid savings, home equity, and retirement savings. Our simple propositions regarding the link between saving and investment action and asset accumulation are as follows: (1) deposit patterns affect asset accumulation, (2) withdrawal patterns affect asset accumulation, and (3) portfolio composition affects asset accumulation. The first two propositions are essentially truisms. The third proposition refers, of course, to the fact that some assets have greater returns than others. This proposition is stated very broadly and has nearly universal acceptance in this form. Here, we focus on a more specific and controversial subquestion—whether homeownership increases the asset levels of low-income households. We choose this question because home equity tends to be the primary asset for low-income households with assets and because there are reasons that low-income, minority, and single-mother households might receive below-average, and even negative, rates of return on housing.

Rates of return on housing are strongly influenced by location and timing of purchase and sale. The supply of and demand for housing vary dramatically by neighborhood, and these variations affect prices. In addition, real estate markets tend to be cyclical, and rates of return are strongly influenced by whether home prices were inflated at the time of purchase and sale. Because residential neighborhoods are highly segregated by race and class, location is a particularly salient variable for the subgroups of interest. Put simply, the homes that low-income families can afford to purchase tend to be in "less-desirable" neighborhoods. As a result of racial and ethnic segregation, minorities tend to have access to even fewer neighborhoods. This spatial concentration may weaken housing markets in these areas, resulting in lower returns (Carr and Kutty 2008; Gyourko, Linneman, and Wachter 1999).

Using Panel Study of Income Dynamics (PSID) data, Reid (2004) examines the housing choices and outcomes over a several-year period for about 5,000 renters. She finds that many renters who purchased homes— especially low-income and minority homebuyers—returned to renting in a relatively short time. The financial returns to homeownership were very small for low- and middle-income minorities and low-income whites. Although some low-income and minority homeowners did experience appreciation, Reid concludes that white and middle- and upper-income households were much more likely to benefit financially from homeownership.

Using data on purchase and sale price for homes that were both purchased and sold, Belsky and Duda (2002) compare the returns for individuals purchasing low-cost homes to those for other buyers. They find that returns from the sale of a home were strongly influenced by the timing of the sale and that many people experienced losses when real estate transaction costs were considered. Those who purchased low-cost homes, however, were more likely to sell at a profit during market upswings and less likely to suffer losses when selling during market downturns. This study is limited to four metropolitan areas and examines repeat sales of short-term owners. It is not clear whether these authors consider the (forgone) cost of rental payments when computing return on the sale of a home.

Evidence clearly indicates that market conditions have a strong effect on rates of return on owner-occupied housing. Beyond this, however, it is difficult to draw a clear conclusion from the literature. To accurately compute the rate of return to homeownership, one might want to consider not only the difference between purchase price and selling price but also real estate transaction costs, forgone earnings from alternative investments, maintenance costs (in comparison to maintenance costs

---

Box 4.4. Summary of Institutional Theory Related to Saving and
Asset Accumulation

Key Assumptions
- Institutions shape saving preferences, saving action, investment choices, and
  saving and asset outcomes.

Key Constructs
- Access
- Information
- Incentives
- Facilitation
- Expectations
- Restrictions
- Security

Explanations for Low Saving and Asset Accumulation
- Certain subpopulations (e.g., low-income and minority households) have limited access to institutional supports for saving and asset accumulation.
- Certain subpopulations (e.g., current and potential recipients of public welfare
  programs with asset limits) face saving disincentives.

---

incurred by renters) (Belsky and Calder 2004), and even forgone rental
assistance. Existing studies vary in their coverage of these factors, and this
at least partly explains mixed findings. Learning more about rates of
return for low-income and minority homebuyers—and finding ways to
help potential homebuyers make informed choices—are important
research objectives because home equity is the primary asset for many
low-income and minority households.

Effects of Individual Constructs on Saving and Investment Action

We turn now to several individual constructs expected to shape saving
and investment action: economic resources and needs, informal social
support, financial literacy, and psychological variables.

Economic Resources and Needs

There is reason to believe that economic resources and needs are important predictors of saving and investment action. By definition, low-income

individuals have limited financial in-flows, so they have less "extra" money to save. It is also difficult for low-income individuals to finance saving by reducing consumption when consumption is near subsistence level. At the most fundamental level, therefore, low income is a persistent obstacle to saving. The large body of evidence showing that low-income families have less wealth than middle- and upper-income families provides strong indirect support for the hypothesis that economic constraints shape saving action, but to our knowledge, few studies have directly tested the hypothesis (probably because this relationship is viewed as a truism). Some specific expenses, however, such as medical expenses, vehicle expenses, and debt payments, probably depress saving in many low-income households.

Medical expenses. Families without health insurance may incur large health expenses, especially when a family member has a chronic condition or experiences a serious acute illness or injury. Quantitative evidence directly linking these expenses to saving outcomes is quite limited. Based on data from 1,855 participants of an individual development account (IDA) program, an asset-building program for low-income households, Banov (2005) examines the effects of medical debt (whether or not an individual has overdue medical payments) on program outcomes. He found that the average monthly IDA deposit (net of unmatched withdrawals) for those with medical debt is about $3.50 (19 percent) less than the average monthly deposit for those without medical debt. And, those with medical debt are about 5 percentage points more likely to drop out of the IDA program (39 percent versus 34 percent). One important limitation of this study is that the dataset does not include indicators of health status, so medical debt may be a proxy for poor health status.

Lack of health insurance also increases the cost of health care and detracts from saving. Banov (2005) finds that health insurance is significantly and positively related to average monthly net deposits and to gross deposits. This suggests that holding health insurance contributes to a family's ability to save. These findings are somewhat difficult to interpret, however, because there is no indicator of out-of-pocket medical expenses, and we cannot assume that people with insurance have low out-of-pocket expenses. (Some insured individuals pay high premiums, for example.)

Vehicle costs. A second potential obstacle to saving is expenses incurred when vehicles break down. Empirical evidence regarding the magnitude of these expenses is difficult to find, but it is common knowledge that low-income families tend to drive older, more problem-prone vehicles. We suspect that annual expenses related to vehicle breakdown are smaller than the other expenses discussed here, but they are mentioned fairly frequently in qualitative studies of low-income families (Finn, Zorita, and Coulton 1994; Hogan et al. 2004; Sherraden et al. 2005), perhaps because they are irregular and somewhat unpredictable and families do not budget for them.

Debt load. The third financial obstacle to saving is partly related to these other two—monthly debt payments, including payments for credit card debt and medical debt. One indicator of problematic debt burden is having total debt payments greater than 40 percent of income. According to data from the Survey of Consumer Finances (SCF), 27 percent of families in the lowest quintile of annual income met this criterion in 2001. This was 2.5 times higher than the figure for all families in the United States (11 percent) (Aizcorbe, Kennickell, and Moore 2003). Another indicator of debt repayment problems is making late debt payments. Data from the 2001 SCF show that 13 percent of debtors in the lowest income quintile were 60 or more days late with at least one loan payment in the previous year, a slight increase from 1998. In the overall population, 7 percent of families were late in making debt payments (Aizcorbe et al. 2003). Debt loads may be particularly problematic for today's young adults (Draut 2006, 2008).

These findings suggest that many low-income households are overburdened with debt. It may be in a household's best interest to pay down debt before attempting to accumulate savings. Reducing debt increases net worth, but debt obligations can nonetheless depress saving, including deposits to incentivized accounts. Although there is little quantitative evidence, one qualitative study found that low-income individuals attribute their difficulty in saving and maintaining assets to burdensome debt payments (Edin 2001).

Informal Social Support

The second individual construct identified here is informal support from social network members—the degree to which social network members encourage or hinder efforts to save and maintain assets. We posit that informal social support affects saving action. For example, encouragement, positive reinforcement, and reminders to save are likely to send the message that saving is desirable and to make saving easier. We also hypothesize that social network members may discourage saving by sending the message that "extra" income should be shared with others.

This second hypothesis flows from a groundbreaking ethnographic study by Stack (1974) showing that frequent demands from social network members make it difficult for blacks to accumulate assets. For cultural reasons, the pressure to share savings with others may be stronger for black families than for white families.[4] The pressure may also be stronger for low-income families of any race, who are more likely than middle- and upper-income families to have social network members who are struggling to meet basic expenses.

In addition to Stack's work cited above, two recent qualitative studies support the hypothesis that network members impede the saving efforts of an individual. In a qualitative study of 30 Hispanic and black families in San Jose, California, and rural Mississippi, Caskey (1997) reports findings similar to Stack's (1974)—some interviewees said they did not save because others would insist they share their savings.[5] In quantitative, multivariate studies, Chiteji and Hamilton (2005) and Heflin and Patillo (2002, 2006) find that families are less likely to have bank accounts when they have poor siblings and parents. Heflin and Patillo also find that these kin characteristics decrease the likelihood of homeownership for whites but not for blacks. And blacks are more likely to have poor siblings and cross-class relationships that are less beneficial (Heflin and Patillo 2006). Chiteji and Hamilton find that poverty in extended families decreases the likelihood of stock owner- ship. Lombe and Ssewamala (2007) find an increase in the amount of help respondents give community members is inversely related to per- formance in an IDA program. All of this research concludes that poverty in the extended family and informal networks can constrain asset accumulation.

There is even less empirical evidence related to the hypothesis that informal support increases saving. One qualitative study of 25 IDA par- ticipants in Minnesota finds that support from family, friends, and com- munity organizations during times of crisis is an important facilitator of saving. In-depth interviews with IDA participants in the American Dream Demonstration (ADD) also suggest that encouragement and saving reminders from IDA staff help people save (Sherraden et al. 2005).

Financial Literacy

Our third individual construct is financial literacy, including both knowl- edge and skills. We hypothesize that financial literacy affects saving and investment action. It seems common sense that people will save more and make better investment decisions when they know how much money is needed to achieve a certain goal, understand compound interest, know how to create a budget, and so forth. In fact, the belief that financial literacy affects saving and investment is the fundamental premise of financial education initiatives.

Empirical studies on this topic are, however, rare. Using nationally representative data from the SCF, Hilgert, Hogarth, and Beverly (2003) find a positive association between overall financial knowledge and following recommended financial practices. They also find positive associations between specific types of financial knowledge and specific types of financial behavior. For example, those who scored high on knowledge of credit management also tended to follow recommended credit-management practices. This study relies on self-reported data regarding financial behavior, however, and does not consider the possibility that financial behavior may affect financial knowledge. Another study uses two-stage least squares regression to control for reverse causality and finds that financial knowledge is positively associated with retirement savings (Kotlikoff and Bernheim 2001). The measure of financial knowledge used may not be a particularly valid indicator of *practical* financial knowledge, however.[6] This study also relies on self-reported financial data.

While more evidence is needed to verify that increasing financial literacy leads to greater saving and smarter investment choices, it is certainly likely that those who lack basic financial knowledge and skills will have more trouble finding and using appropriate saving and investment vehicles. Americans in general are not very educated about financial matters, and evidence shows that low-income people are especially likely to score poorly on "tests" of financial knowledge (Bernheim 1998; Brobeck 2002; Consumer Federation of America 1990). In one study of over 600 low-income people (Anderson, Zhan, and Scott 2004), the average participant answered only 56 percent of the 41 financial knowledge questions correctly. Knowledge of saving and investment strategies was especially low. For example, only 48 percent understood that "investments" are usually riskier than savings accounts. Within older populations, those who plan for retirement have higher amounts of wealth, and these planners exhibit higher levels of financial literacy (Lusardi and Mitchell 2007a).

Few studies have examined the financial literacy of single parents in particular. Because they tend to have less income and wealth and because their households may have less access to financial education, single parents may have less financial knowledge, on average. Conversely, at least one study of participants in a financial management program for low-income people (90 percent women) finds that single parents have *greater* financial knowledge than married participants (Zhan, Anderson, and Scott 2006). This may indicate, consistent with qualitative evidence in Sherraden and others (2005), that married women rely more on their husbands in financial matters, while single women make many financial decisions by themselves.

Psychological Variables

Economists and others have long assumed that personality characteristics and attitudinal variables affect saving and asset accumulation. Here, we hypothesize that three psychological variables—future orientation, motives for saving, and perceived ability to save—affect saving and investment action. We do not claim that that these are the only important psychological variables or even the most important ones, but we offer these hypotheses to illustrate how psychology might affect asset building.

Future orientation. Future orientation can be defined as a willingness to invest in one's future, even when one must postpone pleasure. The rapidly growing literature in behavioral economics assumes or suggests that *many, if not most, people* have trouble postponing pleasant experiences. One implication, of course, is that people have trouble saving because saving requires them to postpone consumption, and numerous theoretical articles have suggested that self-control problems lead to under-saving (Laibson 1997; O'Donoghue and Rabin 1999; Strotz 1956). Consistent with this literature (and common sense), we hypothesize that future orientation shapes saving action, that is, "patient" people deposit more and withdraw less.[7]

Frederick, Loewenstein, and O'Donoghue's (2003) review of estimates of time preference, another term for future orientation, imply that $100 today is more valuable to most people than $150 in one year. At the same time, a key assumption of behavioral theory is that many individuals lack the self-control to reduce current consumption in favor of future consumption. Still, to our knowledge, very few studies attempt to document the prevalence of self-control problems quantitatively. One exception is a study by Ameriks and others (2004). This study's multivariate analysis shows that underconsumption is associated with higher net worth, and overconsumption is associated with lower net worth. The authors argue that this second finding is unlikely to be an artifact of the high levels of education in the sample, but more empirical research would be useful. In addition to this quantitative study, a few qualitative studies provide evidence that individuals—with both low incomes and high incomes—believe that they have trouble postponing consumption (Beverly, Romich, and Tescher 2003; Caskey 1997; Kennickell, Starr-McCluer, and Sunden 1997; Romich and Weisner 2000).

Motives for saving. The notion of saving motives encompasses two phenomena: how important saving is to an individual and the goal or purpose of savings. We hypothesize that those with salient and specific saving motives are more likely to save. Neoclassical economists typically emphasize four motives for saving: (1) maintaining consumption during retirement, (2) preparing for income shocks and other emergencies (precautionary saving), (3) transferring wealth to future generations (bequest motive), and (4) purchasing "big-ticket" items such as consumer durables, education, or a vacation (target saving). The first three are expected to influence long-term saving and the fourth to affect short- to medium-term saving and dissaving (Sturm 1983). Simple descriptive evidence from the 2001 SCF shows that retirement and precautionary motives are the most common motives, followed by education and other types of target saving (Aizcorbe et al. 2003, table 2).

In recent years, economists have given special attention to the role of precautionary saving in asset accumulation. Using the PSID, Carroll and Samwick (1997) find that U.S. households overall save mostly for precautionary reasons until about age 50. Of course, income uncertainty is higher for the poor, so—all else constant—they have an extra-strong precautionary motive. But if precautionary savings matter so much to the poor, why do they have low or no wealth? Simulated outcomes from the model in Hubbard and others (1995) "can replicate observed patterns in household wealth accumulation after accounting explicitly for precautionary saving and asset-based, means-tested social insurance" (360). In particular, their model suggests that holding low (or no) wealth can make sense for low-educated, low-income households because they face a 100 percent tax on savings from asset limits, should their uncertain incomes fall so low that they qualify for asset-tested public assistance.

Perceived ability to save. In addition to future orientation and motives for saving, aspirations and expectations of success are likely to affect saving action. We posit that those who expect saving attempts to be successful are more likely to save (e.g., more likely to deposit, more likely to enroll in saving programs, and so forth). Conversely, those who expect their saving attempts to be "unsuccessful" are less likely to save.

In part, individual saving-related aspirations and expectations are likely to be determined by past experiences, including past asset-accumulation experiences. According to aspirations theory (Lewin et al. 1944), an individual's aspirations are raised (or lowered) according to her success (or failure) in achieving them. Applying this proposition to economic behavior, Katona (1975) suggests that an individual who makes progress toward a savings goal is more likely to raise that goal. Conversely, those whose saving attempts are unsuccessful are likely to lower their saving aspirations. The experiences of social network members may also be important. If an individual has rarely seen someone else achieve a savings goal, she may not believe that she can be successful.

Research has rarely examined these hypotheses directly. In-depth interviews with IDA participants provide some evidence that successes with saving make people feel more confident in their ability to save and increase their intentions to save (Sherraden et al. 2005). In the only quantitative study that we know of, Moore and others (2001) find that perceived inability to save is negatively related to saving in IDAs, but the relationship is not statistically significant ($p = 0.17$). A related variable, the perception that "saving takes too long" is also statistically insignificant ($p = 0.43$). The sample for this regression is relatively small ($N = 166$) and excludes people who had dropped out of IDA programs. If those who dropped out were those who felt the least able to save (as one would expect), the study may underestimate the effects of perceived inability to save.

Effects of Institutional Constructs on Saving and Investment Action

We turn now to seven constructs that we believe are important aspects of institutions designed to promote saving and asset accumulation. The constructs are (1) access, (2) information, (3) incentives and disincentives, (4) facilitation, (5) expectations, (6) restrictions, and (7) security (Beverly and Sherraden 1999; Sherraden et al. 2005; Sherraden and Barr 2005). These seven constructs have emerged from research on IDAs, matched savings accounts for low-income people. As box 4.4 shows, we emphasize effects of these constructs on *saving and investment action*. In other words, we suggest that the effects of institutional constructs on *asset accumulation* are largely indirect, through saving and investment action. There are important exceptions. For example, incentives and security almost certainly have strong direct effects on asset accumulation, perhaps moderating the relationship between portfolio choices and asset accumulation. To keep the framework simple, however, we focus here on the effects of institutional constructs on saving and investment action.

Access

We hypothesize that access affects saving and investment action. Access refers to eligibility and practicality. As discussed below, many households are not "eligible" for programs and policies that encourage asset building—for example, a large portion of the population does not have access to a pension plan in the workplace—and eligibility varies substantially by race and class. Regarding practicality, distance is a major barrier to financial services and other markets in rural areas. Even though markets may exist at a distance, transaction costs in reaching them can make them unavailable. In these circumstances, it is not fully informative to interpret saving and asset-accumulation outcomes as resulting solely from individual characteristics and choices.

The hypothesis that access (eligibility and practicality) affects saving and investment action seems to be common sense but is difficult to test. In studies, "access" is almost inevitably combined with the other institutional constructs. To our knowledge, no study has attempted to identify the effects of access separate from the effects of other institutional characteristics. This may be an important task for future research.

Information

We posit that financial information shapes saving and investment action. This information may be general or specific to a particular financial product or program. For example, to participate successfully in a traditional IRA, a person must know that an IRA is available and that she is eligible. She must also know how to choose an appropriate investment, how to make contributions, how to receive the tax deduction, and, later, how to make withdrawals. Some individuals (probably those who are more educated and more comfortable with financial matters) will seek out this type of information, but many will not obtain information unless it is delivered to them in an accessible format.

The hypothesis that information shapes saving and investment action is, to some extent, a truism: without information about a particular product or program, an individual cannot purchase it or participate in it. Beyond this, however, whether or not information affects financial behavior is an empirical question. Almost all of the related empirical studies examine the effects of financial education (one method of providing financial information) on financial outcomes. One exception is a study that examines the effects of financial communication (e.g., paper and web-based education materials, projection tools, and plan statements) on 401(k) participation and contribution decisions of employees in 26 firms (Nyce 2005). The findings suggest that financial communication, especially web based, has large positive effects on participation and contribution and that the effects may be strongest for low earners. An important strength of this study is the use of administrative data. However, the measures of financial communication are fairly crude,[8] and the study examines participation in just a single saving product. More research on the effects of financial communication is needed.

The remaining studies described here examine financial education. Many of these studies have an important limitation: data on outcomes come from participants' self-report. In order to please research or program personnel, participants may exaggerate their savings or their adherence to recommended financial practices, or they may make "honest" mistakes due to faulty recall.[9] Many existing studies are also subject to selection bias: when financial education is voluntary, those who choose to attend are probably more motivated than others to increase their financial literacy and financial well-being (Caskey 2001), or attendees may seek out financial information because they already have substantial assets (Lusardi 2002).

For many adults in the United States, employers are an important source of information related to retirement saving. A few studies suggest that employer-sponsored financial education seminars increase pension-plan participation rates and contributions. For example, Bayer, Bernheim, and Scholz (1996) find that more frequent corporate-sponsored retirement seminars are associated with both higher participation and higher levels of contributions to 401(k) plans. Similarly, Bernheim and Garrett (2003) find that employees who work for companies that offer financial education are more likely to participate in pension plans and tend to have greater wealth. The effects on wealth are especially strong for those with little wealth. Lusardi (2002) also finds that employer-sponsored retirement seminars have large effects on wealth in low-wealth and low-education samples. All three of these studies rely on self-reports of financial behavior and wealth. In a randomized experiment at a large university, those offered monetary incentives to attend a benefits training seminar were more likely to attend, and subsequently, persons in their department were more likely to have enrolled in a tax-deferred retirement account plan several months later (Duflo and Saez 2003).

Some studies examine the effects of financial education that is specifically targeted to low-income households. A study by Hirad and Zorn (2002) evaluates the effects of prepurchase homeownership counseling and finds that counseling, especially individual and classroom counseling, is associated with a large reduction in the risk of 90-day mortgage delinquency. When using a statistical strategy to control for selection bias, the researchers confirm that counseling (broadly defined) and classroom counseling, in particular, significantly reduce delinquency rates. The effects of individual counseling become insignificant, however. In research on IDAs using ADD data, Clancy, Grinstein-Weiss, and Schreiner (2001) find that up to 12 hours of general financial education is associated with large increases in net IDA savings, but selection bias is a potential problem because the most motivated savers may have completed more financial education.

Finally, a few studies look not at specific financial education programs but at state curriculum mandates related to financial education in public schools.[10] There is evidence that curriculum mandates, especially mandates requiring coverage of personal finance in a specific course, increase financial knowledge and saving rates. For example, Tennyson and Nguyen (2001) use data on 1,600 high school students in 31 states to examine whether state curriculum mandates predict students' scores on a 31-item test of financial knowledge. Controlling for other characteristics of the state, school size, and several individual characteristics, they find that students in states that required coverage of personal finance in a specific course scored significantly higher. Using data from a 1995 survey of about 2,000 respondents between the ages of 30 and 49, Bernheim, Garrett, and Maki (2001) find evidence that curriculum mandates related to coverage of personal finance during high school increase self-reported saving rates in adulthood. These studies are probably not subject to selection bias because students did not choose to be exposed to financial education.

However, it is impossible to assess the accuracy of the self-reported saving rates used by Bernheim and others.

In sum, there is a fair amount of evidence that financial education improves financial outcomes, but more rigorous research is needed (Caskey 2006). Of particular interest are studies that minimize selection bias and examine financial outcomes that may be objectively verified. If additional research confirms that financial information can shape financial behavior, it will be important to determine whether low-income, minority, and single-mother households have access to appropriate financial information. Few studies have examined this question, but there are reasons for concern. Due to job instability and concentration in the low-wage service sector, these subpopulations probably have less access than others to employer-sponsored financial information. Those who did not complete high school are also less likely to have received school-based financial education.

Incentives and Disincentives

We propose that incentives and disincentives shape saving and investment action. Incentives come in at least three forms: nonfinancial rewards, subsidies, and rates of return. Nonfinancial rewards may include peer relationships, status, or opportunities to learn. We focus here on financial incentives because we suspect that, overall, financial incentives tend to be more important than nonfinancial incentives.

Subsidies. Subsidies are direct or indirect "payments" to those who save in particular saving plans or hold particular kinds of wealth. Often these subsidies directly increase wealth, as in the case of matching contributions for deposits into 401(k)s and IDAs (unless people save less in other forms to offset these subsidies). Other times, these subsidies are not deposited into saving vehicles, so recipients may choose whether or not to save them. For example, tax benefits associated with homeownership and IRA contributions reduce tax liability but do not directly increase home equity or IRA savings. Schreiner and Sherraden (2007) argue that matches in IDAs may encourage saving by low-income people for at least three reasons. First, of course, matches increase the reward to saving and may help compensate for the sacrifice required to defer consumption. Second, matches may motivate people to save by translating a given level of saving into a stock of wealth that is large enough to use for a major asset, such as a house or a college education. Third, the match may be the program feature that catches a participant's eye and motivates him to enroll in the first place.

A large number of studies examine the effects of matching contributions, but the evidence is mixed. In perhaps the only randomized experiment designed to test match rates, Duflo and others (2005, 2006) examine the effects of matching contributions on IRA participation and contributions. Over 14,000 H&R Block clients in St. Louis were randomly assigned to one of three groups and then invited to deposit portions of their tax refunds into Express IRAs. One group was eligible for a 20 percent match (on contributions up to $1,000), one group was eligible for a 50 percent match, and the control group received no match. Take-up rates were 17 percent for the 50 percent match group, 10 percent for the 20 percent match group, and 3 percent for the control group. For those who contributed, average contribution levels (excluding the match) were $1,310, $1,280, and $860, respectively. Although there is an important competing hypothesis—because there is evidence that tax professionals had a large influence on whether individuals chose to contribute to the Express IRA—the authors conclude that match rates affected both IRA participation and contributions.

Most of the other evidence on the effects of match rates comes from research on defined contribution pension plans and IDAs. Evidence suggests that the existence of a match increases *participation* and that higher match rates are associated with higher participation. For example, Nyce (2005) examines administrative data on 401(k) participation for over 300,000 employees in 48 firms. In descriptive analysis, he finds that participation rates are higher in firms that have a match than in firms that do not and that participation increases as the match rate increases. Multivariate analysis also suggests that participation rises with the match rate (Kempson, McKay, and Collard 2005; Sherraden et al. 2005).

Evidence on 401(k) participation strongly suggests that the existence of a match (regardless of the match rate) increases the amount of *contributions* (Schreiner and Sherraden 2007). Evidence about the effect of match rate on contributions is mixed, however. Examining this relationship is complicated because programs that offer matches almost always have match caps (i.e., the maximum match allowed for saving), and programs that provide high match rates tend to have low match caps (Schreiner and Sherraden 2007). When match caps exist, data on contributions are "censored" at the match cap, because some people want to make contributions beyond the match cap but are not allowed.

In their examination of match rates using ADD data, Schreiner and Sherraden (2007) conclude (1) that higher match rates "improved inclusion by making more participants 'savers,' " and (2) that many ADD participants were saving for fixed goals (and so saved less when eligible for larger matches because they could reach their goals with lower levels of saving). The analysis also reveals that higher match rates increased asset accumulation per participant when *both* effects of match rates are considered (the positive effect of higher match rates on "inclusion" and the negative effect of higher match rates on net contributions for "savers").

Although incentives may cause people to save more by increasing the reward for saving, they may also encourage people to save less because match money allows them to reach a fixed savings goal with less of their own saving. In addition, people may simply reshuffle assets, that is, move existing assets from another savings vehicle into the match-eligible product instead of saving more. Low-income households, however, are probably less likely than others to reshuffle because they are less likely to have assets to reshuffle. Empirical analysis simulating the effects of private pension plans suggests that pensions do not offset personal saving among less-educated (and presumably lower-income) workers (Bernheim and Scholz 1993). Using ADD data to examine the sources of IDA deposits, Schreiner and others (2001) observe that many IDA participants had no or very low liquid assets at enrollment and that most had too few liquid assets to fund all of their IDA deposits. Based partly on these observations, Schreiner and others conclude that IDAs come from some mix of new savings and shifted assets, but they emphasize that ADD data do not allow them to quantify or even rank these two sources. Findings from a cross-sectional survey of about 300 IDA participants (Moore et al. 2001) are consistent with the conclusion that IDA deposits are a mix of new savings and reshuffled assets (for details, please refer to chapter 5).

Rates of return. Rates of return are also incentives. The fact that investors seek the highest possible rate of return for a given level of risk provides some evidence that financial incentives shape financial decisions. To consider this proposition more carefully, however, one must ask whether incentives affect (1) participation in a particular saving plan or program, (2) levels of contribution to the plan or program, and (3) overall (net) saving. The effect of financial incentives on net saving is the subject of much debate. According to economic theory, an increase in the rate of return will not necessarily increase saving for two reasons. First, changes in the rate of return on savings may simply result in the "reshuffling" of the form of assets with no new saving. Second, for net savers, an increase in the after-tax rate of return has two contradictory effects. Individuals may choose to save more because the price of current consumption increases relative to the price of future consumption (the substitution effect). On the other hand, with higher rates of return, individuals can save less and still enjoy the same amount of future consumption (the "fixed-goal effect," according to Schreiner and Sherraden [2007]).

Common *disincentives* for saving are unattractive or even negative rates of return, often due to inflation, high fees, or investment risk. We have already mentioned reasons that low-income, minority, and single-mother households might receive lower rates of return on owner-occupied housing. Other types of disincentives reduce the need for or even the desirability of assets. Means-tested income transfer programs, such as Temporary Assistance for Needy Families, Food Stamps, and Supplemental Security Income, are expected to create saving disincentives for two reasons: (1) they provide a certain level of income at the time of economic emergencies, and (2) they have restrictive asset means tests (Hubbard et al. 1995; Ziliak 2003).

The first phenomenon is often called the "consumption-floor effect." Income transfer programs create consumption floors because they guarantee a minimum level of income (to some). These consumption floors are expected to reduce the precautionary saving motive (the perceived need to save in preparation for sudden economic losses) and are, therefore, expected to lower saving rates in general. Asset means tests are expected to discourage the accumulation of financial assets because households must spend down or keep their financial assets below asset limits in order to be eligible for transfer benefits. Presumably, asset means tests affect those who are *likely* to participate in these programs as well as those who are currently receiving benefits (Hubbard et al. 1995; Neumark and Powers 1998).

These disincentives, then, are relevant to low-income households (by definition the only households eligible for these programs) and to minority and single-mother households (because they are more likely than non-Hispanic whites and married couples to participate in these programs). Recent studies examining increases in asset limits associated with welfare reform, however, show some inconsistent results. Therefore, it is not yet clear whether loosening asset restrictions will increase saving by low-income households (Hurst and Ziliak 2006; McKernan, Ratcliffe, and Nam 2007; Nam 2008; Sullivan 2006). (For details, please refer to chapter 5 in this book.)

In sum, with regard to saving *incentives,* there is some evidence that matches increase participation in saving programs and even more evidence that matches increase contributions to these programs. Evidence is mixed regarding the effect of matches or other incentives on net saving (across all saving vehicles); contributions to incentivized saving programs are probably a mix of new savings and shifted assets. With regard to *disincentives,* evidence suggests that income transfer programs reduce asset accumulation by low-income households due to the consumption floor and due to their restrictive asset means tests. Regarding the effects of recent increases in welfare asset limits, existing studies provide mixed evidence.

Facilitation

We posit that facilitation shapes saving and investment action. Facilitation refers to any form of assistance in saving, especially making saving "automatic." Common examples are automatic payroll deduction and automatic transfers into saving products. Usually, people must arrange for automatic transfers, but after signing up they no longer have to make conscious decisions to save. Like other researchers (Beverly, McBride, et al. 2003; Maital and Maital 1994; Shefrin and Thaler 1988), we posit that these "precommitment constraints" increase deposits because funds for saving are never "in hand" and are therefore much less likely to trigger spending temptations.

Another type of facilitation involves automatic enrollment into a savings plan. For example, employees in a particular firm might be automatically enrolled in the company's 401(k) plan with a default investment option, unless they actively opt out or choose a different investment option. (These plans are often called "opt-out" plans.) Automatic enrollment is likely to shape saving and investment action because, as behavioral theory suggests, people often postpone financial decisions and remain with the status quo.

A third and perhaps surprising source of facilitation is the federal income tax system. Many households—especially low- and moderate-income households—receive sizeable federal tax refunds. Building on the notion of mental accounting, Thaler and others have argued that people are more likely to save "irregular" income than regular wage and salary income, especially when the irregular in-flows are large (see Shefrin and Thaler 1992; Thaler 1990). This proposition implies that people are more likely to save out of tax refunds than out of wage and salary income, especially when refunds are large. Thus, by providing sizeable refunds to many households (through the earned income tax credit and child tax credit, for example), the income tax system may shape saving action.

Effects of precommitment constraints. In in-depth interviews, IDA participants commonly stated that direct deposit helped them save (Sherraden et al. 2005). Much more rigorous evidence that precommitment constraints increase deposits comes from a test of the Save More Tomorrow plan (SMarT) (Thaler and Benartzi 2004). In this study, 286 workers in a mid-sized manufacturing firm (out of 315 eligible workers) agreed to meet with an investment consultant hired by the firm to discuss saving in the company pension plan. Of these, 79 immediately agreed to increase their contributions to the pension plan. The remaining 207 were invited to enroll in the SMarT plan, which allowed workers to precommit to automatically save their 3 percent annual raises in the company pension plan. More than three-fourths—162 employees—enrolled in the SMarT plan. After four annual pay raises, these employees had increased their average saving rates from 3.5 percent to 13.6 percent of income. Those who had immediately agreed to increase their contributions to the pension plan—but who did not arrange for automatic annual saving increases— had increased their saving rates only from 4.4 percent to 8.8 percent.

Effects of automatic enrollment. Another rigorous study provides evidence that automatic enrollment affects saving and investment action. Madrian and Shea (2000) examine 401(k) participation and contribution rates in a company that began automatically enrolling employees in their 401(k) plan. Before the change, employees had to sign up to participate in the 401(k) plan. After the change, employees had to actively opt out of the plan if they did not want to participate. Although none of the economic features of the plan changed, participation was significantly higher under automatic enrollment. Participants were also likely to stay with the default contribution rate and fund allocation.

Effects of the federal income tax system. There is some evidence that the federal income tax system facilitates saving and asset purchases. Three studies provide quantitative but largely indirect evidence. Using multivariate analysis and a nationally representative sample of consumer units from the Consumer Expenditure Survey, Barrow and McGranahan (2000) find an increase in expenditures on durable goods among earned income tax credit (EITC) recipients in February, the modal month of refund receipt. Similarly, data from ADD show that net IDA deposits increase substantially in tax season (Schreiner and Sherraden 2007). In a survey of 650 Chicago households expecting to receive a federal refund and EITC benefits, Smeeding, Phillips, and O'Connor (2000) find that 50 percent of respondents plan to save at least a portion of the tax refunds. Actual behavior may differ from planned behavior, of course, so quantitative data on actual refund use would be more informative.

At least three qualitative studies provide additional evidence that federal refunds are used to purchase and maintain assets (in addition to purchasing goods and services for immediate consumption, paying bills, and paying down debt). In in-depth interviews with almost 200 low-income single mothers in Chicago and Charleston, South Carolina, Edin (2001) finds that some mothers use refunds to make property tax and insurance payments, to finance car expenses, and even to make down payments on homes. In in-depth interviews with a random sample of 42 participants in New Hope, a demonstration program for low-income working adults, Romich and Weisner (2000) find that some of their respondents use refunds to buy appliances and furniture, repair cars, or make down payments on cars and homes.

Finally, some scholars have argued that people *deliberately* use the income tax system as a kind of saving plan. Millions of households withhold more than the taxes they owe. More evidence is needed to determine whether this is because they want a lump-sum refund and are willing to forgo earnings on the money to receive one (Neumark 1995), whether they overwithhold to avoid the penalties of underwithholding (Highfill, Thorson, and Weber 1998), or whether they overwithhold inadvertently. To our knowledge, the only empirical evidence on this question comes from three small qualitative studies (Edin 2001; Olson and Davis 1994; Romich and Weisner 2000), showing that some low-income households choose not to receive the EITC in advance so that they can accumulate a lump sum for special purposes.

Expectations

Expectations are implicit or explicit suggestions about desired saving, investment, or asset accumulation. They are embodied in institutional features such as match caps (amount of money that earns matching deposits), saving targets, and social pressure of peers and staff of saving programs.

For example, the fact that up to $4,000 in contributions to a traditional IRA is tax deductible may set up an expectation that individuals save $4,000 a year for retirement. We hypothesize that people respond to these implicit and explicit expectations, that expectations shape saving and investment action.

A small but growing body of research supports our hypothesis that expectations shape saving action. Milligan (2003) finds that a one dollar increase in the match cap in the Canadian Registered Retirement Savings Plan is associated with a 50 cent increase in saving. In ADD research, Schreiner and Sherraden (2007) find that a one dollar increase in the IDA match cap is associated with a 57 cent increase in net IDA savings. Both of these studies control for censoring at the match cap. Also in ADD, a number of in-depth interviewees said that they saved more or saved more regularly because they were expected to deposit a specific amount each month. There is also evidence that IDA participants viewed the match cap as a savings goal (Sherraden et al. 2005). On the other hand, very few eligible individuals maximize an IRA deduction or a 401(k) match, and this suggests that many people do *not* view caps as expectations— or are unable or unwilling to conform to these expectations.

Restrictions

Restrictions are prohibitions, rules that restrict access to or use of assets. Most subsidized saving policies have restrictions. For example, money in 529 college savings plans must be used for college education, and 401(k) savings are not available until retirement.[11] We hypothesize that restrictions shape saving action, specifically by helping people resist temptations to spend savings. This hypothesis is consistent with a growing literature in behavioral economics about self-control problems and the tendency to overspend (Laibson 1997; Thaler 1994; Thaler and Shefrin 1981). In addition, the fact that people deposit money in simple restricted accounts (such as Christmas Club accounts) that do not provide higher interest rates than basic savings accounts suggests that some people believe restrictions help them accumulate savings.

IDA participants have said that they like the restrictions on IDA withdrawals (Moore et al. 2001; Sherraden et al. 2005).[12] In in-depth interviews with about 30 participants in a matched saving program for low-income individuals in England, Kempson and others (2005) find that a majority liked the fact that they could not access their savings immediately.[13] Most of these individuals said, however, that they would *not* favor restrictions on the use of their money. Low participation rates in IRAs, 401(k)s, 529 plans, and other restricted saving vehicles probably indicate that a substantial proportion of American households are not comfortable with restrictions, at least as currently structured and as currently bundled with other institutional characteristics. More research is needed to determine what types of restrictions people are willing to accept.

In one of the few rigorous studies of the effects of restrictions, Ashraf, Karlan, and Yin (2006) randomly assigned current clients at a small rural bank in the Philippines to one of three groups. One group was invited to open an account with strong withdrawal restrictions. One group was encouraged to save using existing bank products but was not offered the new product. The control group received no further contact. The fact that 28 percent (about 200) of those who were eligible chose to open the restricted account, even though they were not compensated with higher interest rates, provides evidence that some people believe restrictions help them save. Additional evidence suggests that the restricted account increased savings. Over time, those who were eligible for the account increased their bank account balances more than those in the other groups, and this savings did not appear to have been moved from other accounts in the same bank. The increased savings is small in nominal terms but substantial as a percentage of prior formal savings.

Security

Security refers to freedom from unreasonable risk in saving and asset holding. All households need a safe place to put their money. We propose that security shapes saving and investment action, specifically that people are more likely to deposit, less likely to withdraw, and more likely to have a diverse portfolio when they can participate in a variety of secure saving policies, programs, and products. Security can be considered at two levels: micro and macro. Micro security refers to protection from risks of lost assets for a particular household and in the shorter term. Macro security refers to protection from risks for the political economy as a whole and in the longer term.

Micro security includes both risk of property loss and investment risk. Property-loss risk refers to threats of misplacement, theft, and destruction (e.g., through catastrophes such as fire or flood). For most middle- and upper-income savers in the United States, security from property-loss risk of savings is taken for granted with deposits into a financial institution. Not everyone in the world has ready access to and trust in such institutions, however. Where such access and trust cannot be taken for granted, (lack of) security may be the dominant institutional construct in explaining saving action and savings outcomes.

At the micro level, a second type of risk is investment risk. The topic of investment risk is well developed in microeconomics, usually in relation to rates of return. It is commonly understood that, in competitive markets, riskier investment options, over time, can offer higher rates of return. Therefore, some degree of investment risk is desirable for asset accumulation over the long term, and "security" from this risk can have negative consequences.

Discussion of security would not be complete without also mentioning macro risks to which all asset accumulations are vulnerable. Macro risks have to do with the competence and integrity of the political system, integrity of the financial markets, and management of the macro economy. Whenever assets accumulate, as in a defined contribution retirement plan, these assets may be subject to depletion through mismanagement or corruption. Fortunately, the United States has exceptionally strong, efficient, and transparent financial markets, so macro risks in financial markets are relatively limited. Fiscal and monetary policies greatly affect investment returns. Indeed, inflation risk is often the single greatest threat to long-term asset accumulation.

At this point, the body of evidence related to our hypothesis that security affects saving and investment action is small and indirect. African Americans have much lower net worth than whites and hold smaller portions of their investments in financial securities and larger portions in real estate. As scholars ranging from W. E. B. Dubois (1935) to Melvin Oliver and Thomas Shapiro (1995) have noted, blacks historically have had reason not to trust financial institutions and security investments, preferring literally to keep their money closer to home.

Effects of Intergenerational and Interhousehold Transfers on Investment Action and Asset Accumulation

In addition to individual and institutional constructs, our conceptual framework suggests that intergenerational and interhousehold transfers shape asset building. In particular, we posit that interhousehold transfers affect investment action (the mix of assets held) and asset accumulation. Transfers take a variety of forms. They may involve living people (inter vivos transfers), or they may occur at death (bequests). They may consist of money, material assistance, or time. Transfers may be consumed or saved. Transfers that are saved increase the recipient's wealth. Even transfers that are consumed can indirectly facilitate asset accumulation. For example, parental assistance with educational expenses can allow a young adult to graduate from college with little or no debt. The absence of debt in turn makes it easier for the graduate to save and makes her more attractive to mortgage lenders (Shapiro 2004).

One common phenomenon is for parents or other family members to give money to young adults for a down payment on a first home. This down payment assistance may make homeownership possible for some families. In all likelihood, it reduces the recipient's monthly mortgage payment—by reducing the mortgage amount and perhaps by eliminating private mortgage insurance—and so frees up money for saving (Shapiro 2004). And when down payment assistance allows families to purchase homes in neighborhoods that they otherwise could not afford, it can improve their neighborhood environments, their social standing, and their children's educational opportunities. Shapiro argues that these transfers can have lasting effects: "These head-start assets set up different starting lines, establish different rules for success, fix different rewards for accomplishments, and ultimately perpetuate inequality" (3). As discussed below, low-income families are less likely to receive substantial down payment assistance.

Another phenomenon is worth mentioning here: the availability of financial help from others may *reduce* saving for some individuals. For example, individuals who believe that family members will provide money in the event of job loss might be less motivated to accumulate precautionary savings. On the whole, we suspect that bequests and inter vivos transfers increase the wealth of recipients, but more empirical evidence on this topic is needed.

Existing evidence strongly suggests that inter vivos transfers and bequests, in the aggregate, are substantial. For example, using SCF data, Gale and Scholz (1994) estimate that the annual flow of intended intergenerational transfers (including inter vivos transfers, trust accumulations, and life insurance payments to children) equaled about $63 billion in 1986 (in 1986 dollars) and that the annual flow of bequests equaled an additional $105 billion. Using PSID data from the mid- to late 1980s, Wilhelm (2001) estimates that 22 percent of the U.S. population has ever received a bequest, with an average inheritance amount of over $140,000. Schoeni and Ross (2005) use 1988 PSID data to look at transfers to young adults and consider the benefits of shared housing and help with college tuition and other educational expenses as well as cash gifts. They find that young adults received substantial amounts of material support, perhaps as much as $38,000 (in 2001 dollars) between the ages of 18 to 34.

Although it seems plausible that these transfers affect saving action and asset accumulation, researchers have rarely examined how transfers are used by recipient families, that is, whether transfers are saved or used in ways that free up other money for saving. There is some indirect evidence that interhousehold transfers make home purchase possible for some families. Data from the 1986 SCF indicate that those who received an intergenerational transfer of $3,000 or more during a three-year period were more likely to have purchased their first home during this period than those who had neither received nor given a transfer (16 percent versus 6 percent) (Gale and Scholz 1994). And data from the 1988 PSID show that receipt of money assistance is positively correlated with home purchase (Schoeni 1997). Some qualitative evidence also suggests that down payment assistance sometimes makes the difference between becoming a homeowner or remaining a renter (Shapiro 2004). If home purchase in turn increases wealth for these families, then transfers have indirectly increased asset accumulation. More research on this topic is needed.

Studies on interhousehold transfers also show that higher-income households and whites are much more likely than others to receive sizeable transfers of money and material assistance. For example, Gale and Scholz (1994) find that recipients of transfers of at least $3,000 had higher average income (and higher net worth), and were more likely to be white, than those who neither gave nor received a transfer. Wilhelm (2001) also finds that 28 percent of those in the highest permanent income quintile had ever received a bequest, compared with 13 percent in the lowest quintile. Higher-income families also tended to receive much larger amounts. For inter vivos gifts, the likelihood of receiving a transfer did not vary much by income, but higher-income recipients tended to receive larger gifts. In research on transfers to young adults, Schoeni and Ross (2005) find that youth in the top quartile of family income received almost three times as much assistance as youth in the bottom two quartiles.

Other studies confirm that whites are more likely than blacks and Hispanics to expect and to receive inheritances (Gittleman and Wolff 2004; Menchik and Jianakoplos 1997; Wolff 2002). One study estimates that, for the period between 1984 and 1994, differences in the likelihood of receiving an inheritance raised the rate of wealth accumulation of whites relative to blacks more than differences in the rate of return to capital and more than differences in saving rates (Gittleman and Wolff 2004). Although some studies find that race differences in the likelihood of giving or receiving a transfer disappear once variables like income, wealth, and education are controlled (Jayakody 1998; Sarkisian and Gerstel 2004), as long as blacks and Hispanics tend to have lower income, wealth, and education, minorities will likely be at a disadvantage in wealth accumulation.

Fewer studies have examined the likelihood of single mothers to receive interhousehold transfers. If unmarried mothers do not have partners, their extended families are likely to be smaller than those of married couples, so the probability of receiving interhousehold transfers is probably lower. And Hao (1996) suggests that *never-married* single mothers are unlikely to receive financial support from their parents for two reasons. First, if parents do not approve of out-of-wedlock births they may withdraw financial support. Second, many never-married mothers come from poor families that are unable to provide financial support.

Using data from the National Survey of Families and Households, Hao (1996) finds that married families with children receive the most private transfers (including all loans and gifts from kin and nonkin), while never-married single mothers receive the least. Hao also finds that the positive association between private financial transfers and family wealth is stronger among married-couple families. On the other hand, Schmidt and Sevak (2004) find that inheritance does not explain the difference in net worth between single-mother households and married households.

How Public Policy Shapes Saving- and Asset-Related Institutional Constructs

In this section, we describe how public policy currently shapes institutional constructs, illustrating how institutional supports for saving tend to be delivered in "bundles." We also describe existing federal asset-related programs and policies that are targeted to low-income households.[14]

Bundles of Institutional Constructs

Applied social theory and research is complicated by many "real world" factors, one of which is "bundling" of multiple constructs within a single policy, program, or other intervention. Seldom does an intervention represent a single theoretical construct. In asset-based policies, for example, the constructs discussed above—access, information, incentives, facilitation, expectations, restrictions, security—rarely appear alone but instead are usually bundled together in some form.

The challenges for researchers are to (1) identify the constructs that may be present, (2) develop measures for each of them, (3) assess each construct in an applied setting, and (4) employ analytical procedures to sort out which constructs may be causing the outcome(s) of interest. In quantitative research, a typical approach would be to use multiple regression, controlling for many individual and program characteristics, to assess which factors predict an outcome—such that the results are statistically significant and effect sizes are large enough to matter for program or policy purposes.

An analytical step beyond this would be to test for interaction effects among constructs of interest. It could be, for example, that information and expectations both independently predict a savings outcome, but have even greater predictive power when they occur together. Or it could be that incentives are not predictive in themselves, but the interaction of incentives with access has a strong effect. Testing interactions is one pathway for beginning to understand effectiveness of various *bundles of constructs* that may be represented in a policy or program.

It seems likely that bundles of constructs for saving action tend to come in common forms. For example, there may be a form that provides mostly security in a "rainy day" fund (e.g., a passbook savings account in the private sector). Other forms may have strong elements of incentives, facilitation, expectations, and restrictions designed for long-term asset accumulation (e.g., a 401(k) retirement-savings plan). Thus, some bundles may be better for particular purposes. If inclusive (universal and progressive) asset accumulation is the goal, structured saving *plans* that represent large bundles of key constructs are likely to be the most effective policy package (Clancy and Sherraden 2003; Clancy, Orszag, and Sherraden 2004; Schreiner and Sherraden 2007). Current examples of savings plans—all of which are created by public policy—include 401(k) plans in the private sector, 403(b) plans in the nonprofit sector, the Thrift Savings Plan for federal employees, and 529 college savings plans.

Currently, asset-building bundles tend to be delivered through employment settings and through the tax system. Federal expenditures on the initiatives that provide these bundles of supports are large (e.g., mortgage interest deduction from income tax). For the most part, those who have jobs with benefits, those who are homeowners, and those who are investors have access to these bundles. In the next three subsections, we describe the major bundles of institutional supports and show that low-income, minority, and single-mother households have less access to these bundles than others.

Bundles of institutional supports provided through employment. The primary institutional supports delivered through employment settings come through retirement benefits, both defined benefit and defined contribution plans. These retirement plans support asset building in several ways. Perhaps most importantly, they provide incentives for asset accumulation. Employer matches directly increase wealth (unless recipients offset these matches by saving less in other forms). When employer contributions require a corresponding employee contribution, they also create potential incentives for saving. The federal government provides an additional subsidy and incentive by deducting employee contributions from income (in income tax calculations).

These employer-sponsored savings plans also provide facilitation, especially through the use of payroll deductions and direct deposit. When participation is mandatory, deciding to save and acting on this decision require no mental effort. Even when participation is voluntary, the use of automatic transfers allows individuals to precommit, and this greatly reduces the mental effort required to save. The automatic-enrollment, or "opt-out," plans described above provide even greater facilitation, by automatically enrolling individuals in voluntary plans unless they elect otherwise.

Employer-sponsored retirement accounts are almost always restricted. In many defined benefit plans, funds are not available until workers reach a certain age. In most defined contribution plans, funds can be accessed prior to retirement for qualified uses, such as health costs; early withdrawals for nonqualified uses are subject to substantial penalties. Although a sizeable proportion of families do withdraw funds before retirement, especially when changing jobs,[15] on the whole, these restrictions probably help protect savings for use in retirement. In recent years, there has been emerging interest in using payroll deductions and direct deposit to support savings that would be independent of retirement restrictions.[16]

Employees who have access to employer-sponsored savings plans often have access to financial education as well, especially if they work for medium-size or large firms. These educational initiatives—often newsletters or optional group seminars—attempt to motivate and inform employees.

Subsidies, facilitation, restriction, and education all send the message that saving and asset accumulation are desirable. The terms of matching contributions may also set up specific expectations for saving. If a worker receives the maximum employer contribution when she contributes 5 percent of her earnings to a 401(k) plan, for example, then the plan may create an expectation that employees save 5 percent of earnings. Similarly, the terms of automatic-enrollment plans may communicate specific expectations about saving for retirement.

Low-income individuals are less likely than middle- and upper-income individuals to have access to these benefits. The percentage of full-time private workers employed at firms that sponsor pension plans increases substantially with earnings (42 percent among those with earnings less than $20,000 versus 80 percent among those earning more than $60,000) (Purcell 2001). Minorities and women also tend to have less access to employer-sponsored pension plans than non-Hispanic whites and men. For example, in 2003, 57 percent of white workers and 53 percent of black workers were covered by these pension plans; 57 percent of male workers were covered, compared to 56 percent of female workers (Purcell 2006).

When low-earning workers do have access to pension plans, they are less likely to participate. Among full time-time private sector workers, only 68 percent of workers earning less than $20,000 participate in a pension program when eligible, while 94 percent of those earning more than $60,000 participate (Purcell 2001). Limited ability to save is almost certainly one important reason for lower participation rates. And, when low-income households are able to save, they may choose to save for more immediate goals than retirement (and may thus prefer less-restricted saving vehicles). Institutional variables probably also play a role. The tax-favored treatment of pension contributions is worth less to households in lower tax brackets than households in higher tax brackets, and worth nothing at all to households with no income tax liability.

Bundles of institutional supports provided through homeownership. Homeownership also comes with a bundle of institutional supports. In this case, facilitation and restriction are probably most important. When an individual takes out a mortgage to purchase a home, she has a contractual obligation to make monthly payments, and the portion of each payment that goes to principal directly increases her wealth. Since most people will go to great lengths to avoid mortgage default, little or no mental energy or extra effort is required to "save" monthly in the form of home equity. Also, because people will go to great lengths to avoid default and because the transaction costs of selling a home are very high, home equity is quite illiquid. These "restrictions" help protect home equity.

In addition to facilitation and restrictions, there are incentives and subsidies for homeownership. Interest payments on home mortgages and state and local property taxes for owner-occupied homes may be deducted from income (if deductions are itemized). These tax benefits reduce the cost of homeownership (and send the message that home-ownership is "good") and so may encourage people to purchase homes.[17] In some time periods in some locations, home values have appreciated dramatically. The reverse is also true. Falling home prices and rising fore-closure rates, which began in 2007, have eroded the equity previously built up by homeowners. Fluctuations in the housing market do pose risks, but the long-term nature of homeownership and the past market performance of real estate has generally supported "passive" asset accu-mulation for households that build up home equity as they pay down their mortgage loans. The exclusion of capital gains on the sales of prin-ciple residences from federal income tax also provides an incentive and subsidy for homeownership.[18]

The impact of the housing downturn of 2007 and 2008 will require fur-ther assessment, but it is likely that owner-occupied housing will remain the primary asset for many low-income, minority, and single-mother households. These groups will continue to have less access to homeown-ership and receive fewer benefits from ownership than others do. The two primary prerequisites for homeownership are assets (to make a down payment) and evidence of "credit worthiness" (to qualify for a mortgage). For a conventional loan, mortgage lenders typically require a down pay-ment equal to 10 to 20 percent of the purchase price.[19]

A first-time homebuyer typically has two main sources for her down payment: her own personal savings or transfers from others. Mayer and Engelhardt (1996) find that 21 percent of first-time buyers received gifts for down payments in the late 1980s and early 1990s. For recipients, this assistance was substantial: the average gift equaled 51 percent of the total down payment. Using 1996 PSID data, Shapiro (2004) reports that 54 per-cent of white and 88 percent of black first-time homebuyers said that their down payments came entirely from their own savings. These figures suggest that a substantial proportion of white buyers (and a smaller pro-portion of black buyers) receive down payment assistance. These figures may underestimate the importance of transfers because an individual's savings may have come from earlier gifts or bequests.

In addition to down payments, a potential homebuyer must demonstrate the ability to repay her mortgage, and evidence suggests that low-income, minority, and single-mother households have limited access to mainstream credit.[20] Lenders' assessment of "credit worthiness" depends upon level of income, stability of income, savings, and credit history (Belsky and Calder 2004). By definition, low-income households do not fare as well as others on the first criterion. In addition, many low-income, minority, and single-mother households have fairly volatile incomes because they work seasonally, because they have experienced unemployment, or because some or all of their earnings come from informal employment. Further, these households are less likely to have savings.

Credit history provides additional insight to lenders about an applicant's credit worthiness. Those who have been identified as "credit risks" are unlikely to qualify for mainstream credit. Some of the factors that lead to this label are having a debt-to-income ratio above a certain threshold, a history of missed payments, or a history of personal bankruptcy. Low-income individuals are more likely than others to be identified as credit risks.

Other households may be unable to demonstrate credit worthiness because they have little or no documented credit history. Those without bank accounts and credit cards are particularly likely to have this problem (Belsky and Calder 2004). Low-income and minority households are less likely than others to have bank accounts and credit cards (Aizcorbe et al. 2003; Bucks et al. 2006; Hogarth, Anguelov, and Lee 2005). Single-mother households are slightly less likely than others to have bank accounts and credit cards (Hogarth and Lee 2000).[21] Racial discrimination may serve as an additional barrier to homeownership for minority households. Using PSID data, Charles and Hurst (2002) find that blacks are twice as likely as whites to have applications for home mortgages rejected, even when they control for wealth and proxies for credit history.

We have already argued that homeownership may be a risky investment for low-income households. In addition, low-income households benefit less than others from homeownership because the subsidies for homeownership are delivered through the tax system. To benefit from the deductions for mortgage interest payments and state and local property taxes, a household must itemize deductions. According to 1998 data from the SCF, only 13 percent of homeowners in the bottom 40 percent of the income distribution itemized (Glaeser and Shapiro 2002). In addition, these deductions are not refundable, so households benefit only if they owe taxes. Families that owe taxes but are in the lowest tax brackets benefit less than families in higher tax brackets. Finally, the homes owned by low-income households are likely to be modestly priced, and deductions for mortgage interest payments and property taxes are more valuable for expensive homes (or large mortgages) than for modestly priced homes (or small mortgages).

Empirical evidence confirms that these deductions disproportionately benefit higher-income families. The value of the mortgage interest deduction was over $65 billion in 2006 and according to the Joint Committee on Taxation (2007), almost three-quarters of the benefits of this deduction accrued to households with annual incomes of $100,000 or more. Roughly 4 percent of the benefits accrued to households with incomes below $50,000. Results from the simulation cited by Woo, Schweke, and Buchholz (2004) predict that in 2006 the bottom 60 percent of taxpayers by income will receive less than 5 percent of the combined benefits from the mortgage interest and property tax deductions. The top 1 percent of taxpayers by income is expected to receive almost 11 percent of the combined benefits.

Bundles of institutional supports provided through other types of saving and investment. Finally, a bundle of institutional supports is available to "investors," that is, to those who hold specific, fairly sophisticated saving and investment vehicles. Of particular interest here are individual retirement accounts, such as traditional IRAs, Roth IRAs, and Keogh plans. The most important institutional supports provided by these programs are incentives, restrictions, and expectations.

Incentives are provided through the tax system. For example, contributions to traditional IRAs are deductible (although withdrawals are taxable). Contributions to Roth IRAs are not deductible, but earnings and allowed withdrawals are not taxed.

Traditional IRAs and Keogh plans are restricted. For example, withdrawals taken from a traditional IRA before age 59.5 are subject to a 10 percent penalty unless used for higher education or first-time home purchase, or unless the account holder becomes disabled. The maximum deductible contributions for these individual retirement programs may also set up expectations for saving. Unlike employer-sponsored retirement plans, participation in individual retirement plans must be initiated and structured by individuals. Thus, accessing these institutional supports requires effort and financial sophistication as well as wealth.

Low-income households are eligible for traditional and Roth IRAs, but the participation rate is extremely low. According to estimates by Burman and others (2004, table 6), in 2004 only 0.2 percent of tax units in the lowest income quintile contributed to a traditional IRA and only 0.3 percent contributed to a Roth IRA. The comparable figures for all tax units were 2.7 percent and 2.8 percent. Low-income filers were also much less likely than high-income filers to contribute the maximum amounts. Financial constraints and the desire to save for shorter-term goals almost certainly limit participation by low-income households.

Low-income, minority, and single-mother households probably have limited access to the federal subsidies related to long-term capital gains, life insurance and annuities, and capital gains transferred through estates. These groups tend to hold more conservative saving and investment products; the tax-preferred products require greater financial sophistication and greater risk tolerance than vehicles like savings accounts and certificates of deposit. Also, these subgroups are much less likely than others to leave sizeable bequests.

Institutional Supports Provided through Targeted Asset-Building Initiatives

The previous paragraphs show that low-income households are much less likely than others to benefit from the policy bundles just described. The federal government, however, has a number of asset-building policies and programs that are targeted specifically to low-income households. Here we briefly describe some of the major targeted asset-building initiatives and then discuss the extent to which these targeted programs provide institutional supports. Federal asset-building initiatives for low-income households include both discretionary spending programs and tax expenditures. Targeted policies exist in at least four categories: homeownership, IDAs, small business development, and tax credits.

Homeownership. In recent years, the U.S. Department of Housing and Urban Development (HUD) has focused increasingly on promoting homeownership for lower-income households. Before the fall of housing prices and rise in mortgage defaults and foreclosures that began in 2007, funds spent on targeted homeownership programs represented a small portion of HUD's overall discretionary budget authority (about $2 billion out of

$37 billion in recent years). This figure is expected to increase as the federal government commits more resources to housing counseling and homeowner assistance.

Prior to these efforts the largest HUD program promoting homeownership was the HOME Investment Partnerships Program. HOME can be used to support homeownership and provide rental assistance. State and local officials have flexibility to determine how to best address their community's low-income housing needs, and in recent years, the percentage of funds devoted to homeownership has increased. Support for homeownership includes down payment and rehabilitation assistance. In 2003, a new set-aside within HOME, the American Dream Downpayment Initiative, was authorized. These funds provide grants of up to $10,000 to low-income, first-time homebuyers for down payments and closing costs. Funds may also be used for some rehabilitation and home repair of housing acquired with assistance.

Another source of federal assistance is the Community Development Financial Institutions Fund (operating under the Treasury department). This fund promotes economic revitalization and community development by investing in and providing assistance to community development financial institutions. These institutions, in turn, provide loans, investments, financial services, and technical assistance to underserved populations and communities.

A third important source of federal assistance is the Federal Housing Administration (FHA). FHA has recently expanded its suite of products, but its primary mission is to provide mortgage insurance on loans made by FHA-approved lenders. A significant portion of low-income borrowers use FHA products when purchasing a home, and these products help reduce the barriers to homeownership. The FHA generates money for the federal government through fees.

Individual development accounts. While IDA programs are relatively new, they have received modest support from the federal government through the Assets for Independence Act (AFIA) and the Office of Refugee Resettlement. Enacted in 1998 and funded at about $25 million a year since, AFIA created the first federally funded national demonstration program for IDAs. Through AFIA, the Office of Community Services in the Department of Health and Human Services (HHS) awards five-year grants to nonprofit organizations and to government or financial institutions partnering with nonprofits. Grant recipients must provide an equal amount of funding from private sources. Federal funds may be used to administer programs and to provide matching funds for IDA deposits. IDA funds must be used to purchase a first home, pay for higher education, or capitalize a small business. Over 180 agencies and community-based groups across the nation have been awarded grants for AFIA projects. In these AFIA projects, participants have established over 21,000 IDAs and have saved a total of $14.6 million.

In a separate program, the HHS Office of Refugee Resettlement (ORR) awards grants to nonprofit organizations providing IDAs to refugees. Since 1999, approximately $66 million has supported over 13,000 IDA accounts through ORR. While there is no specific budget line to support refugee IDA programs, they have been funded through the ORR discretionary budget. This budget item has been reduced in recent years and no IDA program announcement has been issued since FY 2003.

Small business development. The federal government offers a number of programs to support small business capitalization, mostly through activities of the U.S. Small Business Administration. Only a few of these programs—including the Microenterprise Development Initiative, the Microloan program, and the Program for Investment in Microentrepreneurs—are targeted to lower-income borrowers. Most of these programs are small and primarily provide loans and technical assistance to microenterprises.

Tax credits. As noted above, several large tax expenditures support asset building for primarily middle- and upper-income households. Two tax expenditures, the saver's credit and the EITC, are targeted to low-income households. A third, the child tax credit (CTC), is available to a broader segment of the population but also benefits low-income households. We describe these here.

The saver's credit was created in 2001 to encourage low-income people to save for retirement. It provides up to a 50 percent tax credit for up to $1,000 in contributions to retirement accounts, including 401(k) plans and IRAs. This credit, however, is nonrefundable, so it benefits only those with federal tax liability.

The EITC is a federal income tax credit for low-income workers. In tax year 2004, working families with children were eligible for the EITC if they had incomes below about $30,000 to $36,000 (depending on number of children in the family and filing status). In tax year 2003, the average EITC for families with children was $2,100 (Center on Budget and Policy Priorities 2004). The EITC is refundable, so an individual receives a refund if the credit amount exceeds her tax liability.

The EITC was not explicitly designed to encourage asset building. There is evidence, however, that it does facilitate asset accumulation, especially when linked to initiatives explicitly designed to encourage saving and asset accumulation. As discussed earlier, behavioral theory suggests, and some empirical evidence confirms, that people view lump-sum refunds differently than wage and salary income and may be more likely to save or purchase assets with refund payments. This has led both for-profit and not-for-profit organizations to offer a variety of saving products at the time of tax preparation, including low-fee bank accounts (Beverly, Romich, et al. 2003), IRAs (Duflo et al. 2005; Tufano and Schneider 2004), and IDAs. Another program encouraged EITC recipients to "split" their refunds, directing part to a savings account and receiving the rest in the form of a check for consumption (Beverly, Schneider, and Tufano 2006).

The CTC is also a federal income tax credit worth up to $1,000 to eligible tax filers for each qualifying child. In tax year 2004, eligibility began to phase out at $75,000 for single heads of household and $110,000 for couples filing jointly. The CTC is only partially refundable. Like the EITC, it is not explicitly an asset-building initiative, but it does affect the potential of a lower-income family to build assets by reducing its tax liability and perhaps increasing the size of its tax refund.

Assessment of targeted asset-building initiatives. It is not yet possible to say, with confidence, whether targeted asset-building programs described above substantially increase the assets of participants. This important question requires detailed information about a variety of assets and some reasonable estimate of how asset levels would have changed in the absence of the programs. In the absence of more information about impact, we describe here the scope of these targeted initiatives and the level of institutional support provided.

In terms of dollars spent and number of people participating, the low-income-targeted initiatives described here are much smaller than the programs and policies that largely benefit middle- and upper-income households. In fiscal year 2009, the Office of Management and Budget estimates that over $100 billion will be spent on deductions of mortgage interest payments. In contrast, for the same fiscal year, less than $2 billion was requested for the HOME Investment Partnerships Program and $24 million was requested for the Assets for Independence demonstration program, while tax expenditures for the Saver's Credit were expected to be about $900 million (Cramer, O'Brien, and Lopez-Fernadini 2008).

The targeted initiatives also provide substantially less institutional support for saving and asset accumulation. With regard to *access,* most of the targeted programs have eligibility requirements that exclude many low-income households. For example, IDA programs often require that participants be employed. The EITC is available only to individuals with earnings, and childless workers are eligible for only a very small credit. Small business programs are available only to those who have or are starting their own businesses. In addition, to participate in homeownership, IDA, or small business programs, an individual must fill out an application form and probably meet with a case manager. The process may be time consuming and intrusive, and so, may create a barrier to participation for some.

With regard to *information,* it is difficult to say whether information needed to participate successfully in targeted programs is more available or less available than information related to homeownership and retirement-saving benefits. One study suggests that less than two-thirds of low-income parents knew about the EITC in 1999 (Phillips 2001). To our knowledge, there is no empirical evidence about knowledge of the other targeted programs described here. Presumably, social service agencies provide information about these targeted programs to potential participants, but individuals who are not connected to these agencies may have no source of information about these programs.[22] Moreover, the motives or incentives for providing information differ for targeted programs, compared to homeownership and retirement-saving initiatives. For the targeted programs, the motivation to educate comes from the "goodwill" of nonprofit organizations and staff members, that is, from the desire to provide resources to disadvantaged families. For homeownership and retirement-saving initiatives, there are individuals and organizations—realtors, lenders, and investment companies, for example—that receive clear benefits when new "participants" are recruited. Also related to information is the fact that most of these targeted programs require some degree of financial sophistication. It takes financial knowledge and confidence, for example, to purchase a home or start a small business.

Of the targeted programs described here, IDAs have the most obvious *incentives* for saving. These incentives are generous in percentage terms, but benefits are capped and the dollar amount transferred can be far less generous than, say, retirement pension benefits. In addition, federally funded IDA programs are small in budgetary terms and in terms of people served. Also, to receive federal money, nonprofit organizations must provide match money, a requirement that does not exist (indeed, is irrelevant) in the tax-expenditure programs supporting homeownership and retirement savings. Future funding for these programs is uncertain because AFIA is a demonstration program, and the Office of Refugee Resettlement has not allocated additional funding to IDAs in recent years. The saver's credit also provides an incentive for saving, but this program is limited in scope because only filers with federal income tax liability benefit.[23]

With regard to *facilitation*, automatic enrollment is not often available for these targeted programs. For some, automatic transfers can be arranged if the participant has a bank account or, in the case of the saver's credit, access to a 401(k) plan. The EITC and CTC provide some facilitation, to the extent that income tax refunds are more "save-able" than more regular income. In some IDA programs, staff actively encourage and sometimes assist participants in making a monthly saving deposit.

Most of the targeted programs discussed here have *restrictions*. For example, financial assistance from homeownership programs may be used only for homeownership, support from microenterprise programs is restricted to small business efforts, matching funds for IDA deposits may be used only for approved purposes, and deposits that qualify for the saver's credit go into restricted retirement accounts. There are no restrictions associated with the use of the EITC and the CTC (consistent with the fact that these are not explicitly designed as asset-building programs).

Very likely, for most participants, these targeted programs are perceived as *secure*. Although there are risks involved with investing in a small business, purchasing a home, and contributing to a retirement-savings plan, receiving additional support for these activities through these targeted programs creates no additional risk.

In sum, these targeted programs provide much less institutional support for saving and asset accumulation than the homeownership and retirement-saving initiatives that operate through the tax system and through employers. In large part, this is due to substantial differences in size and scope. Targeted programs reach far fewer people, they are primarily available only to those with earnings, and the financial benefits provided are typically much lower in dollar terms. Like the "nontargeted" initiatives, targeted programs provide restrictions and security, and some provide incentives and expectations. But these institutional supports are available only to the small portion of the low-income population that applies for assistance and satisfies eligibility requirements.

The end result is likely to be that targeted programs have modest effects, in the aggregate, on asset building.

Suggestions for Future Research

This summary of empirical evidence reveals a number of gaps in knowledge. Of special interest are gaps that limit ability to design programs and policies that facilitate saving and asset building in low-income households. Following are some research questions that may provide additional policy-relevant knowledge.

- Under what conditions is homeownership a good asset-building strategy for low-income households? What are effective strategies for helping potential homeowners make wise choices about ownership?
- Does health insurance coverage facilitate saving and asset building for low-income households?
- Does financial education change financial knowledge, attitudes, and behaviors in ways that lead to increased saving and asset accumulation in low-income households? Does well-targeted financial information that is delivered automatically to individuals (e.g., is not available just to those who choose to attend a financial seminar) produce these outcomes?
- What match structure (i.e., match rate and match cap) maximizes participation in incentivized saving programs? What match structure maximizes contributions? What match structure maximizes net saving (across all saving vehicles)? Do these findings vary by income or education level?
- Does loosening the asset tests in income transfer programs lead to increased saving and asset holding?
- Under what circumstances do people want restrictions? Under what circumstances do they want liquidity? Do these patterns vary by income or education level?

Some of the most promising avenues for future research would require new policy interventions not just new or improved data sources. New interventions would be indicated in at least two scenarios. First, there may be no existing initiative with the institutional characteristic, or *bundle* of characteristics, of interest. For example, if researchers would like to examine responses to a savings account for education provided automatically to all children at birth and with match money for low-income households, then a new intervention would be needed. Second, new interventions are highly desirable, if not required, when researchers want to examine—very rigorously—how actual behavior responds to varying institutional characteristics; no existing program has systematically varying institutional characteristics. For example, the most rigorous way to test effects of match structure is to randomly assign individuals to groups that are offered different match structures.

As suggested by our example, an important line of experimental or quasi-experimental research would involve match structure. This research focus is promising because existing studies suggest that people (across the income spectrum) respond to financial incentives, but these studies do not identify "optimal" match structures. Like questions about match structure, questions about the demand for restrictions and liquidity would be best answered with an experiment or quasi-experiment designed around a new intervention. Questions about financial education and financial information could be answered with new interventions, or research plans might be carefully designed around existing interventions. In lieu of interventions with impact assessments, some insights could be gained from carefully constructed survey questions that ask individuals how they feel about saving products with different restrictions and whether they would save in them.

Other avenues for future research would not require new interventions but might require new data. For example, to identify conditions under which homeownership is a good asset-building strategy, researchers would probably require a new dataset that combines (1) information on neighborhood characteristics from existing census data, (2) information about individual and household characteristics (including net worth) from survey data, and (3) information on real estate transactions from survey data or, preferably, from administrative records. In short, data requirements to answer research questions identified here vary substantially, but some of these research pursuits would require a large financial investment.

In closing, we emphasize one rather obvious but often overlooked point. For the purpose of designing programs and policies that facilitate asset building in low-income households and in households of color, there is an imperative for research that draws samples that include these populations in sufficient numbers for meaningful statistical analyses.

NOTES

1. For example, a worker signing up for a 401(k) investment option may assume that the default option is the best choice for him; otherwise, this choice would not have been defined as the default.

2. The use of mental accounting means, in part, that people think about funds differently depending on their source. For example, regular wage and salary income may be defined as funds for consumption, while irregular income, such as money from a temporary job or from a tax refund, may be defined as savings or "treat" money.

3. Programs that enroll people automatically are sometimes called "opt-out" programs because eligible individuals are enrolled in the program unless they take the initiative to opt out.

4. Existing studies have focused on black-white differences. Future research needs to study other racial and ethnic minorities.

5. Reinforcing the importance of social context, some interviewees also said that any savings they managed to accumulate would be quickly depleted because network members would refuse to help during a financial crisis as long as the family had savings (Caskey 1997).

6. The measure was created from only six knowledge questions, including, "what is the current Dow Jones Industrial average?"; "for people who pay federal income taxes, what is the lowest income tax bracket?"; and "what is the 30-year conventional mortgage rate right now?"

7. Some have argued that poor people and other "out groups" (such as racial and ethnic minorities) live for the present and cannot or choose not to postpone pleasure (see, for example, the discussion in Katz 1990). Others have argued that low-income people and minorities have below-average life expectancies and, thus, fewer incentives to save. Others claim that minorities have learned through negative experiences that rewards do not often arrive as promised and, therefore, have fewer incentives to postpone pleasure. Thus, there has been much speculation (but little research) on the determinants of future orientation. When people discuss future orientation, time preference, and perhaps to a lesser extent, self-control, we suspect they are thinking of fairly stable personality characteristics. Our opinion is that *some* people are consistently patient or impatient, regardless of the opportunities and constraints they face. For most people, however, we believe that willingness to postpone pleasure is substantially influenced by external factors, especially institutional factors, such as information, incentives, expectations, and so on.

8. The variables describing firms' 401(k) communication programs measure (1) how often plan information is provided to employees, (2) how often financial education materials are provided, (3) the proportion of employees with access to projection information, and (4) the percentage of communication materials that is available on the Internet.

9. Some studies of financial education use a post-test to examine *intended* behavior of participants. As both psychology and behavioral economics emphasize, however, intentions often do not directly translate into action. In fact, one study finds that only 14 percent of those who said, after a one-hour employer-sponsored retirement seminar, that they planned to enroll in the 401(k) plan actually did so. About 30 percent of those who said they planned to increase their contribution rate actually did so (Choi et al. 2002). We do not discuss studies that use only measures of intended behavior as outcomes.

10. In addition to the studies cited here, there is at least one study of a well-known financial education program for high school students, the National Endowment for Financial Education's High School Financial Planning Program (Danes and Haberman 2004). This study relies on a survey of students administered by teachers who had implemented the curriculum. We do not discuss these results because the response rates were very low and because we believe these data are particularly vulnerable to social desirability bias and other types of bias.

11. Very often, money in restricted accounts may be used for other purposes, but financial penalties are imposed.

12. In ADD in-depth interviews, some said that, without restrictions, their IDA savings would have been drawn upon by family and friends. This finding is consistent with evidence from Chiteji and Hamilton (2005) and Stack (1974) that poor people and people of color may have difficulty accumulating assets due to social network demands. Thus restrictions on savings may have negative social consequences. We cannot evaluate this, except to report that some IDA participants express appreciation for the restrictions.

13. Participants could withdraw their money at any point, but this resulted in the loss of match money.

14. In this section, we focus largely on public policies that are explicitly designed to encourage asset building. We do not discuss social insurance programs, such as Social Security, Unemployment Insurance, and Disability Insurance, although these programs almost certainly have important effects on asset holding. Social insurance programs protect assets by providing cash assistance when income declines due to age, unemployment, or injury, for example. These programs might also offset private saving, however, because people who know they are eligible for social insurance benefits may be less motivated to save on their own for emergencies and retirement.

15. Engelhardt (2002) estimates that less than 43 percent of preretirement lump-sum distributions from defined contribution plans are rolled over to an IRA, transferred to another employer, or converted to an annuity.

16. Cramer (2006) has proposed encouraging employers to automatically enroll their employees into nontax-advantaged, flexible savings accounts.

17. Glaeser and Shapiro (2002) argue that the home mortgage interest deduction does not increase homeownership because it disproportionately benefits those who would own homes even in the absence of the deduction.

18. Excluded gains were limited to $250,000 for individuals and $500,000 for married couples in the 2004 tax year.

19. Borrowers who take out conventional mortgages with less than a 20 percent down payment usually must purchase private mortgage insurance. Government-sponsored mortgage programs, such as those affiliated with the Federal Housing Administration, provide mortgages to eligible households with down payments of only 2 to 3 percent (Mayer and Engelhardt 1996).

20. Many low-income individuals qualify for credit from subprime lenders, but these loans tend to have higher interest rates and higher penalties for default (Belsky and Calder 2004). Immergluck and Wiles (1999) and others after them have described a "dual mortgage market" in which mainstream lenders serve higher-income white neighborhoods and subprime lenders serve lower-income and minority communities. Furthermore, the aggressive marketing of subprime loans trapped many families in loans they could

not maintain and led to the rise of default and foreclosure rates which began to appear in 2007, precipitating a broader decline in the housing market.

21. Making matters even more complicated for these households is the fact that it is difficult for an individual with poor credit to open a savings or checking account (Belsky and Calder 2004). Thus, it can be difficult for an individual to recover from past credit problems. Hogarth and others (2005) examine barriers to basic account ownership in detail.

22. Low-income filers who use a tax preparation service do not need to know about the EITC to receive it, but those who file their own returns must know to claim it. And, some households without tax liability may not file because they are unaware that they are eligible for the credit.

23. Gale, Iwry, and Orszag (2004) estimate that only about one out of every 1,000 returns that qualify for the saver's credit based on income has enough tax liability to receive the maximum possible credit (if the maximum eligible contribution were made).

REFERENCES

Aarts, Henk, Peter M. Gollwitzer, and Ran R. Hassin. 2004. "Goal Contagion: Perceiving is Pursuing." *Journal of Personality and Social Psychology* 87(1): 23–37.

Aizcorbe, Ana M., Arthur B. Kennickell, and Kevin B. Moore. 2003. "Recent Changes in U.S. Family Finances: Evidence from the 1998 and 2001 Survey of Consumer Finances." *Federal Reserve Bulletin* 89(1): 1–32.

Ameriks, John, Andrew Caplin, John Leahy, and Tom Tyler. 2004. "Measuring Self-Control." Cambridge, MA: National Bureau of Economic Research.

Anderson, Steven G., Min Zhan, and Jeff Scott. 2004. "Targeting Financial Management Training at Low-Income Audiences." *Journal of Consumer Affairs* 38(1): 167–77.

Ando, Albert, and Franco Modigliani. 1963. "The 'Life Cycle' Hypothesis of Saving: Aggregate Implications and Tests." *American Economic Review* 53(1): 55–84.

Ashraf, Nava, Dean S. Karlan, and Wesley Yin. 2006. "Tying Odysseus to the Mast: Evidence from a Commitment Savings Product in the Philippines." *Quarterly Journal of Economics* 121(2): 635–72.

Banov, Rachel. 2005. "The Effect of Health Insurance on Savings Outcomes in Individual Development Accounts." St. Louis, MO: Washington University in St. Louis, Center for Social Development.

Barrow, Lisa, and Leslie McGranahan. 2000. "The Effects of the Earned Income Credit on the Seasonality of Household Expenditures." *National Tax Journal* 53(4, part 2): 1211–44.

Bayer, Patrick J., B. Douglas Bernheim, and John Karl Scholz. 1996. "The Effects of Financial Education in the Workplace: Evidence from a Survey of Employers." Cambridge, MA: National Bureau of Economic Research.

Belsky, Eric, and Allegra Calder. 2004. "Credit Matters: Low-Income Asset Building Challenges in a Dual Financial Service System." Joint Center for Housing Studies Working Paper BABC 04-1. Cambridge, MA: Harvard University.

Belsky, Eric S., and Mark Duda. 2002. "Asset Appreciation, Timing of Purchase and Sales, and Returns to Low-Income Homeownership." In *Low-Income Homeownership: Examining the Unexamined Goal,* edited by Nicolas P. Retsinas and Eric S. Belsky (208–38). Cambridge, MA: Joint Center for Housing Studies; Washington, DC: Brookings Institution Press.

Bernheim, B. Douglas. 1994. "Personal Saving, Information, and Economic Literacy." In *Tax Policy for Economic Growth in the 1990s* (53–78). Washington, DC: American Council for Capital Formation.

———. 1998. "Financial Illiteracy, Education, and Retirement Saving." In *Living with Defined Contribution Plans,* edited by Olivia S. Mitchell and Sylvester J. Schieber (69–97). Philadelphia: University of Pennsylvania, Wharton School, Pension Research Council.

Bernheim, B. Douglas, and Daniel M. Garrett. 2003. "The Effects of Financial Education in the Workplace: Evidence from a Survey of Households." *Journal of Public Economics* 87(7–8): 1487–519.

Bernheim, B. Douglas, and John Karl Scholz. 1993. "Private Saving and Public Policy." *Tax Policy and the Economy* 7: 73–110.

Bernheim, B. Douglas, Daniel M. Garrett, and Dean M. Maki. 2001. "Education and Saving: The Long-Term Effects of High School Financial Curriculum Mandates." *Journal of Public Economics* 80: 435–65.

Bertrand, Marianne, Sendhil Mullainathan, and Eldar Shafir. 2004. "A Behavioral-Economics View of Poverty." *American Economic Review* 94(2): 419–23.

———. 2006. "Behavioral Economics and Marketing in Aid of Decision-Making among the Poor." *Journal of Public Policy and Marketing* 25(1): 8–24.

Beverly, Sondra, and Michael Sherraden. 1999. "Institutional Determinants of Saving: Implications for Low-income Households and Public Policy." *Journal of Socioeconomics* 28: 457–73.

Beverly, Sondra G., Amanda Moore McBride, and Mark Schreiner. 2003. "A Framework of Asset-Accumulation Stages and Strategies." *Journal of Family and Economic Issues* 24(2): 143–56.

Beverly, Sondra G., Jennifer L. Romich, and Jennifer Tescher. 2003. "Linking Tax Refunds and Low-Cost Bank Accounts: A Social Development Strategy for Low-Income Families?" *Social Development Issues* 25(1/2): 235–46.

Beverly, Sondra G., Daniel Schneider, and Peter Tufano. 2006. "Splitting Tax Refunds and Building Savings: An Empirical Test." In *Tax Policy and the Economy,* vol. 20, edited by James M. Poterba (111–62). Cambridge, MA: MIT Press.

Brobeck, Stephen. 2002. "Developing a National Strategy to Advance Financial Literacy." Washington, DC: Consumer Federation of America.

Bucks, Brian K., Arthur B. Kennickell, and Kevin B. Moore. 2006. "Recent Changes in U.S. Family Finances: Evidence from the 2001 and 2004 Survey of Consumer Finances." *Federal Reserve Bulletin* 92(1): 1–38.

Burman, Leonard E., William G. Gale, Matthew Hall, and Peter R. Orszag. 2004. "Distributional Effects of Defined Contribution Plans and Individual Retirement Arrangements." *National Tax Journal* 57(3): 671–701.

Carr, James H., and Nandinee Kutty. 2008. *Segregation: The Rising Costs for America.* New York: Routledge.

Carroll, Christopher D. 1997. "Buffer-Stock Saving and the Life Cycle/Permanent Income Hypothesis." *Quarterly Journal of Economics* 12(1): 1–55.

Carroll, Christopher D., and Andrew A. Samwick. 1997. "The Nature of Precautionary Wealth." *Journal of Monetary Economics* 40(1): 41–71.

Caskey, John P. 1997. "Beyond Cash-and-Carry: Financial Savings, Financial Services, and Low-Income Households in Two Communities." Swarthmore, PA: Swarthmore College.

———. 2001. "Can Lower Income Households Increase Savings with Financial-Management Education?" *Cascade* 46:1–4, 10–11, 18.

———. 2006. "Can Personal Financial Management Education Promote Asset Accumulation among the Poor?" Policy Brief 2006-PB-06. Indianapolis: Networks Financial Institute at Indiana State University.

Center on Budget and Policy Priorities. 2004. *The Earned Income Tax Credit: Boosting Employment, Aiding the Working Poor.* Washington, DC: Center on Budget and Policy Priorities.

Charles, Kerwin Kofin, and Erik Hurst. 2002. "The Transition to Home Ownership and the Black-White Wealth Gap." *Review of Economics and Statistics* 84(2): 281–97.

Chiteji, Ngina, and Darrick Hamilton. 2005. "Family Matters: Kin Networks and Asset Accumulation." In *Inclusion in the American Dream: Assets, Poverty, and Public Policy,* edited by Michael Sherraden (87–111). New York: Oxford University Press.

Chiteji, Ngina S., and Frank P. Stafford. 1999. "Portfolio Choices of Parents and Their Children as Young Adults: Asset Accumulation by African-American Families." *American Economic Review* 89(2): 377–80.

Choi, James, David Laibson, Brigitte Madrian, and Andrew Metrick. 2002. "Defined Contribution Pensions: Plan Rules, Participant Decisions, and the Path of Least Resistance." *Tax Policy and the Economy* 16: 67–114.

Clancy, Margaret, and Michael Sherraden. 2003. "The Potential for Inclusion in 529 Savings Plans: Report on a Survey of States." St. Louis, MO: Washington University in St. Louis, Center for Social Development.

Clancy, Margaret, Michal Grinstein-Weiss, and Mark Schreiner. 2001. "Financial Education and Savings Outcomes in Individual Development Accounts." St. Louis, MO: Washington University in St. Louis, Center for Social Development.

Clancy, Margaret, Peter Orszag, and Michael Sherraden. 2004. "College Savings Plans: A Platform for Inclusive Saving Policy?" St. Louis, MO: Washington University in St. Louis, Center for Social Development.

Cohen, Stewart. 1994. "Consumer Socialization: Children's Saving and Spending." *Childhood Education* 70(4): 244–46.

Conley, Dalton. 1999. *Being Black, Living in the Red: Race, Wealth, and Social Policy in America.* Berkeley: University of California Press.

Consumer Federation of America. 1990. *Consumer Knowledge: The Results of a Nationwide Test.* Washington, DC: Consumer Federation of America.

Cramer, Reid. 2006. "AutoSave: A Proposal to Reverse America's Savings Decline and Make Savings Automatic, Flexible, and Inclusive." Washington, DC: New America Foundation.

Cramer, Reid, Rourke O'Brien, and Alejandra Lopez-Fernadini. 2008. "The Assets Report 2008: A Review, Assessment, and Forecast of Federal Assets Policy." Washington, DC: New America Foundation.

Danes, Sharon M., and Heather Haberman. 2004. "2003–2004 Evaluation of the NEFE HSFPP." Greenwood Village, CO: National Endowment for Financial Education.

Deaton, Angus. 1991. "Saving and Liquidity Constraints." *Econometrica* 59(5): 1221–48.

Draut, Tamara. 2006. *Strapped: Why America's 20- and 30-Somethings Can't Get Ahead.* New York: Doubleday.

———. 2008. *Economic State of Young America.* New York: Dēmos: A Network for Ideas and Action. http://www.demos.org/pubs/esya_5_7_08.pdf. (Accessed July 26, 2008.)

Dubois, W. E. Burghardt. 1935. *Black Reconstruction: An Essay toward a History of the Part Which Black Folk Played in the Attempt to Reconstruct Democracy in America, 1860–1880.* New York: Harcourt, Brace and Company.

Duesenberry, James S. 1949. *Income, Saving and the Theory of Consumer Behavior.* Cambridge, MA: Harvard University Press.

Duflo, Esther, and Emmanuel Saez. 2003. "The Role of Information and Social Interactions in Retirement Plan Decisions: Evidence from a Randomized Experiment." *Quarterly Journal of Economics* 118(3): 815–42.

Duflo, Esther, William Gale, Jeffrey Liebman, Peter Orszag, and Emmanuel Saez. 2005. "Saving Incentives for Low- and Middle-Income Families: Evidence from a Field Experiment with H&R Block." Washington, DC: Retirement Security Project.

———. 2006. "Saving Incentives for Low- and Middle-Income Families: Evidence from a Field Experiment with H&R Block." *Quarterly Journal of Economics* 121(4): 1311–46.

Edin, Kathryn J. 2001. "More than Money: The Role of Assets in the Survival Strategies and Material Well-Being of the Poor." In *Assets for the Poor: The Benefits of Spreading Asset Ownership,* edited by Thomas M. Shapiro and Edward N. Wolff (206–31). New York: Russell Sage Foundation.

Engelhardt, Gary V. 2002. "Pre-retirement Lump-Sum Pension Distributions and Retirement Income Security: Evidence from the Health and Retirement Study." *National Tax Journal* 55(4): 665–85.

Finn, Cathleen M., Paz M. B. Zorita, and Claudia Coulton. 1994. "Assets and Financial Management among Poor Households in Extreme Poverty Neighborhoods." *Journal of Sociology and Social Welfare* 21(4): 75–94.

Frederick, Shane, George Loewenstein, and Ted O'Donoghue. 2003. "Time Discounting and Time Preference: A Critical Review." *Journal of Economic Literature* 40(2): 351–401.

Friedman, Milton. 1957. *A Theory of the Consumption Function.* Princeton, NJ: Princeton University Press.

Furnham, Adrian. 1985. "Why Do People Save? Attitudes to, and Habits of, Saving Money in Britain." *Journal of Applied Social Psychology* 15(4): 354–73.

Gale, William G., and John Karl Scholz. 1994. "Intergenerational Transfers and the Accumulation of Wealth." *Journal of Economic Perspectives* 8(4): 145–60.

Gale, William G., J. Mark Iwry, and Peter R. Orszag. 2004. "The Saver's Credit: Issues and Options." *Tax Notes* 103(5): 597–612.

Gittleman, Maury, and Edward N. Wolff. 2004. "Racial Differences in Patterns of Wealth Accumulation." *Journal of Human Resources* 39(1): 193–227.

Glaeser, Edward L., and Jesse M. Shapiro. 2002. "The Benefits of the Home Mortgage Interest Deduction." Cambridge, MA: Harvard Institute of Economic Research.

Greenstein, Robert. 2005. *The Earned Income Tax Credit: Boosting Employment, Aiding the Working Poor.* Washington, DC: Center on Budget and Policy Priorities.

Gyourko, Joseph, Peter Linneman, and Susan Wachter. 1999. "Analyzing the Relationships among Race, Wealth, and Home Ownership in America." *Journal of Housing Economics* 8(2): 63–89.

Hao, Lingxin. 1996. "Family Structure, Private Transfers, and the Economic Well-Being of Families." *Social Forces* 75(1): 269–92.

Heflin, Colleen M., and Mary Patillo. 2002. "Kin Effects on Black-White Account and Home Ownership." *Sociological Inquiry* 72(2): 220–39.

———. 2006. "Poverty in the Family: Race, Siblings, and Socioeconomic Heterogeneity." *Social Science Research* 35(4): 804–22.

Highfill, Janet, Douglas Thorson, and William V. Weber. 1998. "Tax Overwithholding as a Response to Uncertainty." *Public Finance Review* 26(4): 376–91.

Hilgert, Marianne A., Jeanne M. Hogarth, and Sondra G. Beverly. 2003. "Household Financial Management: The Connection between Knowledge and Behavior." *Federal Reserve Bulletin* 89(7): 309–22.

Hirad, Abdighani, and Peter M. Zorn. 2002. "Prepurchase Homeownership Counseling: A Little Knowledge is a Good Thing." In *Low-Income Homeownership: Examining the Unexamined Goal,* edited by Nicholas P. Retsinas and Eric S. Belsky (146–74). Cambridge, MA: Joint Center for Housing Studies; Washington, DC: Brookings Institution Press.

Hogan, M. Janice, Catherine Solheim, Susan Wolfgram, Busisiwe Nkosi, and Nicola Rodrigues. 2004. "The Working Poor: From the Economic Margins to Asset Building." *Family Relations* 53(2): 229–36.

Hogarth, Jeanne M., and Jinkook Lee. 2000. "Use of Financial Services and the Poor." St. Louis, MO: Washington University in St. Louis, Center for Social Development.

Hogarth, Jeanne, Christoslav Anguelov, and Jinkook Lee. 2005. "Who Has a Bank Account? Exploring Changes over Time, 1989–2001." *Journal of Family and Economic Issues* 26(1): 7–30.

Howard, Christopher. 1997. *The Hidden Welfare State: Tax Expenditures and Social Policy in the United States.* Princeton, NJ: Princeton University Press.

Hubbard, R. Glenn, Jonathan Skinner, and Stephen P. Zeldes. 1994. "Expanding the Life-Cycle Model: Precautionary Saving and Public Policy." *American Economic Review* 84(2): 174–79.

———. 1995. "Precautionary Saving and Social Insurance." *Journal of Political Economy* 103(2): 360–99.

Hurst, Erik., and James P. Ziliak. 2006. "Do Welfare Asset Limits Affect Household Saving? Evidence from Welfare Reform." *Journal of Human Resources* 41(1): 46–71.

Immergluck, Daniel, and Marti Wiles. 1999. *Two Steps Back: The Dual Mortgage Market, Predatory Lending, and the Undoing of Community Development.* Chicago: Woodstock Institute.

Jayakody, R. 1998. "Race Differences in Intergenerational Financial Assistance: The Needs of Children and the Resources of Parents." *Journal of Family Issues* 19(5): 508–33.

Joint Committee on Taxation. 2007. "Estimates of Federal Tax Expenditures for Fiscal Years 2007–2011." Paper prepared for the U.S. House of Representatives Committee on Ways and Means and the Committee on Finance. Washington, DC: U.S. Government Printing Office.

Katona, George. 1975. *Psychological Economics.* New York: Elsevier.

Katz, Michael. 1990. *The Undeserving Poor.* New York: Pantheon.

Keister, Lisa A. 2003. "Religion and Wealth: The Role of Religious Affiliation and Participation in Early Adult Asset Accumulation." *Social Forces* 82(1): 175–207.

———. 2004. "Race, Family Structure, and Wealth: The Effect of Childhood Family on Adult Asset Ownership." *Sociological Perspective* 47(2): 161–87.

Kempson, Elaine, Stephen McKay, and Sharon Collard. 2005. "Incentives to Save: Encouraging Saving among Low-Income Households." Bristol, UK: University of Bristol, Personal Finance Research Centre.

Kennickell, Arthur B., Martha Starr-McCluer, and Annika E. Sundén. 1997. "Saving and Financial Planning: Some Findings from a Focus Group." *Financial Counseling and Planning* 8(1): 1–8.

Kotlikoff, Laurence J., and B. Douglas Bernheim. 2001. "Household Financial Planning and Financial Literacy: The Need for New Tools." In *Essays on Saving, Bequests, Altruism, and Life-Cycle Planning,* edited by Lawrence J. Kotlikoff (427–78). Cambridge, MA: MIT Press.

Laibson, David. 1997. "Golden Eggs and Hyperbolic Discounting." *Quarterly Journal of Economics* 112(2): 443–77.

Lewin, Kurt, Tamara Dembo, Leon Festinger, and Pauline S. Sears. 1944. "Level of Aspiration." In *Personality and the Behavior Disorders,* edited by Joseph McVicker Hunt (333–78). New York: Ronald Press Company.

Lombe, Margaret, and Fred M. Ssewamala. 2007. "The Role of Informal Social Networks in Micro-Savings Mobilization." *Journal of Sociology and Social Welfare* 34(3): 37–51.

Lusardi, Annamaria. 2002. "Preparing for Retirement: The Importance of Planning Costs." *National Tax Association Proceedings* (148–54). Washington, DC: National Tax Association.

Lusardi, Annamaria, and Olivia S. Mitchell. 2007a. "Baby Boomer Retirement Security: The Roles of Planning, Financial Literacy, and Housing Wealth." *Journal of Monetary Economics* 54(1): 205–24.

———. 2007b. "Financial Literacy and Retirement Preparedness: Evidence and Implications for Financial Education." *Business Economics* 42(1): 35–44.

Madrian, Brigitte C., and Dennis F. Shea. 2000. "The Power of Suggestion: Inertia in 401(k) Participation and Savings Behavior." *Quarterly Journal of Economics* 116(4): 1149–87.

Maital, Shlomo, and Sharone L. Maital. 1994. "Is the Future What It Used to Be? A Behavioral Theory of the Decline of Saving in the West." *Journal of Socio-economics* 23(1/2): 1–32.

Mayer, Christopher J., and Gary V. Engelhardt. 1996. "Gifts, Down Payments, and Housing Affordability." *Journal of Housing Research* 7(1): 59–77.

McKernan, Signe-Mary, Caroline Ratcliffe, and Yunju Nam. 2007. *The Effects of Welfare and IDA Program Rules on the Asset Holdings of Low-Income Families.* Poor Finances: Assets and Low-Income Households Report. Washington, DC: Office of the Assistant Secretary for Planning and Evaluation, U.S. Dept. of Health and Human Services. http://aspe.hhs.gov/hsp/07/PoorFinances/assets/index.htm. (Accessed July 26, 2008.)

Menchik, Paul L., and Nancy Ammon Jianakoplos. 1997. "Black-White Wealth Inequality: Is Inheritance the Reason?" *Economic Inquiry* 35: 428–42.

Milligan, Kevin. 2003. "How Do Contribution Limits Affect Contributions to Tax-Preferred Savings Accounts?" *Journal of Public Economics* 87: 253–81.

Modigliani, Franco, and A. K. Ando. 1957. "Tests of the Life Cycle Hypothesis of Savings." *Bulletin of the Oxford Institute of Statistics* 19: 99–124.

Modigliani, Franco, and Richard Brumberg. 1954. "Utility Analysis and the Consumption Function: An Interpretation of Cross-Section Data." In *Post-Keynesian Economics,* edited by Kenneth K. Kurihara (388–436). New Brunswick, NJ: Rutgers University Press.

Moore, Amanda, Sondra Beverly, Mark Schreiner, Michael Sherraden, Margaret Lombe, Esther Y. N. Cho, Lissa Johnson, and Rebecca Vonderlack. 2001. "Saving, IDA Programs, and Effects of IDAs: A Survey of Participants." St. Louis, MO: Washington University in St. Louis, Center for Social Development.

Nam, Yunju. 2008. "Welfare Reform and Asset Accumulation: Asset Limit Changes, Financial Assets, and Vehicle Ownership." *Social Science Quarterly* 89(1): 133–54.

Neumark, David. 1995. "Are Rising Earnings Profiles a Forced-Saving Mechanism?" *Economic Journal* 105: 95–106.

Neumark, David, and Elizabeth Powers. 1998. "The Effect of Means-Tested Income Support for the Elderly on Pre-retirement Saving: Evidence from the SSI Program in the U.S." *Journal of Public Economics* 68(2): 181–206.

Nyce, Steven A. 2005. "The Importance of Financial Communication for Participation Rates and Contribution Levels in 401(k) Plans." Philadelphia: University of Pennsylvania, Wharton School, Pension Research Council.

Nyhus, Ellen K., and Paul Webley. 2001. "The Role of Personality in Household Saving and Borrowing Behavior." *European Journal of Personality* 15: S85–S103.

O'Donoghue, Ted, and Matthew Rabin. 1999. "Procrastination in Preparing for Retirement." In *Behavioral Dimensions of Retirement Economics,* edited by Henry J. Aaron (125–56). Washington DC: Brookings Institution Press.

Oliver, Melvin L., and Thomas M. Shapiro. 1995. *Black Wealth/White Wealth: A New Perspective on Racial Inequality.* New York: Routledge.

Olson, Lynn M., and Audrey Davis. 1994. "The Earned Income Tax Credit: Views from the Street Level." Evanston, IL: Northwestern University, Center for Urban Affairs and Policy Research.

Phillips, Katherin Ross. 2001. "Who Knows about the Earned Income Tax Credit?" Washington, DC: The Urban Institute. *Assessing the New Federalism* Brief B-27. http://www.urban.org/url.cfm?ID=310035. (Accessed July 9, 2008.)

Pollak, Robert A. 1998. "Notes on How Economists Think." Chicago: Joint Center for Poverty Research.

Purcell, Patrick J. 2001. *Pension Sponsorship and Participation: Summary of Recent Trends.* Washington, DC: Congressional Research Service.

———. 2006. "Retirement Plan Participation and Contributions: Trends from 1998–2003." *Journal of Pension Planning and Compliance* 32: 37–62.

Reid, Carolina Katz. 2004. "Achieving the American Dream? A Longitudinal Analysis of the Homeownership Experiences of Low-Income Households." Center for Studies in Demography and Ecology Working Paper 04-04. Seattle: University of Washington.

Romich, Jennifer L., and Thomas Weisner. 2000. "How Families View and Use the EITC: Advance Payment Versus Lump Sum Delivery." *National Tax Journal* 53(4, part 2): 1245–65.

Samwick, Andrew Alan. 2006. "Saving for Retirement: Understanding the Importance of Heterogeneity." *Business Economics* 41(1): 21–27.

Sarkisian, Natalia, and Naomi Gerstel. 2004. "Kin Support among Blacks and Whites: Race and Family Organization." *American Sociological Review* 69(6): 812–37.

Schmidt, Lucie, and Purvi Sevak. 2004. "Gender, Marriage, and Asset Accumulation in the United States." Williamstown, MA: Williams College.

Schoeni, Robert. 1997. "Private Interhousehold Transfers of Money and Time: New Empirical Evidence." *Review of Income and Wealth* 43(4): 423–48.

Schoeni, Robert F., and Karen E. Ross. 2005. "Material Assistance from Families during the Transition to Adulthood." In *On the Frontier of Adulthood: Theory, Research, and Public Policy,* edited by Richard A. Settersten Jr., Frank F. Furstenberg Jr., and Rubén. G. Rumbaut (396–416). Chicago: University of Chicago Press.

Schreiner, Mark, and Michael Sherraden. 2007. *Can the Poor Save? Saving and Asset Building in Individual Development Accounts.* New Brunswick, NJ: Transaction Publishers.

Schreiner, Mark, Michael Sherraden, Margaret Clancy, Lissa Johnson, Jami Curley, Michal Grinstein-Weiss, Min Zhan, and Sondra Beverly. 2001. "Savings and Asset Accumulation in Individual Development Accounts." St. Louis, MO: Washington University in St. Louis, Center for Social Development.

Seidman, Laurence S. 2001. "Assets and the Tax Code." In *Assets for the Poor: The Benefits of Spreading Asset Ownership,* edited by Thomas M. Shapiro and Edward N. Wolff (324–56). New York: Russell Sage Foundation.

Shapiro, Thomas M. 2004. *The Hidden Cost of Being African American: How Wealth Perpetuates Inequality.* New York: Oxford University Press.

———. 2006. "Race, Homeownership and Wealth." *Washington University Journal of Law and Policy* 20: 53–74.

Shefrin, Hersh M., and Richard H. Thaler. 1988. "The Behavioral Life-Cycle Hypothesis." *Economic Inquiry* 26(4): 609–43.

———. 1992. "Mental Accounting, Saving, and Self-Control." In *Choice over Time,* edited by George Loewenstein and Jon Elster (287–330). New York: Russell Sage Foundation.

Sherraden, Margaret, Amanda Moore McBride, Elizabeth Johnson, Stacie Hanson, Fred M. Ssewamala, and Trina R. Shanks. 2005. *Saving in Low-Income Households: Evidence from Interviews with Participants in the American Dream Demonstration.* St. Louis, MO: Washington University in St. Louis, Center for Social Development.

Sherraden, Michael. 1991. *Assets and the Poor: A New American Welfare Policy.* Armonk, NY: M. E. Sharpe.

———. 2005. "Inclusion in Asset Building." Testimony for Hearing on Building Assets for Low-Income Families, Subcommittee on Social Security and Family Policy, Senate Finance Committee, April 28. St. Louis, MO: Washington University in St. Louis, Center for Social Development.

Sherraden, Michael, and S. Michael Barr. 2005. "Institutions and Inclusion in Saving Policy." In *Building Assets, Building Credit: Bridges and Barriers to Financial Services in Low-Income Communities,* edited by Nicolas P. Retsinas and Eric S. Belsky (286–315). Washington, DC: Brookings Institution Press.

Smeeding, Timothy M., Katherin Ross Phillips, and Michael O'Connor. 2000. "The Earned Income Tax Credit: Expectation, Knowledge, Use, and Economic and Social Mobility." *National Tax Journal* 53(4, part 2): 1187–1209.

Spilerman, Seymour. 2000. "Wealth and Stratification Processes." *Annual Review of Sociology* 26(1): 497–524.

Stack, Carol B. 1974. *All Our Kin: Strategies for Survival in a Black Community.* New York: Harper and Row.

Strotz, Robert H. 1956. "Myopia and Inconsistency in Dynamic Utility Maximization." *Review of Economic Studies* 23(3): 165–80.

Sturm, Peter H. 1983. "Determinants of Saving: Theory and Evidence." *OECD Economic Studies* 1: 147–96.

Sullivan, James X. 2006. "Welfare Reform, Saving, and Vehicle Ownership: Do Asset Limits and Vehicle Exemptions Matter?" *Journal of Human Resources* 41(1): 72–105.

Tennyson, Sharon, and Chau Nguyen. 2001. "State Curriculum Mandates and Student Knowledge of Personal Finance." *Journal of Consumer Affairs* 35(2): 241–62.

Thaler, Richard H. 1990. "Saving, Fungibility and Mental Accounts." *Journal of Economic Perspectives* 4(1): 193–205.

———. 1994. "Psychology and Savings Policies." *American Economic Review* 84(2): 186–92.

———. 2000. "From *Homo economicus* to *Homo sapiens.*" *Journal of Economic Perspectives* 14(1): 133–41.

Thaler, Richard H., and Shlomo Benartzi. 2004. "Save More Tomorrow: Using Behavioral Economics to Increase Employee Saving." *Journal of Political Economy* 112(1, part 2): S164–S187.

Thaler, Richard H., and Hersh M. Shefrin. 1981. "An Economic Theory of Self-Control." *Journal of Political Economy* 89(2): 392–401.

Thaler, Richard H., Amos Tversky, Daniel Kahneman, Alan Schwartz. 1997. "The Effect of Myopia and Loss Aversion on Risk Taking: An Experimental Test." *Quarterly Journal of Economics* 112(2): 647–61.

Tufano, Peter, and Daniel Schneider. 2004. "H&R Block and Everyday Financial Services." Cambridge, MA: Harvard Business School Publishing.

Tversky, Amos, and Daniel Kahneman. 1991. "Loss Aversion in Riskless Choice— A Reference-Dependent Model." *Quarterly Journal of Economics* 106(4): 1039–61.

Wärneryd, Karl-Erik. 1996. "Personality and Saving." VSB-CentER Savings Project Progress Report 39. Tilburg University, the Netherlands: CentER for Economic Research.

Wilhelm, Mark O. 2001. "The Role of Intergenerational Transfers in Spreading Asset Ownership." In *Assets for the Poor: The Benefits of Spreading Asset Ownership,* edited by Thomas M. Shapiro and Edward N. Wolff (132–64). New York: Russell Sage Foundation.

Wolff, Edward N. 2002. "Inheritances and Wealth Inequality, 1989–1998." *American Economic Review* 92(2): 260–64.

Woo, Lillian G., F. William Schweke, and David E. Buchholz. 2004. *Hidden in Plain Sight: A Look at the $335 Billion Federal Asset-Building Budget.* Washington, DC: Corporation for Enterprise Development.

Yamokoski, Alexis, and Lisa Keister. 2006. "The Wealth of Single Women: Marital Status and Parenthood in the Asset Accumulation of Young Baby Boomers in the United States." *Feminist Economics* 12(1–2): 167–94.

Zhan, Min, Steven G. Anderson, and Jeff Scott. 2006. "Financial Knowledge of the Low-Income Population: Effects of a Financial Education Program." *Journal of Sociology and Social Welfare* 33(1): 53–74.

Ziliak, James P. 2003. "Income Transfers and Assets of the Poor." *Review of Economics and Statistics* 85(1): 63–76.

5

Effects of Asset Tests and IDA Programs

Yunju Nam, Caroline Ratcliffe, and Signe-Mary McKernan

Assets can bolster long-term economic gains of households by enabling long-term investment for the future (e.g., education and homeownership). At the same time, assets can cushion households against sudden income losses or expenditure spikes. Savings held as financial assets, however, can make low-income households ineligible for benefits from means-tested programs. Most means-tested programs, including Temporary Assistance for Needy Families (TANF) and the Food Stamp program (FSP), restrict eligibility to households with assets that fall below a threshold. These asset restrictions, or "asset tests," are designed to limit program benefits to those most in need. These restrictions, however, can have the unintended consequence of discouraging low-income households from saving and, therefore, impose barriers to long-term development among low-income households.

Since the early 1990s, federal and state governments have introduced policies and program rules to encourage savings and asset building among low-income households. First, they have relaxed asset rules for means-tested programs such as TANF and the FSP. Relaxed asset limits may encourage low-income households to save and accumulate assets, because they are less likely to lose public benefits because of their savings or vehicle assets. In addition, federal and state governments have been supporting individual development account (IDA) programs. IDAs are restricted savings accounts that provide matched funds at the time of withdrawal if the savings are used for a set goal that is likely to promote long-term development (e.g., higher education, homeownership, or entrepreneurship).

This chapter reviews and evaluates the state of our knowledge on the effects of government asset-related policies and program rules on low-income households' participation in means-tested programs and asset holdings. Specifically, we address three questions: (1) What are the effects of asset tests for means-tested programs on low-income households' program participation? (2) What are the effects of asset tests on low-income households' asset holdings? and (3) What are the effects of IDA programs on low-income households' asset holdings?

We begin by providing background on federal and state asset policies that are most likely to affect low-income households. Next, for each of the research questions, we discuss the mechanism by which we expect asset policies to affect low-income households' behavior (i.e., their program participation and asset building) and review the existing empirical literature. Finally, we discuss limitations of existing research and identify future research questions to advance our understanding of the relationship between public policies and the well-being of low-income households.

Background

Federal and state governments have adopted asset-building policies for low-income households since the early 1990s. Examples include the relaxation of asset limits in means-tested programs and the introduction of IDA programs. The Family Support Act of 1988 permitted states to apply for federal waivers to raise the Aid to Families with Dependent Children (AFDC) program's asset limits. Without a federal waiver, states could not raise these limits above the federal limits of $1,500 on vehicle assets and $1,000 on countable assets (i.e., the sum of financial assets—cash on hand, values in saving and checking accounts, bonds, stocks—and vehicle values that exceed the vehicle asset limit). The 1996 welfare reform legislation, which replaced AFDC with TANF, abolished the federal asset limits for welfare, allowing states to create their own limits (Corporation for Enterprise Development 2002; Rowe and Versteeg 2005; Savner and Greenberg 1995).

Taking advantage of the federal policy changes, many states increased limits imposed on countable assets in unrestricted accounts and vehicle assets. Between 1993 and 2003, average unrestricted asset limits to qualify for AFDC/TANF more than doubled in real terms (from $1,139 to $2,587), and 25 states implemented policies to exempt at least one vehicle when determining program eligibility (table 5.1). States also liberalized asset tests by creating restricted account programs. Restricted accounts have separate and higher asset limits than unrestricted accounts, but withdrawals are limited to only certain uses such as education, retirement, homeownership, or business start-up. Whereas only one state allowed welfare recipients to have restricted accounts in 1993, 28 states introduced restricted accounts by 2003. The average limit on assets in restricted accounts, among states with these accounts, also increased over time from $1,139 in 1993 to $7,683 in 2003.

In comparison to TANF, asset limits in the FSP were liberalized more slowly. Countable asset limits remained unchanged during the 1980s and 1990s (at $3,000 and $2,000 for households with and without an elderly member, respectively). Also, the federal vehicle asset limit increased by only $150 (in nominal dollars) during this period (from $4,500 to $4,650), although the federal government did allow a few states to ease vehicle asset limits via waivers.

The federal government took significant steps to liberalize FSP asset limits through the Agricultural Appropriation Act of 2001 (PL 106-398) and the Food Security and Rural Investment Act of 2002 (PL 107-171). These two pieces of legislation allowed states to align FSP asset limits with those of other public assistance programs such as TANF. As a result, the number of states that allowed the exemption of at least one vehicle increased dramatically from 3 states in 1999 to 30 states in 2003 (table 5.1). At the same time, states began to extend categorical eligibility for food stamps to units that receive TANF services (not just TANF cash benefits). Many states use this expansion of categorical eligibility as a way to ease vehicle asset limits. By 2003, 36 states offered expanded categorical eligibility (table 5.1).

During the 1990s, federal and state governments also began to adopt IDA programs to encourage low-income, low-wealth households to accumulate assets for their long-term economic development. IDA programs create accounts for participants to save for specific purposes, such as higher education, homeownership, and entrepreneurship. An important feature of IDA programs is the matching funds they provide at the time of withdrawal if savings will be used for one of the pre-set goals (Corporation for Enterprise Development 2002; Sherraden 1991, 2001).

Table 5.1. State AFDC/TANF, Food Stamp, and State IDA Program Rules, Number of States with Rule and Mean Value of Rule by Year

Program rule variable	1991	1993	1995	1997	1999	2001	2003
AFDC/TANF							
Unrestricted asset limit (mean asset limit, $)	$1,199	$1,139	$1,353	$2,366	$2,730	$2,652	$2,587
Vehicle asset limit (mean asset limit, $)	$1,798	$5,150	$5,745	$9,967	$10,748	$10,562	$10,333
Vehicle asset limit, at least one vehicle (# of states)	0	0	2	19	22	24	25
Restricted account asset limit (mean asset limit, $)	$0	$1,139	$4,368	$7,509	$7,686	$7,836	$7,683
Restricted account asset limit (# of states)	0	1	4	14	20	23	28
FSP							
FSP vehicle asset limit, at least one vehicle (# of states)	0	0	1	3	3	2	30
Expanded categorical eligibility (# of states)	0	0	0	0	0	38	36
IDA							
State IDA programs (# of states)	0	0	0	4	9	24	24
Maximum match rate (mean, $)	$0.00	$0.00	$0.00	$1.88	$1.86	$2.25	$2.30
Match cap (mean, $)	$0	$0	$0	$5,099	$3,576	$12,585	$12,823
Eligibility beyond welfare recipients (# of states)	0	0	0	3	7	20	19

Sources: Urban Institute, Welfare Rules Database; U.S. Department of Agriculture, Food Stamp Rules Database; Center for Social Development, State IDA Policy Information and 2005 Survey on State IDA Programs.

AFDC/TANF = Aid to Families with Dependent Children/Temporary Assistance for Needy Families

FSP = Food Stamp program

IDA = Individual Development Account

Notes: Means do not include zeros. All dollar values are expressed in year 2000 dollars, as calculated using the implicit price deflator for personal consumption expenditures.

Recognizing the potential effectiveness of IDA programs based on evaluation results of privately funded IDA programs such as the American Dream Demonstration, some states instituted IDA programs through legislation, executive orders, or administrative decisionmaking during the mid-1990s (Warren and Edwards 2005). State IDA initiatives were facilitated by subsequent federal legislation. The welfare-to-work law of 1997 permitted grantees to use TANF funds for IDA programs. Further, the Assets for Independence Act (AFIA) of 1998 created the first federally funded national demonstration programs for IDAs. AFIA mandates the Office of Community Services in the Department of Health and Human Services to award five-year grants to nonprofit organizations and to government or financial institutions partnering with nonprofits for IDA programs (Corporation for Enterprise Development 2002). By 2003, 24 states had IDA programs that were at least partially funded by the state government (table 5.1).[1] Among states with IDA programs, the average match rate was roughly two to one across the years, while the average match cap (the maximum amount of savings that is eligible for the match) increased in the early 2000s and was almost $13,000 in 2003.

Effect of Means-Tested Program Rules on Program Participation

Restrictive asset eligibility rules may deter low-income households from participating in means-tested public assistance programs even when they are experiencing economic hardship. Low asset limits in means-tested programs may simply disqualify some low-income households from participating. In addition, asset tests can make the public assistance program application process complicated and burdensome to low-income households, especially those whose resources are close to the cutoff point (Bartlett, Burstein, and Hamilton 2004; McConnell and Ponza 1999; O'Brien 2006; Pavetti, Maloy, and Schott 2002). These costs associated with verifying eligibility can lead to reduced participation. In fact, qualitative studies show that program participants and applicants do find it time consuming and burdensome to collect all required documents for asset tests, such as bank statements and vehicle information (O'Brien 2006; Pavetti et al. 2002). Requiring this information be reported to program staff may also be perceived as intrusive and too personal.

Asset tests may also discourage eligible low-income households from applying for benefits because they misunderstand asset eligibility rules. Households may believe they are not eligible for benefits or question their eligibility. Further, households with aspirations of accumulating assets in the near future may not want to apply for benefits (McConnell and Ponza 1999; O'Brien 2006). Research does, in fact, suggest that a substantial proportion of eligible households are uncertain about their eligibility. According to Bartlett and others (2004), over half of the FSP-eligible non-participants believed themselves ineligible for benefits or were not sure of their eligibility. Asset tests played a role in their misunderstandings about FSP eligibility—15 percent thought the value of a vehicle would disqualify them and 12 percent thought the value of their financial assets would disqualify them. Further, qualitative interviews with TANF recipients suggest that they were misinformed about program rules; the majority believed that TANF asset limits were much lower than the actual limits (O'Brien 2006).

Although existing qualitative research provides insight into the ways asset tests affect program participation, it does not provide information about the magnitude of these effects. Several empirical studies have examined the effects of asset limits on AFDC/TANF receipt (Blank and Ruggles 1996; Hurst and Ziliak 2006; Sullivan 2006) and Food Stamp receipt (Blank and Ruggles 1996; Daponte, Sanders, and Taylor 1999; Hanratty 2006; Ratcliffe, McKernan, and Finegold 2008; Rosso 2003; Wemmerus and Gottlieb 1999). Most of these studies are, however, based on descriptive analyses. Exceptions include three analyses of FSP receipt (Hanratty 2006; Ratcliffe et al. 2008; Wemmerus and Gottlieb 1999).

In estimating the extent to which asset tests may affect low-income households' public assistance program participation, the descriptive analyses generally compare potential recipients' asset holdings with asset limits in the particular public assistance programs being studied (Blank and Ruggles 1996; Daponte et al. 1999; Hurst and Ziliak 2006; Rosso 2003; Sullivan 2006). Using a sample of single mothers from the 1986 and 1987 panels of the Survey of Income and Program Participation (SIPP), Blank and Ruggles (1996) show that only a small percentage of income-eligible households were made ineligible for AFDC and food stamp benefits because of asset tests. The percentage of months single mothers were ineligible for AFDC increased from 57 percent when only income was considered to 60 percent when assets were also taken into account (Blank and Ruggles 1996). The percentages for the FSP were 48 percent and 55 percent, respectively (Blank and Ruggles 1996).

Hurst and Ziliak (2006) use the Panel Study of Income Dynamics (PSID) to examine liquid-asset holdings among likely welfare recipients, defined as single mothers with less than 16 years of schooling. They find, for example, that more than half of likely welfare recipients had zero liquid assets and that liquid-asset values were generally low among those with some liquid assets. Based on their analysis, they conclude that countable asset tests are not likely to affect the means-tested program participation of the majority of likely welfare recipients. An analysis by Sullivan (2006), based on SIPP data from 1992 through 1999, shows similar results on the countable asset limit. However, Sullivan shows that vehicle ownership is relatively common among potential and current welfare recipients and suggests that the vehicle asset limit in place under AFDC might have been more binding than countable asset limits, and thus more likely to affect participation. Among single mothers with a high school degree or less, for example, 58 percent owned a vehicle and the mean vehicle equity value was $1,862, almost 25 percent higher than the former AFDC vehicle asset limit of $1,500 (Sullivan 2006).

Analyses of a broader population of low-income households (i.e., not only single mothers) suggest that asset tests do make households ineligible for benefits, and thus, are likely to lead to lower program participation. Daponte and others (1999) conducted detailed FSP eligibility screening among food pantry service users with incomes below 185 percent of the poverty threshold. They found that 17.5 percent of households not participating in the FSP were determined to be ineligible because their countable assets exceeded asset limits. In addition, a study by Rosso (2003), which uses November 1999 SIPP data, shows that a significant percentage of households that were income-eligible for the FSP failed to pass asset tests. Our calculations, using data presented in table 1 (Rosso 2003), show that 30.1 percent of these households failed to pass asset tests. Finally, research suggests that the liberalization of vehicle asset limits in the early 2000s made 2.7 million more individuals eligible for food stamps in 2002 than would have been eligible under the old asset rules (Cunnyngham 2004).

Wemmerus and Gottlieb (1999) is a rare experimental study that examines the effects of liberalized asset limits on FSP participation in North Carolina's Vehicle Exclusion Limit Demonstration. The study shows that the exclusion of the first automobile from FSP eligibility increased the program participation rate by 2.3 percent. This demonstration also indicates that it takes time to see the full impact of the eligibility change; the

FSP participation rate increased most between 12 and 18 months after the new rule was implemented.

Two recent empirical studies use SIPP data (1996 and 2001 panels), state variation in FSP asset limits, and a multivariate framework to examine the effects of asset limits on food stamp receipt. Consistent with Wemmerus and Gottlieb (1999), Ratcliffe and others (2008) find that exempting at least one vehicle from asset tests increases low-income households' FSP receipt. Hanratty (2006), however, finds that the effects of vehicle exemption rules on low-income families' food stamp receipt were not statistically significant. While the literature provides evidence that relaxing vehicle asset limits increased FSP receipt (Ratcliffe et al. forthcoming; Wemmerus and Gottlieb 1999), relaxing TANF vehicle asset limits was found to have no statistically significant effect on low-income households' FSP receipt (Ratcliffe et al. 2008).

In summary, information about the relationship between asset limits and TANF receipt is quite limited. To our best knowledge, every study on cash assistance program participation (AFDC and TANF) relies on descriptive statistics. These studies suggest that most current and potential welfare recipients are unlikely to be bound by the old countable asset limit because their asset possession is much lower than the limit (Blank and Ruggles 1996; Hurst and Zilliak 2006; Sullivan 2006). At the same time, the literature suggests that welfare benefit receipt is more likely affected by vehicle asset limits (than countable asset limits) because vehicle ownership is relatively common among potential and current welfare recipients (Sullivan 2006). While informative, descriptive studies have limitations in demonstrating the effects of asset limits on welfare program participation. These analyses, for example, do not provide information on how individuals respond behaviorally to changes in asset limits.

The literature provides more information on the relationship between FSP rules and FSP participation. Analyses suggest that a substantial proportion of income-eligible households are made ineligible for the FSP because of their asset holdings (Daponte et al. 1999; Rosso 2003), although the estimated effects are more modest when the sample is limited to single mothers (Blank and Ruggles 1996). Three studies go beyond descriptive analyses to examine the effect of FSP vehicle asset exemptions on FSP participation. Two studies find that vehicle exemptions increased FSP participation (Ratcliffe et al. 2008; Wemmerus and Gottlieb 1999), while one study finds no statistically significant relationship (Hanratty 2006).

Effects of Means-Tested Programs and Program Rules on Asset Holding

Means-tested public assistance programs are believed to lower saving rates among poor households for two reasons: (1) they guarantee a certain level of consumption by providing benefits at the time of economic emergencies (consumption-floor effect) and (2) they have restrictive asset tests. The consumption floor in income transfer programs is expected to influence saving rates by reducing precautionary saving motives. That is to say, the availability of income from the government is expected to reduce a household's need to save for a sudden economic loss (e.g., losing a job) and, therefore, to lower saving rates among current and potential beneficiaries of these programs. Restrictive asset tests are also expected to discourage low-income households from accumulating financial assets. This is because households may spend down their assets or keep them below asset limits to become eligible for means-tested program benefits (Hubbard, Skinner, and Zeldes 1995).

The consumption-floor effect of income-maintenance programs is salient even among middle-income households, as shown in the case of Unemployment Insurance (Carroll, Dynan, and Krane 2003; Engen and Gruber 2001), but its effect is stronger for low-income households, mainly due to their lower lifetime earnings (Hubbard et al. 1995; Ziliak 2003). The literature on the consumption-floor effects of specific income transfer programs (such as Unemployment Insurance, Supplemental Security Income [SSI], AFDC, and Food Stamps) suggests that households' financial assets tend to decrease with increases in the likelihood of benefit receipt, expected benefit levels from income transfer programs, and the generosity of state benefits (Bird and Hagstrom 1999; Engen and Gruber 2001; Gruber and Yelowitz 1999; Neumark and Powers 1998; Ziliak 2003).

Existing empirical studies also find that asset tests affect the asset accumulation of low-income households (Gruber and Yelowitz 1999; Hubbard et. al 1995; Ziliak 2003). Ziliak (2003) finds that the effect of asset-tested transfer income on liquid assets is more than twice that of transfer income not asset tested, suggesting that asset tests impose an additional barrier to financial asset accumulation independent of the consumption-floor effect. Two empirical studies show strong effects of Medicaid and SSI asset limits on low-income households' asset holding. Gruber and Yelowitz's (1999) examination of the Medicaid program suggests that the presence of asset tests leads to a reduction in total household net worth. Specifically, they find that a $1,000 increase in estimated benefits from Medicaid (Medicaid-eligible dollars) in the presence of an asset test reduces household assets by 4.4 percent, while in the absence of an asset test, household assets decrease by only 1.8 percent. Similarly, Neumark and Powers (1998) suggest that elderly low-income households may lower their liquid assets as they approach retirement and the eligibility age for SSI to pass the asset test.

Five studies examine the effects of AFDC/TANF asset limits on asset holdings (Hurst and Ziliak 2006; McKernan, Ratcliffe, and Nam 2007; Nam 2008; Powers 1998; Sullivan 2006). All of these studies use temporal and state variations in asset-limit policies to identify the effects of program rules on asset building. The earliest of these studies (Powers 1998) examines the effect of the Omnibus Budget Reconciliation Act of 1981 that lowered AFDC countable and vehicle asset limits in some states by generally requiring states with asset limits above the new federal level to lower them. The other studies investigate the effects of liberalized asset-limit policies since the early 1990s. Four of these studies (Hurst and Ziliak 2006; Nam 2008; Powers 1998; Sullivan 2006) focus only on AFDC/TANF program rules, while McKernan and others include program rules from the FSP, IDAs, and the earned income tax credit.[2]

The findings from this literature are inconclusive. Of five empirical studies, Hurst and Ziliak (2006) and Sullivan (2006) find that relaxing AFDC/TANF asset-test rules did not increase households' liquid-asset holdings or net worth, Powers (1998) and Nam (2008) find positive effects of generous asset-test rules, and McKernan and others (2007) report mixed effects.

Using PSID data, Hurst and Ziliak (2006) test whether relaxed AFDC/TANF asset-test rules (measured with the dollar amount of countable and vehicle asset limits) increase asset holdings of likely welfare recipients (single mothers with less than 16 years of schooling). They find that higher asset limits are not associated with a significant increase in net worth and liquid assets among single-mother families. Sullivan's study reports findings consistent with Hurst and Ziliak, based on data from the 1992, 1993, and 1996 SIPP panels.

Powers (1998) and Nam (2008), on the other hand, find that higher asset limits are positively associated with single mothers' asset holdings. Using 1978 and 1983 data from the National Longitudinal Survey of Young Women, Powers finds that a decrease of one dollar in countable asset limits for AFDC families reduced a female head's net worth (excluding vehicle equity) by 25 cents.

Different findings between Powers and two other recent studies (Hurst and Ziliak 2006; Sullivan 2006) can be explained by different observation periods and characteristics of the studied asset-rules changes. Powers's analysis is based on data collected before welfare reform (1978–1983) when economic, political, and social environments were different from the period that the other two studies examine. In addition, she investigates a policy change that tightened asset limits, whereas the other two studies examine liberalized asset-limit policy. That is to say, Powers investigates a policy change that would have immediate impact on the target population of welfare recipients (i.e., welfare recipients could spend down their savings quickly when they were likely to lose their eligibility due to decreased asset limits), while the other studies examine a policy shift that would have taken time to affect the target population (i.e., saving up in response to increased limits could not be done easily and rapidly among low-income households).

Nam (2008) uses the same data and time period as Hurst and Ziliak (2006), but reaches different conclusions by using a different program measure. Nam expands on Hurst and Ziliak's analysis by estimating models that measure the length of time since states adopted new asset limits. Incorporating these "length of time" measures into the analysis allows Nam to capture and test whether it takes time for current and potential welfare recipients to learn about and adapt to program rule changes. She finds that the earlier a state raised its countable asset limit, the more likely were female-headed households with children to have positive savings and a bank account. Nam (2008) and Hurst and Ziliak (2006) also examine different measures of savings. Nam examines a nonlinear measure of saving (natural logarithm) and finds that the amount of saving is significantly higher for those living in states with higher asset limits when taking into account the possibility of their making positive saving. Hurst and Ziliak, on the other hand, examine a linear measure and find no effect of asset limits on savings.

The McKernan, Ratcliffe, and Nam study (2007) differs from the other three by including a comprehensive list of public assistance program rules. For example, their analysis includes a new type of AFDC/TANF asset-limit policy (restricted account asset limits) that treats savings for special purposes (e.g., education, homebuying, or business start-up) more favorably than traditional unrestricted countable asset limits. Like Nam (2008), they examine both the dollar amounts of asset limits and years since new asset limits have been adopted. Using five SIPP panels (1990,

1992, 1993, 1996, and 2001), their findings are consistent with Hurst and Ziliak (2006) and Sullivan (2006), showing that higher asset limits on unrestricted accounts, measured in dollar amounts, are associated with neither increased liquid assets nor increased net worth for low-education (high school degree or less) single mothers or families. They show, however, that generous restricted-account asset limits increase liquid-asset holdings. Similar to Nam (2008), they find that the number of years since the adoption of new unrestricted asset limits is associated with increased liquid-asset holdings. The number of years since the adoption of a new restricted account limit, however, does not have a significant association with increased liquid-asset holdings.

The research on the effect of TANF program rules on vehicle ownership is also mixed. Sullivan (2006) and Hurst and Ziliak (2006) find evidence that relaxing AFDC/TANF asset limits leads to higher vehicle ownership. However, these studies come to different conclusions about which policy change promotes vehicle ownership: Hurst and Ziliak attribute it to increases in countable asset limits, whereas Sullivan links it with the liberalization of vehicle asset limits. At the same time, Nam (2008) and McKernan and others (2007) find no evidence that vehicle ownership increases after generous asset limits are adopted. The difference in results across these studies could be explained by different samples and model specifications.

McKernan and others (2007) also examine the effects of relaxed FSP vehicle asset limits on families' asset holdings. Their analyses include FSP vehicle asset exemptions and expanded categorical eligibility. They find that generous FSP vehicle asset limits significantly increase single mothers' vehicle ownership and vehicle equity. Expanded categorical eligibility is also expected to increase vehicle asset holding, because it relaxes asset tests by making families that receive TANF services (not just TANF cash benefits) eligible for food stamps, even if the FSP has more stringent asset tests. Also, according to staff at the U.S. Department of Agriculture, many states use categorical eligibility as a backdoor way to ease vehicle asset limits. Consistent with this intended use of expanded categorical eligibility, McKernan and others (2007) find positive effects of extended categorical eligibility on both low-education single mothers and families.

In summary, theoretical literature hypothesizes that means-tested income transfer programs will reduce low-income households' asset accumulation through the consumption-floor effects and through restrictive asset tests (Bird and Hagstrom 1999; Engen and Gruber 2001; Gruber and Yelowitz 1999; Neumark and Powers 1998; Ziliak 2003). Early empirical studies support this hypothesis, especially for asset-test effects (Gruber and Yelowitz 1999; Hubbard et al. 1995; Powers 1998; Ziliak 2003). However, evidence is mixed on whether recent policy changes liberalizing asset-limit rules have achieved the goal of increasing low-income households' asset holding (Hurst and Zilliak 2006; McKernan et al. 2007; Nam 2008; Sullivan 2006). Many of the existing asset-limit rules in means-tested programs are inconsistent and confusing, which could limit the impact of liberalizing them.

Effect of IDA Programs on Asset Holdings

Sherraden (1991) first proposed IDAs as an institutional construct to promote saving and asset accumulation among low-income households. IDA programs create accounts for participants to save for specific purposes, such as higher education, homeownership, and business start-up. In addition, they provide matching funds at the time of withdrawal (i.e., matched withdrawals), if savings will be used for one of these set goals. Suggesting that assets are a critical element of poor households' long-term economic and social development, Sherraden developed an asset- and capacity-based approach as a new antipoverty strategy to complement traditional income-maintenance programs. Based on the institutional theory of asset building, Sherraden (1991) argues that the poor can save with appropriate institutional structures and public policies that facilitate their saving despite their low level of resources.[3] Because traditional asset-building policies, such as tax-advantaged retirement accounts and tax breaks for mortgage interest, have not worked for the poor as well as they have for middle- and high-income households, IDAs are deliberately structured to encourage the poor to "see saving as an option that is easy to choose and will likely have positive consequences" (Schreiner and Sherraden 2007, 5).

According to Schreiner and Sherraden (2007), IDAs introduce various institutional mechanisms to address the two major impediments to saving among the poor: their low economic resources relative to their consumption needs and their inaccurate belief that saving is not an achievable goal and that asset accumulation would not bring positive outcomes. A key savings mechanism is matched savings, which provides a much higher return than traditional investments such as interest earned from banks or investment gains from the stock market. Accordingly, IDAs motivate the poor to save. In addition, high financial returns yielded by the match increase the economic resources available to the participants when they withdraw their savings for their goals. Another mechanism identified by Schreiner and Sherraden (2007) is the constraint of matches to set goals (e.g., homebuying). This constraint may help participants resist the temptation to withdraw funds for short-term consumption needs. Other mechanisms, including financial education and constructive messages delivered through IDA program staff or peer groups, may boost participants' confidence in their ability to save and increase their financial knowledge (Schreiner and Sherraden 2007).

What do we know about the effect of IDA program rules on asset holdings? Qualitative studies show that the majority of IDA participants saved in IDAs and some of them did so regularly. In fact, in-depth interviews show that low-income IDA participants were able to save even at a time of financial challenge, such as a job layoff (Hogan et al. 2004; Shobe and Christy-McMullin 2005). These studies also show the important role of program components other than matches: many interviewees valued financial education classes and social supports from IDA staff members and fellow participants (Hogan et al. 2004; Shobe and Christy-McMullin 2005).

Several studies based on IDA monitoring data also show that low-income households can save. A majority of IDA participants made deposits into their IDAs, and a substantial proportion succeeded in making matched withdrawals (Losby and Robinson 2004; Schreiner and Sherraden 2007; U.S. Department of Health and Human Services 2004). According to American Dream Demonstration Account Monitoring data, a slim majority of program participants (53 percent) saved at least $100 in their ADD accounts. Among participants who succeeded in saving $100 or more, the average net deposit was $537, the average monthly deposit was $21, and about 35 percent made matched withdrawals. The average value of matched withdrawals (including matches) was $2,711 (Schreiner et al. 2005). Another large-scale demonstration authorized by the AFIA, along with some smaller-scale studies that monitored IDA participants' savings behavior, produced similar results (Losby and Robinson 2004; U.S. Department of Health and Human Services 2004).[4]

Account-monitoring studies, however, have drawbacks in their methodology. First, they do not have information on non-IDA assets and, therefore, do not measure whether deposits into IDAs are new savings or substitutions of savings that would have gone into other savings vehicles. Second, assets accumulated in IDAs may not be attributed purely to IDA effects because participants may have saved in the absence of the IDA.

In an experimental study that controlled for selection into an IDA program by assigning applicants randomly into treatment and control groups, Mills, Gale, and others (2008) find that the IDA program did not significantly increase net worth or business ownership (among treatment-group members in comparison with control-group members). IDA participants also did not significantly differ from control-group members in terms of getting more postsecondary education or vocational training during the study period. IDA program participation, however, significantly increased homeownership among renters who lived in unsubsidized housing at the time of the baseline survey. Participation in an IDA program was also associated with a significant decline in nonretirement financial assets, especially among unsubsidized renters. These results suggest that program participants might have liquidated their financial assets for home purchases (e.g., down payments and closing costs).

Measuring IDA program effects by comparing outcomes of AFIA program participants with a matched comparison group, Mills, Lam, and others (2008) find that AFIA participants experienced significantly higher rates of homeownership and business ownership three years after opening an account. The authors found no significant effect on net worth or participation in means-tested programs.

It has not been tested, however, whether IDA programs promote homeownership among participants in the long run or just accelerate their home purchases to fully utilize program incentives. Long-term effects of IDA programs have not yet been examined due to data limitations. For example, Mills, Gale, and others (2008a) only had four years of follow-up data.

McKernan and others (2007) is the first study (known to the authors) to use a nationally representative sample to examine the effects of IDA programs on low-income households' asset accumulation. Using the individual-level data from the SIPP and state policy data, they examine the relationship between state IDA program rules and asset holdings (liquid assets, vehicle assets, and net worth) of low-education single mothers and low-education families. Results from their study suggest that more generous state IDA policies increase liquid-asset holdings. Specifically, setting a higher amount eligible for the match and having had more years pass since the adoption of a state IDA program both showed a positive association with liquid-asset holdings of low-education families. The authors find no evidence that state IDA program rules are statistically significantly related to vehicle ownership. This finding is consistent with the fact that most state IDA programs do not allow participants to use their IDA savings for vehicle purchases. Finally, IDA program rules are found to have a mixed relationship with net worth. The maximum match rate is associated with an increase in net worth, while the maximum amount qualified for a match is weakly associated with a decrease in net worth. While the study's IDA program findings are quite robust, the authors recommend using caution in interpreting the IDA results because the SIPP does not measure IDA program participation.[5] As a result, the number of IDA program participants captured in the data is uncertain and could be small.

In summary, the existing literature produces mixed results on the effect of IDAs on asset building. IDA account-monitoring data suggest that low-income households are able to save in their IDAs (Schreiner and Sherraden 2007; U.S. Department of Health and Human Services 2004). Two studies of IDA participants (Mills, Lam, et al. 2008; Mills, Gale, et al. 2008) suggest that IDA programs had no effect on participants' net worth. Mills, Gale, and others (2008a) do, however, find evidence that the composition of the assets changed. Specifically, they find that the IDA programs reduced liquid assets but increased homeownership among a certain group of participants (i.e., renters). However, Mills, Lam, and others (2008) find no significant effect of the AFIA IDA program on liquid assets. At the same time, a multivariate study based on a nationally representative sample (McKernan et al. 2007) suggests that state IDA programs have increased liquid-asset holdings, with mixed results on net worth.

The difference in findings on liquid assets across the studies could be due to timing. IDA programs may increase participants' liquid assets in the short run as participants put savings into their IDAs. Then, when participants withdraw their money from their IDAs to receive the match (and use the money for one of the set goals), liquid assets would fall. The design of the McKernan and others (2007) study, for example, is such that IDA participants would be captured at any point in the participation process. The analyses by Mills, Lam, and others (2008) and Mills, Gale, and others (2008), on the other hand, capture IDA participants three and four years after enrollment in the program. Due to limitations in study design and observation period, previous research, however, is unable to answer whether IDA programs have positive long-term impacts on participants' economic development.

Conclusion

The limited and largely descriptive research to date finds that asset tests, especially vehicle asset tests, keep a substantial portion of low-income households from participating in the Food Stamp program and some low-income households from participating in TANF. Research also suggests that misunderstanding and confusion about asset limits leads potentially eligible recipients to believe they are ineligible, and therefore, they fail to apply for benefits. Further, asset tests may deter some low-income households from participating in public assistance programs even when they experience economic hardship. But what role, if any, do asset tests play in keeping moderate-income households from benefits not intended for them? Given other program rules, asset limits may do little to prevent the less needy from participating, yet they make eligibility determinations more burdensome and costly. The benefits from liberalizing asset tests may be offset by the cost of weaker targeting of benefits on the most needy. However, the costs of mistargeted benefits are not well understood and could be relatively low, especially when compared with costs of administering asset tests. For example, the Virginia Department of Planning and Budget estimated that the elimination of TANF asset limits would increase the caseload only slightly, since only 0.5 percent of applicants had been denied due to their assets. At the same time, its cost-benefit estimation suggests that the asset-limit elimination would save the state money; it was predicted to "increase the assistance provided by $127,200 for 40 families and provide $323,050 savings in administrative staff time annually" (Rand 2007, 629). Further research is required to determine the magnitude of these costs in other states or at the federal level.

Research on the effects of asset tests on asset holding is more mixed. Early empirical studies find that asset tests reduce asset holdings, but later studies disagree on whether recent policy changes liberalizing asset-limit rules have increased asset holding. Existing studies illustrate the need for future research to develop new measures of policy change when quantifying asset policy. Findings based on the level of change (e.g., the dollar amount of asset-limit change) differ from those based on the timing of change (e.g., the number of years since a policy change). It takes time for asset limits and IDA programs to affect participation and asset holdings. The effects of recent policy changes could be limited because current asset policies are misunderstood. Potentially eligible recipients may believe they are ineligible and so unnecessarily spend down their assets before applying for benefits.

These findings suggest that asset tests could be simplified and clarified. Since people often need a reliable car to get to work, further relaxing and simplifying vehicle asset limits—by exempting at least one vehicle in all states—may increase employment and job stability, and thus, improve the well-being of low-income families.

Given the potential for restricted asset accounts (such as those in IDA programs) to improve asset holdings, states could simplify and make more equitable program rules related to restricted asset accounts. State means-tested policies on restricted asset accounts are inconsistent, inequitable, and confusing. Similar types of assets are treated differently. For example, only savings in federally funded IDA accounts are exempt in some states but not savings in other similar IDA programs or college and homeown-ership savings programs (Rand 2007). And only savings in some types of retirement accounts (e.g., defined benefit but not defined contribution) are exempt in other states (Neuberger, Greenstein, and Orszag 2006). States could simplify and clarify restricted asset account rules by exempt-ing retirement accounts—such as 401(k) plans and individual retirement accounts—as well as other restricted savings accounts, such as those for education, homeownership, and small business ownership.

Current asset policies are often confusing for current and potential participants and likely costly to enforce. Asset tests vary widely across government social programs (Chen and Lerman 2005), contributing to confusion and administrative costs. The rules could be clarified and sim-plified by making them more consistent across means-tested programs, across states, and across similar asset types.

NOTES

1. The following four criteria are used to define IDA programs reported in table 5.1: (1) the program matches savings when they are withdrawn for defined purposes; (2) the program is funded at least partially from state government, including programs within TANF and welfare-to-work programs (but excluding programs funded solely by private foundations); (3) the program is established through state legislation or administrative rule making; and (4) the program is actually implemented.

2. Sullivan (2006) examines the possible interaction between AFDC/TANF and FSP asset rules with an alternative asset-policy measure; he sets a state's countable and vehicle asset limits as the lower limit of each type across these two programs. He reports that the results of this analysis are consistent with his main finding.

3. For details of institutional theory of asset building, please see chapter 4.

4. IDA program characteristics also affect participants' saving performance. Higher match rates tend to increase participants' likelihood of saving $100 or more in IDA accounts, but match rates greater than two are associated with lower levels of net savings among those who save more than $100. Higher match caps (the highest level of deposits eligible for matches) increase net IDA savings. Up to 10 hours of financial education is associated with high monthly net savings (Schreiner and Sherraden 2007).

5. No national datasets collect information on IDA program participants or saving in IDAs, as discussed in the appendix. Accordingly, it is impossible to investigate what percentage of low-income households actually participate in IDA programs and what portions of their liquid assets and net worth are saved in IDAs.

REFERENCES

Bartlett, Susan, Nancy Burstein, and William Hamilton. 2004. *Food Stamp Program Access Study: Final Report.* E-FAN-03-013-3. Report to the U.S. Department of Agriculture, Economic Research Service. Cambridge, MA: Abt Associates.

Bird, Edward J., and Paul A. Hagstrom. 1999. "The Wealth Effects of Income Insurance." *Review of Income and Wealth* 45(3): 339–52.

Blank, Rebecca, and Patricia Ruggles. 1996. "When Do Women Use Aid to Families with Dependent Children and Food Stamps?" *Journal of Human Resources* 31(1): 57–89.

Carroll, Christopher D., Karen E. Dynan, and Spencer D. Krane. 2003. "Unemployment Risk and Precautionary Wealth: Evidence from Households' Balance Sheets." *Review of Economics and Statistics* 85(3): 586–604.

Chen, Henry, and Robert I. Lerman. 2005. "Do Asset Limits in Social Programs Affect the Accumulation of Wealth?" Washington, DC: The Urban Institute. Opportunity and Ownership Project Brief 4. http://www.urban.org/url.cfm?ID=311223. (Accessed July 25, 2008.)

Corporation for Enterprise Development. 2002. "State Asset Development Report Card." http://www.cfed.org/sadrc/index.php. (Accessed July 25, 2008.)

Cunnyngham, Karen. 2004. *Trends in Food Stamp Program Participation Rates: 1999 to 2002.* Washington, DC: Mathematica Policy Research.

Daponte, Beth O., Seth Sanders, and Lowell Taylor. 1999. "Why Do Low-Income Households Not Use Food Stamps? Evidence from an Experiment." *Journal of Human Resources* 34(3): 612–28.

Engen, Eric M., and Jonathan Gruber. 2001. "Unemployment Insurance and Precautionary Saving." *Journal of Monetary Economics* 47: 545–79.

Gruber, Jonathan, and Aaron Yelowitz. 1999. "Public Health Insurance and Private Savings." *Journal of Political Economy* 107(6): 1249–74.

Hanratty, Maria J. 2006. "Has the Food Stamp Program Become More Accessible? Impacts of Recent Changes in Reporting Requirements and Asset Eligibility Limits." *Journal of Policy Analysis and Management* 25(3): 603–21.

Hogan, M. Janice, Catherine Solheim, Susan Wolfgram, Busisiwe Nkosi, and Nicola Rodrigues. 2004. "The Working Poor: From the Economic Margins to Asset Building." *Family Relations* 53(2): 229–36.

Hubbard, R. Glenn, Jonathan Skinner, and Stephen P. Zeldes. 1995. "Precautionary Saving and Social Insurance." *Journal of Political Economy* 103(2): 360–99.

Hurst, Erik, and James P. Ziliak. 2006. "Do Welfare Asset Limits Affect Household Saving? Evidence from Welfare Reform." *Journal of Human Resources* 41(1): 46–71.

Losby, Jan L., and Jill R. Robinson. 2004. *Michigan IDA Partnership: Year 3 Program Evaluation Report.* Washington, DC: ISED Solutions.

McKernan, Signe-Mary, Caroline Ratcliffe, and Yunju Nam. 2007. *The Effects of Welfare and IDA Program Rules on the Asset Holdings of Low-Income Families.* Poor Finances: Assets and Low-Income Households Report. Washington, DC and St. Louis, MO: The Urban Institute and Washington University, Center for Social Development.

Mills, Gregory, Ken Lam, Donna DeMarco, Chrisopher Rodger, and Bulbul Kaul. 2008. *Assets for Independence Act Evaluation.* Cambridge, MA: Abt Associates.

Mills, Gregory, William G. Gale, Rhiannon Patterson, Gary V. Engelhardt, Michael D. Eriksen, and Emil Apostolov. 2008. "Effects of Individual Development Accounts on Asset Purchases and Saving Behavior: Evidence from a Controlled Experiment." *Journal of Public Economics* 92(5): 1509–30.

Nam, Yunju. 2008. "Welfare Reform and Asset Accumulation: Asset Limit Changes, Financial Assets, and Vehicle Ownership." *Social Science Quarterly* 89(1): 133–54.

Neuberger, Zoe, Robert Greenstein, and Peter Orszag. 2006. "Barriers to Saving." *Communities and Banking* Summer: 25–27.

Neumark, David, and Elizabeth Powers. 1998. "The Effect of Means-Tested Income Support for the Elderly on Pre-retirement Saving: Evidence from the SSI Program in the U.S." *Journal of Public Economics* 68: 181–206.

O'Brien, Bourke. 2006. *Ineligible to Save? Asset Limits and Savings Behavior of Welfare Recipients.* Washington, DC: New America Foundation.

Pavetti, La Donna, Kathleen Maloy, and Liz Schott. 2002. *Promoting Medicaid and Food Stamp Participation: Establishing Eligibility Procedures That Support Participation and Meet Families' Needs.* Final Report. Washington, DC: Mathematica Policy Research.

Powers, Elizabeth T. 1998. "Does Means-Testing Welfare Discourage Saving? Evidence from a Change in AFDC Policy in the United States." *Journal of Public Economics* 68(1): 33–53.

Rand, Dory. 2007. "Reforming State Rules on Asset Limits: How to Remove Barriers to Saving and Asset Accumulation in Public Benefit Programs." *Clearinghouse REVIEW Journal of Poverty Law and Policy* March–April: 625–36.

Ratcliffe, Caroline, Signe-Mary McKernan, and Kenneth Finegold. 2008. "The Effect of State Food Stamp and TANF Policies on Food Stamp Program Participation." *Social Service Review* 82(2): 291–334.

Rosso, Randy. 2003. *Tables Describing the Asset and Vehicle Holdings of Low-Income Households in 1999.* Washington, DC: Mathematica Policy Research.

Rowe, Gretchen, and Jeffrey Versteeg. 2005. *The Welfare Rules Databook: State Policies as of July 2003.* Washington, DC: The Urban Institute. http://www.urban.org/url.cfm?ID=411183. (Accessed July 25, 2008.)

Savner, Steve, and Mark Greenberg. 1995. *The CLASP Guide to Welfare Waivers: 1992–1995.* Washington, DC: Center for Law and Social Policy.

Schreiner, Mark, and Michael Sherraden. 2007. *Can the Poor Save? Saving and Asset Building in Individual Development Accounts.* New Brunswick, NJ: Transaction Publishers.

Schreiner, Mark, Michael Sherraden, Margaret Clancy, Lissa Johnson, Jami Curley, Min Zhan, Sondra G. Beverly, and Michael Grinstein-Weiss. 2005. "Assets and the Poor: Evidence from Individual Development Accounts." In *Inclusion in the American Dream: Assets, Poverty, and Public Policy,* edited by Michael W. Sherraden (185–215). New York: Oxford University Press.

Sherraden, Michael. 1991. *Assets and the Poor: A New American Welfare Policy.* Armonk, NY: M. E. Sharpe.

———. 2001. "Asset-Building Policy and Programs for the Poor." In *Assets for the Poor: The Benefits of Spreading Asset Ownership,* edited by Thomas M. Shapiro and Edward N. Wolff (302–23). New York: Russell Sage Foundation.

Shobe, Marcia A., and Kameri Christy-McMullin. 2005. "Savings Experiences Past and Present: Narratives from Low-Income African American Women." *Affilia* 20(2): 222–37.

Sullivan, James X. 2006. "Welfare Reform, Saving, and Vehicle Ownership: Do Asset Limits and Vehicle Exemptions Matter?" *Journal of Human Resources* 41(1): 72–105.

U.S. Department of Health and Human Services. 2004. *Interim Report to Congress: Assets for Independence Demonstration Program.* Washington, DC: Office of Community Service, Administration for Children and Families, Department of Health and Human Services.

Warren, Naomi, and Karen Edwards. 2005. *Status of State Supported IDA Programs in 2005.* CSD Policy Report 05-03. St. Louis, MO: Washington University, Center for Social Development.

Wemmerus, Nancy, and Bruce Gottlieb. 1999. *Relaxing the FSP Vehicle Asset Test: Findings from the North Carolina Demonstration.* Washington, DC: Mathematica Policy Research.

Ziliak, James P. 2003. "Income Transfers and Assets of the Poor." *Review of Economics and Statistics* 85(1): 63–76.

6

Benefits and Consequences of Holding Assets

Robert I. Lerman and Signe-Mary McKernan

Assets convey an array of economic and social benefits, but people must sacrifice current consumption to accumulate and retain assets. In doing so, they can raise their long-term incomes, gain economic security, and improve their psychological well-being. In some ways, the availability of assets is especially critical for low-income families. Individuals at the economic margins are much more likely to experience severe material hardships when they lack assets or the ability to borrow to deal with an economic shock, such as unemployment.[1] Yet, until recently, few researchers or policymakers considered how assets affect the lives of poor or near-poor families. The nearly exclusive focus has been on raising current incomes and not on whether families use some of their income to save, invest, and build up assets.

In recent years, some policymakers have begun to favor extending the potential benefits of asset-based policies to low- and lower-middle income families. In any consideration of new policies to do so, we should ask several questions. First, which policies can best stimulate asset holding and sounder balance sheets? Second, if various policies are effective, what are their likely costs and benefits? In particular, can expanding asset ownership yield significant economic and noneconomic gains among those with low incomes? Chapter 4 covers the first question in analyzing the determinants of asset building. This chapter concentrates on the effects of assets, assuming the accumulation process has already taken place.

At the same time, we recognize that the ways people use their assets may depend on how they built up their assets—whether the resources came from savings, from gifts or inheritances, or from an unanticipated jump in asset values. Certainly, the effects of assets will depend on the level of debt, the terms of the debt, and the short-term and long-term composition of debt undertaken to accumulate the assets.

This chapter's assessment of effects of assets is organized around three questions: (1) What are the significant financial benefits of possessing assets? (2) What are the significant nonfinancial benefits of possessing assets? (3) What are the adverse consequences of individual-level asset-building efforts? As we will see, existing studies offer considerable evidence but often less than definitive answers about the extent to which the accumulation and holding of assets benefit low-income families.

Common assumptions about the benefits of policies to encourage asset accumulation have come under great scrutiny as a result of the 2007 collapse of the subprime mortgage market. The view that encouraging homeownership among low-income people is an unmitigated good is no longer universally held. This review takes seriously the potential costs as well as the benefits of the outcomes of asset building among low- and lower middle-income families.

Estimates of the correlation between assets and outcomes are common, but it is difficult to test the *causal* impacts of assets on outcomes. Nonetheless, a substantial empirical literature has emerged in which researchers present strong or suggestive evidence about the effects of assets. Many of the relevant studies use similar datasets and methods. The next section analyzes the strengths and weaknesses of the data and methods commonly used. We then present a framework for classifying the topics before examining theories and empirical studies on each topic.

Data Commonly Used to Study Effects of Assets

The primary emphasis in our review is on studies dealing with large representative samples within the United States. To observe actual effects of assets will nearly always require data over a long time period, certainly more than one year. Ideally, such data come from panels in which respondents are followed over time. Yet even when panel data are available, tracking assets and linking assets to outcomes poses difficult data and methodological challenges.

Survey data used to examine the effects of assets commonly come from the following four surveys: the Panel Study of Income Dynamics (PSID), the Survey of Income and Program Participation (SIPP), the National Longitudinal Survey of Youth (NLSY), and the National Survey of Families and Households (NSFH). This is not surprising as all four datasets are longitudinal, contain a rich set of correlates and outcomes of interest—important strengths for evaluating the effects of asset building—and are nationally representative of the population or a subset of the population of the United States. The appendix in this volume provides more details on these and other asset-related data sources.

Some researchers have used more specialized data sources. These include experimental data from an individual development account (IDA) program in Oklahoma (Mills et al. 2008), the American Housing Survey (Nichols 2005), the Current Population Survey (Kane 1994), the Health and Retirement Study (McGarry and Schoeni 1995), IDA Survey Data (Moore et al. 2001), the National Survey of America's Families (Scanlon and Adams 2005), and Office of Housing Enterprise Oversight housing-price indices (Goetzmann and Spiegel 2002), among others. An online appendix to this book, http://www.urban/.org/books/assetbuilding/, summarizes these and other studies.

The primary strengths of the PSID, SIPP, NLSY, and NSFH are their ability to follow individuals over time and their inclusion of measures of assets and of key outcomes. Longitudinal data are important because they better enable researchers to distinguish between the true effects of assets and the effects of other factors that lead some people to accumulate more assets than others. By using longitudinal data, the researcher can potentially account for selection into asset holding—the possibility that it is the unobserved determinants of assets (such as ambition and determination) and not the assets themselves that improve outcomes. The panel data also help rule out reverse causation—the possibility that observed outcomes (e.g., residential stability) determine asset levels (e.g., homeownership) rather than asset levels determining outcomes. Experimental, longitudinal data, such as that from the IDA program in Oklahoma, are best able to distinguish true asset effects from other factors but are less generalizable to the broader population of families in the United States.

Studying the effects of assets requires rich data on personal and family characteristics and other correlates of assets, as well as on several outcomes of interest. The Survey of Consumer Finances (SCF) is less used in this literature because, while rich in asset data and thus strong in measuring assets, the SCF measures only a modest set of background and outcome variables and provides data on individuals only at one point in time.

Methods Commonly Used in the Literature

Empirical research documenting a positive association between asset holdings and various family outcomes is encouraging in its indication of the benefits of asset holdings. However, these associations do not establish causation, a vital element in predicting whether asset-based policies will induce an array of positive outcomes for families. One important concern that often limits our ability to detect causal impacts is the endogeneity of assets.

Homeownership is a good example. This asset and other assets are embedded in interactive relationships between ownership and outcomes. Owning a home may be the result or the cause of such correlated individual outcomes as good citizenship or parenting (DiPasquale and Glaeser 1999). Technically speaking, a variable is endogenous if it is correlated with the error term of a statistical regression equation for any reason. Practically speaking, the problem of endogeneity arises when other factors (e.g., education, financial literacy) are correlated both with the outcome variable (e.g., good citizenship or parenting) and with the explanatory variable of interest (e.g., homeownership). It may be that high levels of education or other factors are actually causing good citizenship, but the positive correlation between homeownership and citizenship is mistaken for a causal role of assets. When researchers do not take account of all factors other than assets that are correlated with both assets and the outcome, the estimate of the effect of assets on the outcome variable will be biased. In fact, all the measures from the regression may be biased. When a single explanatory variable in a regression (such as asset holding) is endogenous, it generally results in biased estimates of the effects of all explanatory variables in the regression. The result is potentially biased estimates of the effects of asset holding (e.g., homeownership) and all other explanatory variables (e.g., age, race/ethnicity) on the outcome of interest (e.g., economic well-being, child well-being).

Consider the issues that arise when trying to isolate the causal effect of homeownership from other factors that affect both homeownership and other positive outcomes. Suppose parents who own housing systematically differ from parents who rent housing in terms of observable characteristics (such as educational attainment) and unobservable characteristics (such as motivation and altruism). The same characteristics that make some parents more likely to own homes may also make those parents more likely to be good citizens, bring up successful children, or achieve other positive outcomes. As a result, homeownership may be credited for the effect of differences in these characteristics. It is relatively easy to isolate the homeownership effect in the case of observable characteristics, but it is difficult to distinguish homeownership effects from the effects of unobservable differences among households (Green and White 1997).

As a second example, consider a finding that shows that owners are more likely to know the names of their congressional representatives. It may mean (1) that owners are more knowledgeable about politics because they are owners (asset causes knowledge), (2) that knowledgeable persons become owners (knowledge causes assets, also known as reverse causation), (3) both (simultaneous outcomes), or (4) that better-educated people are both more likely to be owners and more likely to be knowledgeable (education, not assets, is responsible for the increased knowledge) (Rossi and Weber 1996). Only methods that control for the endogeneity of asset holding can determine which are the causal relationships.

Three main types of descriptive analyses are used in the literature to measure outcomes for families holding assets (e.g., a home or car): (1) presenting means without a comparison group (Moore et al. 2001), (2) comparing costs or returns on financial investments (Baker 2005; Baker and Baribeau 2003; Duda and Belsky 2002; Goetzmann and Spiegel 2002), and (3) comparing means longitudinally (e.g., before and after home purchase) (Reid 2004). In general, nonexperimental descriptive analyses, as used by these studies, do not control for the endogeneity of assets. However, descriptive analyses that involve comparisons—either cross-sectionally or longitudinally (before or after)—do a better job of controlling for endogeneity than analyses without comparisons.

Four main types of multivariate methods are used in the literature to measure the relationship between asset holding (e.g., homeownership) and outcomes while controlling for other factors. Multivariate methods control for observed factors included in the regression (e.g., age, race/ethnicity) and in some cases unobserved factors and, thus, the endogeneity of asset holding.

Ordinary least squares (OLS), logit, probit, general linear model (GLM), and hierarchical regressions control for observable characteristics included in the regression, but not generally for unobservable characteristics and thus not for the endogeneity of asset holding. OLS, logit, and probit regression models are used by Aaronson (2000), Bynner and Despotidou (2001), Conley (1999), DiPasquale and Glaeser (1999), Green and White (1997), Henretta (1984), Mayer and Jencks (1989), McGarry and Schoeni (1995), Raphael and Rice (2002), Reid (2004), Rossi and Weber (1996), Sullivan (2005), Williams (2003), Woldoff (2006), and Zhan and Sherraden (2003). GLM and hierarchical regressions are used by Scanlon and Adams (2005). Some of these studies use more than one type of method, with a second method attempting to control for endogeneity, and so, are listed below.

Instrumental variables (IV) regression does control for the endogeneity of assets if appropriate instruments are used. IV regression techniques are used by Aaronson (2000), Cho (1999), DiPasquale and Glaeser (1999), Haurin, Parcel, and Haurin (2002), Raphael and Rice (2002), and Sullivan (2005). To be an appropriate instrument, an instrumental variable must be related to the endogenous asset variable (e.g., homeownership) and must not be related to the outcome (e.g., child well-being) except for through the endogenous asset variable.

Individual-level fixed effects regression as used by McGarry and Schoeni (1995) controls for time-invariant unobserved characteristics and thus largely controls for the endogeneity of assets.

Simultaneous equations models control for the endogeneity of assets if proper instruments or covariance restrictions are used. Bivariate probit models with instruments for homeownership (the relative cost of owning versus renting) are used by Green and White (1997). Full information maximum likelihood models are used by Kane (1994), but to control for the endogeneity of parents' education, not parents' homeownership. Simultaneous estimation of a path model of directly observed variables is used by Yadama and Sherraden (1996).

Experimental program designs, such as those used by Mills and others (2008), control for the endogeneity of program participation to encourage asset building by randomly assigning program applicants into treatment or control groups. Because program participation is assigned independently of other characteristics that affect outcomes (such as ability to save or make wise investment decisions), we can ignore these other characteristics and simply measure the difference in outcomes (such as homeownership) of those randomly assigned to participate in the IDA program and those randomly assigned not to participate.

Strengths and Limitations of the Methods

Both descriptive and multivariate methods have their strengths and limitations. Descriptive methods are easy to understand and provide important results about the relationship (positive, negative, or no relationship, or magnitude of the relationship) between assets and outcomes. They are an important first step in empirical research. However, in a non-experimental setting, descriptive methods do not generally control for the endogeneity of asset holding because they do not control for factors other than the relationship between the two variables of interest. Multivariate methods bring the benefits of controlling for additional observed characteristics and allow us to learn about conditional relationships—the relationship between two variables while holding other observed factors constant. However, as noted, not all multivariate methods control for unobserved factors (such as financial literacy and individual preferences) that are key to controlling for the endogeneity of asset holding.

Conceptual Framework and Empirical Evidence for the Effects of Asset Holding

Our framework for relating theories and empirical evidence distinguishes between five potential impacts of asset holding: on economic well-being, social well-being, civic engagement, child well-being, and health and psychological well-being. For each potential effect, we first consider the literature and the main hypotheses and then review the relevant empirical studies. Although we discuss the theories that apply to the population as a whole, we also raise issues that arise in examining the effects of asset holding on low-income, minority, or single-mother households.

Before turning to the individual topics, we clarify the distinction between effects of assets and net worth. Often, policy advocates use the terms interchangeably, but the differences are important. For most purposes, it is expanding net worth, not simply increasing asset ownership, that allows people to raise their long-term incomes. This means increasing the value of what people own in assets by more than the value of what people owe in debt. However, sometimes, an asset may be important even if the result is to provide liquidity for contingencies (either directly from liquid assets or indirectly from loans from asset-based collateral) without raising total net worth. Owning a home or a car could yield positive effects even if the asset values are matched by debt, but these circumstances could also generate negative effects if an economic shock leads to declines in asset values or an inability to service the debt. In what follows, we focus the discussion on asset ownership with the assumption that people are able to accumulate assets beyond their debt obligations.

The chapter deals with both financial assets and nonfinancial tangible assets but recognizes distinctions within and between these classes of assets. Financial assets include stocks, mutual funds, bonds, bank accounts, some life insurance policies, pensions, and cash. Although these are all financial assets, they differ markedly with respect to other characteristics, such as the degrees of liquidity, risk, and expected return. Some of these assets may be offset or financed by debt, either short term or long term. Nonfinancial tangible assets include physical units privately owned by the individual. These include owner-occupied housing, automobiles or other vehicles, consumer durables, land, aspects of privately held businesses, and real estate holdings for investment purposes. The equity or net worth in these assets is their market value less any debt secured by the asset.

Figure 6.1 illustrates the links between assets and outcomes based on our framework, which divides asset effects into influences on economic well-being, social well-being and civic engagement, child well-being, and health and psychological well-being. Note that the relationships are potentially simultaneous in two ways. One is the simultaneity between assets and outcomes; more assets might lead to higher income or better health, which, in turn, might lead to higher levels of assets. Second, the five groups of outcomes may interact with each other; economic well-being might increase residential stability, but residential stability may improve economic well-being.

Asset Holding and Economic Well-Being

Assets can raise economic well-being by increasing current and future levels of income and by reducing the variability of income and consumption. This section looks at several aspects of economic well-being, including income, consumption and material hardship, future assets, and self-sufficiency.

We begin with *income*. Assets can influence income in three main ways. First, financial assets can generate cash income directly through interest and dividend payments as well as through capital gains on sales of stocks

Figure 6.1. Conceptual Framework for the Effects of Asset Accumulation

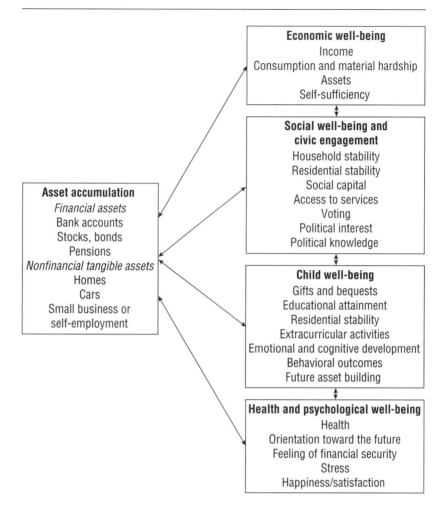

or bonds. Capital gains income materializes when the value of assets increases. Assets also offer a way to increase the level of lifetime income and not just the timing of consumption. Most assets yield a positive return on savings. One can purchase risk-free U.S. Treasury bonds (I-bonds) and even guarantee a positive, though modest, return above the rate of inflation. Given this reality, the assets accumulated by saving $100 today will permit $135 worth of consumption 15 years from now, assuming a real interest rate of 2 percent per year. Of course, if the return exceeds

2 percent, the gain in the real value of lifetime consumption will be more than $35. Thus, those willing to sacrifice and accept a lower level of consumption today can ensure a higher level of total consumption over a lifetime.

Second, physical (nonfinancial, tangible) assets can yield a flow of services (such as housing services) or raise real income by allowing people to pay less for other services (e.g., car instead of taxi). Sometimes, the increase in real income may come about through added leisure, perhaps linked to a decrease in commuting time. Third, assets may allow people to achieve higher incomes by extending their job searches, by financing direct costs of job search (e.g., transportation), by reducing commuting time (Raphael and Stoll 2001), and by investing in education and training. In a sense, the use of assets for these purposes typically represents a reallocation of investments from liquid assets to investments in job search that may or may not yield a high return, this time in the form of higher wage rates.

How assets affect the variability of income depends on an individual's asset portfolio. The investments in job search can lower the time between jobs and thus reduce the variability of income. Some assets involve a natural diversification of income sources. Usually, changes in income from employment are not correlated with income derived from bonds, from the direct use of housing services, or from capital gains in housing. Another possibility is that income from work (based on human capital) can vary positively (or negatively) in response to losses (or gains) from financial and nonfinancial assets (Bodie, Merton, and Samuelson 1992). On the other hand, assets might decline together with earnings. In a town that suffers a large, sudden recession and outflow of jobs, the losses in earnings associated with unemployment are reinforced by capital losses in home values. In general, assets generally lower the variability of total income if they are not highly correlated with other sources of income.

Several studies find support for the idea that assets raise incomes of relatively low-income people. Financial assets and car ownership are associated with positive income and employment outcomes, with some evidence that the relationship is causal. Bynner and Despotidou (2001) find that savings and investments at age 23 are positively associated with labor market experience at age 23 to 33. Moore and others (2001) report that 41 percent of IDA participants said they were more likely to increase work hours and 61 percent said they were more likely to increase their income in other ways. However, neither of these studies controls for the endogeneity of assets. Raphael and Rice (2002) show that car ownership increases employment and hours worked, but not necessarily wages. This evidence is indicative of a causal effect since the authors control for the endogeneity of car ownership. Cho (1999) finds that financial assets are positively associated with the economic well-being of women one year after marital disruption. Estimates by Cho (1999) indicate that other forms of assets, including home equity and the value of business or real property, do not have a statistically significant association with economic well-being.

Consumption is potentially affected by assets in several ways. Assets often raise the level and growth of consumption and typically lower the variability of consumption and material hardship. The increased consumption comes not simply from the asset-induced gains in income. Owning assets allows people to avoid paying extremely high interest rates by reducing the need to borrow and by providing sufficient collateral to be able to borrow at low or moderate interest rates. Having assets to use, liquidate, or borrow against improves the ability of families to limit their borrowing costs.

Assets as buffer stocks (as defined in chapter 1, Asset Definitions) can help smooth consumption in the short term. Of course, almost by definition, saving means forgoing consumption during the phase at which people accumulate assets. In studying asset accumulation among low-income families, Moore and others (2001) find that 30 percent of IDA participants said they had less money for leisure, 8 percent said they had to give up food or other necessities, and 35 percent said they were less likely to save outside their IDAs.

At the same time, buffer stocks from accumulated savings help people avoid large sacrifices in consumption when income falls temporarily below long-term levels (Deaton 1991; Haveman and Wolff 2005). Building up assets to hold as buffer stocks is a primary motivation to save and accumulate assets; people hold these resources as a precaution against some shock, such as disability or unemployment, which suddenly lowers incomes (Skinner 1988; Zeldes 1989). Skinner projects that as much as 56 percent of total lifetime savings arise as families take precautions against income uncertainty and uncertainty about lifespan. Some savings for this purpose may go into private disability or retirement insurance policies, which we may think of as complementing the disability and retirement insurance policies built into the nation's social security system. Skinner suggests another effect of assets accumulated for precautionary purposes:

when people die before adverse shocks use up precautionary savings, the money passes to the next generation as bequests.

Sullivan (2005) finds that households with assets use unsecured debt to borrow when faced with temporary shortfalls in earnings and, thus, maintain consumption. Households with low assets do not borrow—likely because they do not have sufficient access to credit—and their consumption falls. This study controls for reverse causation (that assets affect borrowing, not borrowing affecting assets) by measuring the relationship between assets in an earlier time period and current borrowing.

The role of assets in consumption smoothing may be critical for low-income families. The ability to have access to cash (either from assets or borrowing) may exert a significant effect on the experience of material hardship (Mayer and Jencks 1989). A short-term crisis can have a much more serious and long-term impact when the family suffers hunger, eviction, or the shutoff of utilities than when the family faces a decline in living standards from a much higher starting point, perhaps due to a layoff, disability, or the loss of a spouse who might be providing care for children. Without assets, people who experience hardships will bear high costs to recover and these costs will lower long-term consumption. Mayer and Jencks (1989) show that a family's ability to borrow $500 in the event of an emergency does as much to reduce hardship as tripling family income, all else equal but without controlling for the endogeneity of access to credit. Homeowners report fewer hardships than tenants with the same income and needs, suggesting that homeownership and material hardship are related. But, the study does not control for the endogeneity of homeownership.

Using assets to hedge risks is another way assets can smooth consumption. Consider, for example, the risk of a sudden decline in demand for workers in a particular occupation or industry. Workers can hedge against the potential losses to their permanent incomes should such a risk materialize. One method is to hold a portfolio of assets that move in the opposite direction from assets in their own industry. Taking the opposite strategy, investing in their own firms or assets that move with their own job prospects, is riskier and carries the danger of losing many assets at the very time when workers are most in need (Bodie and Merton 2000).

Accumulating personal assets may be one way to raise the living standards of retirees. In fact, a large share of accumulated assets is earmarked for retirement through the use of defined benefit and defined contribution private pension plans as well as personal savings. In addition, Social

Security and Medicare benefits can be the primary sources of asset values of low- to moderate-income older Americans.

Physical assets can help people hedge against price increases and the associated losses in the real value of consumption. For example, owning a home serves as a hedge against increases in rents and, therefore, lowers the variability of consumption (Sinai and Souleles 2005). Owning a car may hedge against increased prices of transportation associated with taxis, buses, and other transportation. Owning a washing machine may lessen the risk of the higher prices of using laundromats.

Current assets may influence *future assets*. Access to even modest liquid financial assets is often important for an initial purchase, such as paying a down payment on a home or car. The terms by which families can purchase needed goods are usually much less onerous for those with these assets. For example, homebuyers with a down payment of less than 20 percent of the home purchase price typically have to purchase private mortgage insurance. High levels of assets can improve long-term economic well-being by fostering new outlets for the productive use of savings. Those who build up financial or other assets are better able to take advantage of special opportunities when they materialize. Families with assets can, for example, shift their allocations toward a microenterprise or a self-employment activity. Instead of having to borrow, often at high rates, to enter these fields, asset holders can liquidate one investment and enter another.

Auto purchases and auto loans offer an example of how a dearth of assets combined with a weak credit record can lower future assets. Using data on 50,000 applicants to an auto dealership, Adams, Einav, and Levin (2007) find that the mean interest rate paid by buyers was about 26 percent. A key reason for these high rates is that about one-quarter of the value of all loans is not repaid. Repaying loans at 25 percent interest rates weakens an individual's ability to build wealth. If instead, an individual had sufficient assets and credit worthiness to borrow at 9 percent, then a car buyer taking a $10,000 loan could have accumulated $3,440 after the 40-month term of the loan if he or she had saved the difference in monthly interest payments and invested the funds at a 4 percent interest rate.

Experimental evidence shows that IDA programs—savings that are subsidized when withdrawn for sound investment purposes—increase homeownership (Mills and others [2008], likely captures a causal relationship). Homeownership and asset levels are strongly positively related (though no attempts have been made to measure a causal relationship).

Moreover, despite the surprisingly low appreciation rate on house prices of owner-occupied units, the return is actually higher after accounting for such important factors as the implicit rent received from homeownership.

Those with liquid assets can take risks without having to worry about losing key physical assets, like a home or car. Some assets, such as homes, may induce and encourage added savings. Monthly mortgage payments usually involve some repayment of principle as well as interest payments. When a homeowner paints her house or adds a room, she is performing nonmarket work in which all of the added income is invested in raising the home's value.

The asset with the highest net worth for most American families is their home. From a financial perspective, homeownership has four major potential effects compared to renting. First, a home is an investment whose value may rise or fall and lead to large changes in a family's net worth. Second, the financing of homeownership through mortgages that require principal as well as interest payments may be a mechanism for inducing "forced savings." Although renters could in principle save a comparable amount each month, they do not face the same institutional pressure to save.[2] In addition, merely holding onto a home that increases in value with inflation, while the corresponding mortgage debt stays constant (or declines in real terms), results in a buildup of equity. Third, homeownership may act as a hedge against rising rentals in the community. Homeownership with a fixed rate mortgage allows a family to lock in one of its primary expenditures and not face the risks of sudden price increases (Sinai and Souleles 2005). Having the security of fixed living expenses is probably of special importance to low-income families. Fourth, homeownership can raise after-tax income relative to renting because of the tax advantages of homeownership. Of important note, low-income families subject to little or no federal income tax do not reap these advantages. In fact, low-income families may face a financial disadvantage if they move to homeownership—the loss of rental and public housing subsidies (Carasso et al. 2005).

Evaluating the financial return to homeownership is complicated because one must take account of the interest costs of the mortgage payments (Nichols 2005), the benefit of the mortgage interest tax deduction, the stream of implicit rents (net of maintenance and property taxes) conveyed by the home that substitutes for the rent homeowners would otherwise have to pay, and the way homeownership acts as a hedge against rent increases in the market. As discussed in the empirical findings below, accounting for these various components, especially the implicit rent, has large effects on measures of the return to homeownership.

However, some studies on actual returns to homeownership suggest that homeownership does not generate substantial financial returns. Reid (2004) and Goetzmann and Spiegel (2002) find only a 3 to 5 percent annual nominal return to homeownership, using descriptive statistics to compute mean returns in the Panel Study of Income Dynamics and Office of Housing Enterprise Oversight housing-price indices, respectively (online appendix table 6.A.1). Both argue that financial assets, such as the Treasury bill, provide greater financial returns and less risk—and are thus an attractive alternative to homeownership. Goetzmann and Spiegel argue that if homeownership is encouraged, the potential homeowners should be informed of the risks. Bostic and Lee (2007) offer simulations of the potential gains in wealth from homeownership relative to renting based on type of mortgage, down payment, future appreciation, and income level of neighborhood. For housing investments in low-income and middle-income neighborhoods, owners achieve modest gains in wealth after 7–10 years over renters, even in a low-appreciation environment. The benefits are substantially higher for households making higher down payments.

As described above in the conceptual framework, the potential effects of homeownership are not measured by housing-price appreciation alone. One must also account for mortgage costs (Nichols 2005), the benefit of the mortgage interest tax and property tax deduction, and most importantly, the stream of implicit rents (net of maintenance and property taxes) received from the home. A homeowner receives housing services from a home that would otherwise have to be paid by renting or by some alternative housing arrangement. In addition, homeowners can benefit from "forced savings" induced through mortgages that require principal as well as interest payments. Both the riskiness of housing as an asset as well as the hedge that housing provides against future rent increases in the absence of homeownership (Sinai and Souleles 2005) could be considered. On the negative side, the cost of unexpected repairs and the potential losses associated with foreclosure are other risks of homeownership. As Gramlich (2007) points out, foreclosure likely leads to much higher costs on homeowners than does eviction on renters, because homeowners lose their main asset and suffer from blemishes on their credit reports.[3] Thus, measuring the total returns to homeownership is complicated but important in any effort to understand the true effects of homeownership on net worth.

Nichols (2005) estimates a total rate of return that incorporates some of these financial homeownership effects and underscores the importance of accounting for them. He calculates an annualized average rate of return of 8.6 percent for the 1985 through 2002 time period when the appreciation rate, implicit rent, mortgage contract, and mortgage interest tax deduction are all accounted for. The implicit rent makes the largest contribution to the total rate of return. Based on nominal appreciation alone, he calculates an average rate of return of 1.9 percent; adding in implicit rent increases the return to 9.8 percent, subtracting off the cost of the mortgage contract decreases the return to 8.5 percent, and adding the mortgage interest tax deduction increases the rate to 8.6 percent.

The total rate of return may be higher than the 8.6 percent measured by Nichols because his base 1.9 percent appreciation rate is measured by self-reported values from the American Housing Survey rather than market transactions as measured by the Office of Housing Enterprise Oversight housing-price indices. In addition, measures that account for both the housing asset risk and the hedge provided against rent risk may well find that rent risk is greater, as suggested by Sinai and Souleles (2005). Future research on the effects of homeownership on financial returns could incorporate appreciation, implicit rent, mortgage costs, tax implications, and forced savings, as well as rent and housing risk.

The economic returns to homeownership may be lower for low-income and minority families than for moderate- and high-income families (Baker 2005; Baker and Baribeau 2003; Rohe, Van Zandt, and McCarthy 2002; Nichols 2005; and Reid 2004). As Baker (2005) explains, low-income families have taxable incomes too low to benefit from mortgage interest deductions. And low-income families' median period of homeownership is shorter (only four years), meaning that their transaction costs are higher. In addition, low-income and minority households are likely to pay more in mortgage costs, repair costs, and unexpected lending costs associated with excessive points, repayment penalties, and deceptive practices (Renuart 2004). Neighborhood risks are also potentially important, such as a concentration of foreclosures that lower property values (Bostic and Lee 2007). Nichols (2005) estimates that, relative to average households, low-income, low-education, and black households have a higher probability of a negative return on a home and lower rates of return and appreciation. The mortgage contract augments these negative effects possibly because low-income, low-education, and black households make lower down payments and have higher remaining mortgage balances.

On a more positive note for low-income households, Duda and Belsky (2002) calculate that homeownership is relatively less risky for those purchasing low-cost homes rather than more expensive homes. Case and Marynchenko (2002) find that for low-income households in Chicago, Boston, and Los Angeles, homeownership has generally been a good investment, helping families accumulate assets and increase their net worth. Returns to homeownership, however, vary depending on the time period and geographic location (Case and Marynchenko 2002; Rohe et al.). There have been significant periods of decline in Boston and Los Angeles that have led to losses and periods of negative equity for low-income households.

Some evidence indicates that homeownership and home mortgages lead homeowners to save and attain higher asset levels in the future. Although they do not control for the endogeneity of homeownership, Rossi and Weber (1996) find that (1) homeowners have about $6,000 more in savings and about $5,000 more in mutual funds than renters; (2) homeowners are more likely to have credit card debt, installment debt, and personal bank loans; and (3) homeowners are less likely to have education loans and to have bills more than 90 days overdue. Similarly, homeowners in 2004 had total asset holdings 24 times greater than renters ($290,000 versus $12,000), and had debt 12 times greater than renters ($96,000 versus $8,000). Additionally, homeowners were four times less likely to be delinquent on debt and had net worth 46 times greater than renters ($184,000 versus $4,000) (Carasso and McKernan 2006). These relationships between homeownership and assets and net worth, while not causal, support the hypothesis that homeownership leads to substantial financial returns.

Self-sufficiency is another aspect of economic well-being potentially influenced by assets. Assets can increase self-sufficiency by helping families minimize or eliminate their need for income-support programs. A good example is how assets help people respond to temporary shocks. A family with zero or minimal assets might have to apply for income-support program benefits and subsequently be subject to high marginal tax rates and work disincentives. Although welfare programs (TANF) increasingly require work and provide only temporary benefits, this experience may still have stigmatizing and other problematic effects. Unfortunately, the presence of asset tests in these social programs may discourage asset building among low-income families or exclude families from obtaining needed assistance until they liquidate their assets. This issue is examined in chapter 5.

Cho's (1999) results show that financial assets are positively associated with income and negatively associated with welfare receipt for women experiencing marital disruption. These findings indicate that assets may be associated with self-sufficiency. Further research is necessary to examine the link between assets and self-sufficiency and determine whether the link is causal.

Assets can bring individuals a greater sense of personal efficacy and power. They enable people to choose whether to consume their resources today for some valued good or service or, for example, to provide a special grant or a bequest to their children. Asset holders can use their resources for people outside the family as well.

Effects of Asset Holding on Social Well-Being and Civic Engagement

Asset holding can increase household stability by raising the economic stability of household members. Unemployment is a frequent problem for low-income families. When men lose their jobs, they are more likely to divorce (Charles and Stephens 2004). Unemployment can contribute to depression (Liem and Liem 1988), anger, child or spousal abuse, alcohol use, and poor academic and psychological health of children (Kalil and Ziol-Guest 2005). Since many low-income workers are not covered by unemployment insurance, the only way to prevent serious hardships and to mitigate worries about financial outcomes is to draw on assets or borrow, but borrowing is difficult and costly, especially when assets are unavailable (Sullivan 2005). Those with assets can avoid hardship more easily by drawing directly on liquid assets or by using assets as collateral for loans to pay for basic expenses.

Homeownership can mitigate the impact of economic shocks or add to the severity of the shock. Economic shocks may be particularly important for low-income families, which are less likely to have stable income. Homeowners with low mortgage payments have low net housing costs and thus one major need can be met despite losses of other income sources. In addition, homeowners are immune to sudden rent increases linked to an economic boom. For homeowners with substantial mortgages, the responses to an economic shock vary. Losing a job can pose serious problems for homeowners in meeting mortgage payments, just as renters facing job loss have trouble paying rent. When families are unable to meet mortgage payments and banks foreclose on the loans, homeownership can mean significant losses in savings relative to renting and investing in financial assets. Renters, however, can adjust relatively quickly by moving to lower-rent units. For homeowners, the transition is difficult. The home is not a liquid asset that can be quickly sold, but homeowners with equity can either access home equity loans until they return to work or sell their homes.

The high transaction costs of buying and selling homes may limit the ability of homeowners to make quick adjustments to shocks. At the same time, the higher transaction costs of buying over renting a home may reduce turnover and increase residential stability. This higher stability may have implications for neighborhoods and social interactions. One is that areas with high shares of homeowners may have more long-term residents and, thus, greater participation in neighborhood activities. Another potential impact of the higher residential stability induced by homeownership is the increase in the social capital of neighborhoods. Homeowners may expect to stay and have more incentive than renters to invest in making friends with neighbors and their families, thus providing connections to jobs and other opportunities.

Both homeowners' greater permanence in a neighborhood and their incentive to maintain or increase property values may encourage them to expand their involvement in civic organizations, to participate in local anticrime initiatives, to contribute to efforts to keep neighborhoods clean, and to lobby for good local schools. With the rapid rise in homeowner associations and condominiums, homeownership and civic participation are very directly linked to governance through restrictions on voting rights to owners and through management supervised by owners representing all other owners.

DiPasquale and Glaeser (1999) find evidence both in the United States and Germany that homeownership is strongly correlated with variables that attempt to measure good citizenship and social capital, such as civic engagement. The relationship is smaller, but still statistically significant in models that control for the endogeneity of homeownership with individual-level fixed effects. As mentioned, individual-level fixed effects control for time-invariant unobserved characteristics and, thus, largely control for the endogeneity of assets. A large portion of the effect of homeownership comes from the lower mobility of homeowners. In addition, Moore and others (2001) report that about half of current IDA participants said they were more likely to have good relationships with family members. About one-third said they were more likely to be involved in their neighborhoods and about one-third said they were more likely to be respected in their communities. Nembhard and Blasingame (2006) find that wealth is associated with white households' decisions to give money to charity and volunteer. They find that wealth has a greater association with the decision of black households to donate money, but no relationship with their volunteering behavior. Also, Woldoff (2006) finds that nonhousing wealth is positively related to the rate of neighborhood homeownership—a measure for the quality of a neighborhood.

On the other hand, studies by Bynner and Despotidou (2001), Reid (2004), and Rossi and Weber (1996) find mixed evidence on the relationship between assets, social well-being, and civic engagement. Bynner and Despotidou find that voting shows no association with savings and investments, but political interest is positively associated with savings and investments. Reid finds that neighborhood benefits from renting to owning were minimal for low-income whites, though substantial for low-income minorities. Rossi and Weber (1996) find that homeowners are not consistently more likely to be members of social networks, and homeowner versus renter differences on marriage and family behavior are not great. They also find that homeowners and renters do not differ substantially in their general political interest, though homeowners are almost consistently more engaged in local politics than renters.

Both Reid (2004) and Rossi and Weber (1996) base their findings on descriptive analyses and Bynner and Despotidou base their findings on OLS regressions—none of which control for the endogeneity of assets. The strong demographic differences between homeowners and renters revealed by Rossi and Weber (1996) suggest that controlling for both measured and unmeasured differences between homeowners and renters (that is controlling for the endogeneity of homeownership) is important. Future research could examine whether there is a strong relationship between assets and social well-being or civic engagement and whether that relationship is causal.

Finally, having enough assets to have some choice over one's residential location can increase a family's access to high-quality services, since location affects access to high-quality schools, parks, and other community resources. As described above in the empirical findings, few papers have examined the empirical relationship between assets and social well-being and the few that have provide mixed results. This is an opportunity for future empirical research to provide additional measures of the relationship between homeownership and social well-being, while controlling for the endogeneity of homeownership.

Other possible effects of homeownership include psychological benefits, which in turn can affect other outcomes. Homeowners may gain satisfaction and self-esteem from the control they have over key aspects of their living arrangements (Rossi and Weber 1996). Homeownership could lead people to have longer time horizons and a greater orientation to the future because of their expected tenure in the neighborhood and their concerns about neighborhood development and home values. These potential effects, often unobservable, may in turn affect other outcomes such as child well-being and civic engagement.

Effects of Asset Holding on Child Well-Being

The added stability that assets convey may be beneficial to children. Because economic shocks may have less serious consequences for families, parents are better able to deal with family tensions and thus more likely to remain together and avoid large income losses from divorce or separation. The higher residential stability resulting from homeownership can affect schooling outcomes for children. Children may feel more rooted in their communities and maintain friendships when they are less likely to experience residential instability. The stability of schools and friends is likely to encourage increased involvement in extracurricular activities, including access to jobs.

Other assets might also improve educational outcomes for children as well, perhaps by lowering their worries about falling into extreme poverty. Asset holding by parents can help children directly through small grants or loans for a down payment on a car, a deposit on a home or an apartment, and a place to live temporarily.

Asset holding may lead to improvements across generations. Those with assets are better able to make gifts and bequests to their children. For some proponents of asset-based policy (e.g., Oliver and Shapiro 1995; Sherraden 1991), potential effects on the next generation are the primary rationale. The increases in consumption and household and residential stability associated with assets may increase child well-being and children's long-term economic welfare.

Assets may change cognition, which in turn may change behavioral outcomes. As Zhan and Sherraden (2003) find, assets lead to improved educational outcomes for children, and part of the statistical effect operates through parental expectations of children's educational achievement. This is one of the few examples of a specified theory tested in research on asset effects. Holding assets provides an example for children that they can accumulate wealth and that asset accumulation is a normal part of adulthood.

The ownership of homes and other property may promote civic engagement, since the quality of the community and property taxation affect home values. Also, the homeownership-induced increase in residential stability creates incentives for participation because of the ability to enjoy the fruits of any improved community outcomes. Other social benefits from homeownership can accrue to communities and families as well.

The large empirical literature on the relationship between homeownership and child well-being indicates that homeownership improves children's well-being through improved educational attainment and decreased teenage pregnancy, among other potential effects. Homeownership's effects likely work through homeownership's role in increasing residential stability (Aaronson 2000). Green and White (1997) find that homeownership decreases teenage pregnancy and improves children's educational attainment, while controlling for the endogeneity of homeownership. These findings are particularly important for low-income households. Similarly, Conley (1999) finds that parental assets are associated with a decrease in premarital childbearing. Homeownership is also positively associated with improved children's emotional and cognitive development (Haurin et al. 2002), educational attainment (Kane 1994), academic performance (Zhan and Sherraden 2003), increased participation in extracurricular activities (Scanlon and Adams 2005), and decreased behavioral problems (Scanlon and Adams 2005).

Parental homeownership and home values may also be related to children's future homeownership status. Henretta (1984) reports that a parent's homeownership and home value at the time the child last lived at home are positively associated with the future grown child's homeownership and home value, though the relationships differ slightly for blacks and whites. Other findings suggest that homeownership by parents may affect the housing decisions of children through expectations for whites and through expectations and gifts for blacks. These results are consistent with the hypothesis that asset holding affects child well-being through gifts, bequests, and expectations, as described in the conceptual framework.

Besides homeownership, other types of assets are also positively related to child-well being. Zhan and Sherraden (2003) find that savings of $3,000 or above are positively associated with mothers' expectations and children's high school graduation. Williams (2003) shows that household income and wealth are positively associated with children's cognitive development, health, and behavioral development. McGarry and Schoeni (1995) present evidence that wealthy parents are more likely to transfer cash to their children and vice versa. Shapiro and Johnson (2005) report that parental assets allow families to gain educational advantages through enrolling in specialized public schools, moving to high-quality school districts, and enrolling in private schools.

Not all reported empirical relationships between assets and child well-being are positive. According to Zhan and Sherraden (2003), savings are not associated with child academic performance and homeownership is not associated with child academic achievement. Bynner and Despotidou (2001) find that savings and investments at age 23 are not associated with improved parenting outcomes at age 27 as measured by a child's reading. And Haurin and others (2002) report that homeownership is only marginally or not associated with child cognition and child behavior. The paucity of nonpositive relationships in the literature leaves one wondering whether nonpositive relationships are underreported.

Effects of Asset Holding on Health and Psychological Well-Being

Assets may help low-income families create an orientation to the future, an important attribute often less common among the poor than among the middle class. By aspiring to homeownership, for example, the prospect of asset building can lengthen the time horizons of low-income people. Some assets, such as homes, can encourage people to save, as they see how today's sacrifice can raise future living standards. Sherraden (1991) sees assets as sometimes stimulating additional nonmarket productive activity. A good example is when homeowners spend time maintaining and upgrading their homes.

It is possible that holding assets can lead to better physical and mental health. The availability of assets might help people meet unanticipated health care costs and thus encourage people to seek appropriate diagnoses and treatment. Another possibility is that by improving economic security, assets may reduce the stress individuals experience when worried about or experiencing sudden income losses. Finally, building assets may bring people satisfaction and a sense of efficacy in knowing they were able to accomplish something worthwhile. People are likely to be happier if they have the additional security of asset ownership.

The empirical literature yields some evidence that assets positively affect health and psychological well-being. Yadama and Sherraden (1996) find that assets (as measured by savings and, in one instance, house value) have a positive effect on expectations and confidence about the future; influence people to make specific plans with regard to work and family; induce more prudent and protective personal behaviors; and lead to more social connectedness with relatives, neighbors, and organizations. They estimate a simultaneous estimation path model of directly observed variables to control for endogeneity.

Three other papers in the literature measure a positive association between assets and health and psychological well-being. Bynner and Despotidou (2001) find that asset holding is associated with positive health outcomes. According to the study by Moore and others (2001), IDA participants self-report that they felt more confident about their futures (93 percent), more economically secure (84 percent), and more in control of their lives (85 percent) because they have IDAs. Effects on planning were somewhat less common, with about 60 percent of respondents saying they were more likely to make educational and retirement plans. Rossi and Weber (1996) report that homeowners regard themselves as having a greater sense of well-being than renters, but only marginally so.

Adverse Consequences of Asset Holding

Although assets clearly add to economic resources, problems can arise in the process of building and managing assets. One possibility is that building up assets will involve borrowing at rates that exceed the rates of return on assets. If a family borrows at a 10 percent annual interest rate to buy a stock rising at only 3 percent per year, the family's effort to build up assets will leave the family worse off. A second example noted above is that homeownership might hurt families financially if they cannot meet mortgage payments, face high transaction costs, and see little or no gain in the value of their property. High burdens of mortgage payments to income can create especially high amounts of stress (Bostic and Lee 2007). There is evidence that a small share of people neglect pressing current needs in their quest to build assets. Among low-income participants in IDA, Moore and others (2001) report that only 8 percent had to give up food or other necessities, but 9 percent felt more stressful about the future. About 30 percent had less money for leisure when they saved.

Because job losses in an area may be closely associated with declines in house values, homeownership in some settings inhibits job search and geographic mobility. Dietz and Haurin (2003) find that homeowners are less mobile in their job search than are renters because of higher transaction costs of moving and, perhaps, because of greater ties to their neighborhood and community. Stability can be desirable from a housing and social perspective but less desirable if the result is long-term unemployment.

Another problem is that people may invest in very risky assets and lose their savings. In this case, the sacrifices they made to accumulate savings end up as fruitless and potentially discouraging. In the case of recent foreclosures, homeowners are facing losing equity.

Some individuals may spend so much time managing or maintaining their assets that they lose focus on their jobs and family life. Conflict might arise in families as they debate the wisdom of choosing a high- or lower-risk investment. It is possible, though unusual, for people to neglect pressing current needs in their quest to build assets. For most people, this is a less-serious problem than finding the will to make a sure sacrifice today for a potential future benefit. Forcing strict limits on current consumption to accumulate assets may create stress as people face a conflict between pursuing two strong goals. Reid (2004) finds that homeowners run significant risks of returning to renters in the first years of homeownership. These outcomes may take place because many homeowners lack the savings to cope with crises such as unemployment or health problems. Reid also presents estimates that low-income homeowners experience lower levels of house-price appreciation than do higher-income borrowers. Goetzmann and Spiegel (2002) report that nearly all housing markets displayed negative risk-adjusted returns over the past 20 years and warn that devoting too much of an individual's asset/finance portfolio to home investment is risky. As mentioned above, the concern that people devote too much of their finance portfolios to home investment requires further study, especially in light of the important new finding (Sinai and Souleles 2005) that homeownership allows people to avoid the serious risk renters face of sharp increases in market rents. More evidence on the short-term and long-term impacts of homeownership, especially for low-income families, is also an important area for future research.

In general, adverse consequences come about not because of the presence of assets but due to their inappropriate allocation. Some forms of assets, such as retirement assets, are less liquid and are penalized if withdrawn for a greater need or emergency. Thus, people should typically have some liquid assets available as a precaution. Still, even some locked-in assets can sometimes be used as collateral for loans to deal with these sudden needs, and many retirement plans do allow emergency withdrawals.

Suggestions for Future Research and Conclusion

The idea that asset holding generates an array of positive social and economic effects, with or without increases in net worth, is increasingly common. This chapter examines what we know about the relationships between asset holding and economic well-being, social well-being, child well-being, and health and psychological well-being. The empirical findings highlight important and largely positive relationships between asset holding and outcomes measuring economic well-being, child-well being, and health and psychological well-being. The findings on the way assets relate to social well-being and civic engagement are mixed.

Since the majority of empirical studies in the literature do not attempt to control for the endogeneity of assets, most of our knowledge is about the correlation between assets and outcomes; we know less about the causal impacts of asset holding. Moreover, for some outcomes, a limited number of studies exist. These limitations are reflected in the suggestions for future research. Although several studies do provide support for asset-based social policy, the literature measuring the effects of asset holding on outcomes is still in its early stages, especially with regard to effects on low-income families.

Suggestions for Future Research

Measure the causal relationship between asset holding and outcomes. Research demonstrating causal relationships is a gold standard in empirical research, whether in assessing the impacts of asset holdings or in any other area. The literature measuring relationships between asset holding and outcomes has barely begun to measure causal relationships. Without controlling for the endogeneity of assets, we cannot know the causal effect of assets on outcomes. Empirical research measuring causal relationships between asset holdings and outcomes is a high priority for future research.

Measure the total return to homeownership for middle- and low-income groups. Future research measuring financial returns to homeownership could incorporate appreciation, implicit rent, mortgage costs, tax implications, and forced savings, as well as rent and housing risk. Only one of the identified studies measures the total return to homeownership.

Measure the impacts of homeownership, especially for low-income families. More empirical evidence on the short-term and long-term impacts of homeownership for low-income families is another high priority. The general assumption often is that homeownership is good, even for very low income families. Researchers could identify under what circumstances this assumption is accurate or inaccurate.

Further assess the benefits and consequences of asset holding for low-income, low-education, and minority households. In general, more empirical evidence is needed to assess the benefits and consequences of assets for low-income, low-education, and minority households.

Reassess the mortgage interest tax deduction along with other subsidies to asset holding. The mortgage interest tax deduction provides much stronger homeownership incentives for moderate- and high-income families than for low-income families because low-income families are less likely to itemize their tax deductions, and they own less-expensive homes with smaller mortgages and mortgage interest payments. Policy research can reassess the mortgage interest tax deduction and provide suggestions for increasing incentives for homeownership among those low-income families.

Measure the effect of assets on economic mobility and material hardships. Future research has the potential to improve estimates of the mechanisms by which asset accumulation affects economic mobility and material hardships. Theoretically, modest asset levels might limit access to benefit programs and thus have little effect on hardship. Though most studies find assets are helpful in lowering hardship, the evidence is far from conclusive. Such studies require researchers to conduct a long-term follow-up and identify exogenous factors that cause asset holding to vary.

Measure the effect of asset holding on self-sufficiency. Further research in this area would allow for the examination of the link between assets and self-sufficiency and would determine whether the link is causal.

Measure the effects of asset holding on social well-being and civic engagement. Research measuring the causal relationship between asset holding and social well-being and civic engagement would provide valuable insights into the potential effects of asset holding.

Consider the type of assets and mode of financing when measuring effects. Our review suggests that findings on the relationship between assets and outcomes depend on the types of assets considered and the mode of financing assets. For example, financial assets are most important in some studies, while nonfinancial tangible assets such as cars and homes are more important in others. As such, an examination of specific types of assets, if data allow, would enhance understanding in this area. Net worth could also be considered as a specific measure of assets. We found little empirical evidence on the potentially important effects of net worth on outcomes.

Assess the impact of the interaction of financial literacy and assets on social and economic outcomes. The effects of assets may vary systematically with the level of financial knowledge. If so, the gains from assets might be raised significantly with the addition of expanded financial education, especially for low- and middle-income families.

Conclusion

While future research in many promising directions will refine estimates of the effects of assets, the evidence from current research shows that assets improve outcomes in important ways for both adults and children. For families able to ride out housing-market downturns, the returns to homeownership can be large, especially after accounting for the level and variability of rents families would otherwise have to pay if they rented instead of owned their dwellings. Even in low appreciation environments, owners in low- and middle-income neighborhoods achieve modest gains in wealth after 7 to 10 years over renters. But the potential returns to home-ownership go beyond finances. Research finds that homeownership improves outcomes for children of homeowners—such as higher educational attainment and lower teen-pregnancy rates—probably because of homeownership's role in increased residential stability. These findings are particularly important for low-income families. Beyond home-ownership, car ownership is associated with positive employment outcomes, and asset holding in general is associated with positive health and psychological well-being.

Perhaps the best case for holding assets can be made by research that shows what happens when families do not hold assets. Households with low assets are unable to draw on their own assets in an emergency and are often unable to borrow, likely because they do not have sufficient access or credit. As a result, their consumptions falls, sometimes sharply. The ability to borrow in an emergency does as much to reduce hardship as tripling family income. Few assets and a weak credit record mean that even when families are able to borrow, it is in the subprime auto loan or mortgage market, where they pay high interest rates and are at greater risk of predatory lending practices.

Overall, the research findings broadly support the objective of helping families, especially low-income families, build an asset base.

NOTES

1. Some low-income families will turn to social benefit programs, but others are ineligible or reluctant to participate (Currie 2006).

2. Those homeowners with interest-only mortgages are the exception since the provisions of these mortgages do not require principal payments on an ongoing basis.

3. Twenty-five percent of low-income, first-time homebuyers in 2006 had no equity in their homes (Gramlich 2007).

REFERENCES

Aaronson, Daniel. 2000. "A Note on the Benefits of Homeownership." *Journal of Urban Economics* 47: 356–69.

Adams, William, Liron Einav, and Jonathan Levin. 2007. "Liquidity Constraints and Imperfect Information in Subprime Markets." Working Paper 13067. Cambridge, MA: National Bureau of Economic Research.

Baker, Dean. 2005. "Who's Dreaming? Homeownership among Low Income Families." Washington, DC: Center for Economic and Policy Research.

Baker, Dean, and Simone Baribeau. 2003. "Homeownership in a Bubble: The Fast Path to Poverty?" Washington, DC: Center for Economic and Policy Research.

Bodie, Zvi, and Robert C. Merton. 2000. *Finance.* New York: Prentice Hall.

Bodie, Zvi, Robert C. Merton, and William F. Samuelson. 1992. "Labor Supply Flexibility and Portfolio Choice." *Journal of Economy Dynamics and Control* 16: 427–49.

Bostic, Raphael, and KwanOk Lee. 2007. "Homeownership: America's Dream?" Presented at Conference on Access, Assets, and Poverty: The Role of Financial Services among Low- and Moderate-Income Families. National Poverty Center. Washington, DC, October 12.

Bynner, John, and Sofia Despotidou. 2001. "The Effects of Assets on Life Chances." London: Center for Longitudinal Studies, Institute for Education.

Carasso, Adam, and Signe-Mary McKernan. 2006. "The Balance Sheets of Low-Income Households: What We Know about Their Assets and Liabilities." Washington, DC: The Urban Institute. Poor Finances: Assets and Low-Income Households Report, November. http://www.urban.org/url.cfm?ID=411594. (Accessed July 26, 2008.)

Carasso, Adam, Elizabeth Bell, Edgar O. Olsen, and C. Eugene Steuerle. 2005. "Improving Homeownership among Poor and Moderate-Income Households." Washington, DC: The Urban Institute. Opportunity and Ownership Project Brief 2. http://www.urban.org/url.cfm?ID=311184. (Accessed July 26, 2008.)

Case, Karl E., and Maryna Marynchenko. 2002. "Home Price Appreciation in Low- and Moderate-Income Markets." In *Low-Income Homeownership: Examining the Unexamined Goal,* edited by Nicolas P. Retsinas and Eric S. Belsky. Cambridge, MA: Joint Center for Housing Studies; Washington, DC: Brookings Institution Press.

Charles, Kofi, and Melvin Stephens Jr. 2004. "Job Displacement, Disability, and Divorce." *Journal of Labor Economics* 22(2): 489–522.

Cho, Esther Y. 1999. "The Effects of Assets on the Economic Well-Being of Women after Marital Disruption." Center for Social Development Working Paper 99-6. Saint Louis, MO: Center for Social Development, Washington University in Saint Louis.

Conley, Dalton. 1999. *Being Black, Living in the Red: Race, Wealth, and Social Policy in America.* Berkeley: University of California Press.

Currie, Janet. 2006. "The Take-Up of Social Benefits." In *Public Policy and the Income Distribution,* edited by Alan J. Auerbach, David Card, and John M. Quigley (80–148). New York: Russell Sage Foundation.

Deaton, Angus. 1991. "Saving and Liquidity Constraints." *Econometrica* 59(5): 1221–48.

Dietz, Robert D., and Donald R. Haurin. 2003. "The Social and Private Micro-Level Consequences of Homeownership." *Journal of Urban Economics* 54: 401–50.

DiPasquale, Denise, and Edward L. Glaeser. 1999. "Incentives and Social Capital: Are Homeowners Better Citizens?" *Journal of Urban Economics* 45: 354–84.

Duda, Mark, and Eric S. Belsky. 2002. "Asset Appreciation, Timing of Purchases and Sales, and Returns to Low-Income Homeownership." In *Low-Income Homeownership: Examining the Unexamined Goal,* edited by Nicholas P. Retsinas and Eric S. Belsky (208–38). Cambridge, MA: Joint Center for Housing Studies; Washington, DC: Brookings Institution Press.

Goetzmann, William N., and Matthew Spiegel. 2002. "Policy Implications of Portfolio Choice in Underserved Mortgage Markets." In *Low-Income Homeownership: Examining the Unexamined Goal,* edited by Nicholas P. Retsinas and Eric S. Belsky (257–74). Cambridge, MA: Joint Center for Housing Studies; Washington, DC: Brookings Institution Press.

Gramlich, Edward M. 2007. *Subprime Mortgages: America's Latest Boom and Bust.* Washington, DC: Urban Institute Press.

Green, Richard, and Michelle White. 1997. "Measuring the Benefits of Homeowning: Effects on Children." *Journal of Urban Economics* 41: 441–61.

Haurin, Donald R., Toby L. Parcel, and R. Jean Haurin. 2002. "The Impact of Homeownership on Child Outcomes." In *Low-Income Homeownership: Examining the Unexamined Goal,* edited by Nicolas P. Retsinas and Eric S. Belsky (427–46). Cambridge, MA: Joint Center for Housing Studies; Washington, DC: Brookings Institution Press.

Haveman, Robert, and Edward N. Wolff. 2005. "Who Are the Asset Poor? Levels, Trends, and Composition, 1983–1998." In *Inclusion in the American Dream: Assets, Poverty, and Public Policy,* edited by Michael Sherraden (61–86). New York: Oxford University Press.

Henretta, John C. 1984. "Parental Status and Child's Home Ownership." *American Sociological Review* 49(1): 131–40.

Kalil, Ariel, and Kathleen M. Ziol-Guest. 2005. "Single Mothers' Employment Dynamics and Adolescent Well-Being." *Child Development* 76(1): 196–211.

Kane, Thomas. 1994. "College Entry by Blacks Since 1970: The Role of College Costs, Family Background, and the Returns to Education." *Journal of Political Economy* 102(5): 878–911.

Liem, Ramsey, and Joan H. Liem. 1988. "Psychological Effects of Unemployment on Workers and Their Families." *Journal of Social Issues* 44(4): 87–105.

Mayer, Susan, and Christopher Jencks. 1989. "Poverty and the Distribution of Material Hardship." *Journal of Human Resources* 24(1): 88–114.

McGarry, Kathleen, and Robert F. Schoeni. 1995. "Transfer Behavior in the Health and Retirement Survey." *Journal of Human Resources* 30(Supplement): S184–226.

Mills, Gregory, William G. Gale, Rhiannon Patterson, Gary V. Engelhardt, Michael D. Eriksen, and Emil Apostolov. 2008 "Effects of Individual Development Accounts on Asset Purchases and Saving Behavior: Evidence from a Controlled Experiment." *Journal of Public Economics* 92(5–6): 1509–30.

Moore, Amanda, Sondra Beverly, Mark Schreiner, Michael Sherraden, Margaret Lombe, Esther Y. N. Cho, Lissa Johnson, and Rebecca Vonderlack. 2001. "Saving, IDA Programs, and Effects of IDAs: A Survey of Participants." St. Louis, MO: Washington University in St. Louis, Center for Social Development.

Nembhard, Jessica Gordon, and Anthony A. Blasingame. 2006. "Wealth, Civic Engagement and Democratic Practice." In *Wealth Accumulation and Communities of Color in the United States,* edited by Jessica Gordon Nembhard and Ngina Chiteji (294–325). Ann Arbor: University of Michigan Press.

Nichols, Joseph B. 2005. "Mortgage Contracts and the Heterogeneity in the Total Return on Housing." Division of Research and Statistics, Board of Governors of the Federal Reserve System, Washington, DC.

Oliver, Melvin L., and Thomas M. Shapiro. 1995. *Black Wealth/White Wealth: A New Perspective on Racial Inequality.* New York: Routledge.

Raphael, Stephen, and Lorien Rice. 2002. "Car Ownership, Employment, and Earnings." *Journal of Urban Economics* 52(1): 109–30.

Raphael, Stephen, and Michael A. Stoll. 2001. "Can Boosting Minority Car Ownership Rates Narrow Inter-Racial Employment Gaps?" *Brookings-Wharton Papers on Urban Affairs* 2: 99–137.

Reid, Carolina Katz. 2004. "Achieving the American Dream? A Longitudinal Analysis of the Homeownership Experiences of Low-Income Households." Center for Studies in Demography and Ecology Working Paper 04-04. Seattle: University of Washington.

Renuart, Elizabeth. 2004. "An Overview of the Predatory Lending Process." *Housing Policy Debate* 15(3): 467–502.

Rohe, William M., Shannon Van Zandt, and George McCarthy. 2002. "Social Benefits and Costs of Homeownership." In *Low-Income Homeownership: Examining the Unexamined Goal,* edited by Nicolas P. Retsinas and Eric S. Belsky (381–406). Cambridge, MA: Joint Center for Housing Studies; Washington, DC: Brookings Institution Press.

Rossi, Peter H., and Eleanor Weber. 1996. "The Social Benefits of Homeownership: Empirical Evidence from National Surveys." *Housing Policy Debate* 7(1): 1–35.

Scanlon, Edward, and Deborah Adams. 2005. "Home Ownership and Youth Well-Being." In *Inclusion in the American Dream: Assets, Poverty, and Public Policy*, edited by Michael Sherraden (128–45). New York: Oxford University Press.

Shapiro, Thomas M., and Heather Beth Johnson. 2005. "Family Assets and School Access: Race and Class in the Structuring of Educational Opportunity." In *Inclusion in the American Dream: Assets, Poverty, and Public Policy*, edited by Michael Sherraden (112–27). New York: Oxford University Press.

Sherraden, Michael. 1991. *Assets and the Poor: A New American Welfare Policy*. Armonk, NY: M. E. Sharpe.

Sinai, Todd, and Nicholas S. Souleles. 2005. "Owner-Occupied Housing as a Hedge against Rent Risk." *Quarterly Journal of Economics* 120(2): 763–89.

Skinner, Jonathan. 1988. "Risky Income, Life Cycle Consumption, and Precautionary Savings." *Journal of Monetary Economics* 22(2): 237–55.

Sullivan, James X. 2005. "Borrowing During Unemployment: Unsecured Debt as a Safety Net." Notre Dame, IN: University of Notre Dame.

Williams, Trina Rachelle. 2003. "The Impact of Household Wealth and Poverty on Child Development Outcomes: Examining Asset Effects." Ph.D. diss., Washington University: St. Louis.

Woldoff, Rachael A. 2006. "Living Where the Neighbors Are Invested: Wealth and Racial/Ethnic Differences in Individuals' Neighborhood Home Ownership Rates." In *Wealth Accumulation and Communities of Color in the United States*, edited by Jessica Gordon Nembhard and Ngina Chiteji (267–93). Ann Arbor: University of Michigan Press.

Yadama, Gautam, and Michael Sherraden. 1996. "Effects of Assets on Attitudes and Behaviors: Advance Test of a Social Policy Proposal." *Social Work Research* 20(1): 3–11.

Zeldes, Stephen P. 1989. "Optimal Consumption with Stochastic Income: Deviations from Certainty Equivalence." *Quarterly Journal of Economics* 104(2): 275–98.

Zhan, Min, and Michael Sherraden. 2003. "Assets, Expectations, and Educational Achievement." *Social Service Review* 77(2): 191–211.

7

Directions for Research

Michael Sherraden and Signe-Mary McKernan

In this chapter, a review of key research findings and identification of gaps in knowledge may illuminate the book's contributions and provide a foundation for further research. Research can and should be carried out on many different topics, from definitions to impacts, from individuals to communities. While this emerging body of theory and research appears promising, there is much that we do not yet know, and policy should be informed to every extent possible by specified theory and sound evidence.

Asset Definitions

To begin, definitions and measures of assets and asset poverty in existing theories and empirical studies reveal tenuous links between theories and measures, links that can and should be strengthened. The manner in which assets are conceptualized and measured has implications for understanding what is meant by asset poverty. In chapter 1, Nam and her colleagues consider three distinct perspectives. The *consumption model* defines financial assets and physical property as a storehouse for future consumption. In this model, saving is viewed as deferred consumption that allows for households to adjust to fluctuations in their financial resources over the life course. In *social-stratification theory*, assets are viewed as an indicator of class status and a major vehicle for transmitting class across generations. Assets are understood as a critical mechanism for maintaining the current socioeconomic structure and existing inequalities. From an *assets-for-development* perspective, assets promote the capacity of individuals to achieve goals beyond satisfaction of consumption needs. Assets-for-development focuses on investing to achieve life goals in education, property ownership, enterprise, and other areas. From this perspective, asset-building interventions may be effective tools for promoting individual and household development. Together, these three perspectives lay the groundwork for developing more appropriate measures of assets and asset poverty that can inform future research and policy development.

To take one example, it will be important to explore the possibility of an asset threshold that may provide stability and support future household development. There is empirical evidence of such an asset threshold in developing countries (Carter and Barrett 2006), and this concept, if supported by evidence, has the potential to focus policy where resources can matter most. Somewhat related to this is the concept of a transformative asset—an asset that can change the development course of an individual or a family, such as purchase of a home in a better neighborhood (Shapiro 2004). It seems likely that both threshold and transformative assets may be useful concepts for informing policy. If so, it seems likely that particular assets may play special roles (e.g., a washer and dryer at home may yield high efficiency returns or a computer and Internet access may lead to educational development of children).

Existing measures do not capture these multiple and complex aspects of assets. Basic definitions are not yet in place to inform the social-stratification and development perspectives in asset accumulation. Going forward, there is a great deal of work to do in conceptualizing, testing, and refining measures of assets and asset poverty so that these measures can advance understanding of assets in low-income households and serve as fundamental tools in informing, shaping, and assessing social policy.

Assets Holdings and Liabilities

Existing data reveal that the typical low-income family does not own a home, save in a retirement account, or have any business equity. In addition, many low-income families (35 percent) do not own a car. Homeownership and retirement accounts are key asset holdings for the typical middle-income family. These differences in asset holdings of low- and middle-income families suggest directions for future research and policy. Future research should evaluate the benefits of holding any or all of these assets for low-income families and help identify, for example, the numbers and types of low-income families that may benefit from owning a home. Findings from the current subprime mortgage fallout can inform this research. Overall, public policy researchers should examine the incentives and barriers low-income families face in acquiring different assets and what difference these assets make in their well-being and development.

Portraits of asset and debt holdings are far from complete. Further research is needed before we can fully understand the balance sheets of low-income families and how best to use them to understand and improve well-being. Portraying the assets of low-income families by age group would better account for the role that the life cycle plays in asset accumulation. Creating more detailed portraits of families of interest, such as welfare participants and nonparticipants, for policy purposes could reveal ways that welfare policies and programs affect asset building. Assessing the role that different assets and liabilities play in overall wealth could help answer questions such as whether families are better off owning a home or a savings account, having secured versus unsecured debt, or holding consumption versus investment debt. Research on these subjects has considerable potential to inform and influence public policy.

Asset Building across the Life-Course Framework

A life-course framework that examines how individual lives unfold and how they are affected by particular experiences over time is a useful tool for studying the process of asset building. Although research linking the life-course perspective with asset holding is preliminary, several factors have been identified that help explain a range of outcomes, including the effect of intergenerational transfers, race, income, and stages of the life cycle. These variables can account for the effects of expected events, such as aging or changes in family composition, and unexpected ones, such as illness or job loss. It is the dynamic interaction of all these factors, especially among different socioeconomic groups, that offers an informative picture of asset building over the life course. Initial research reveals that these dynamics are distinct for households with low incomes or fewer resources. But even then, the experience of such a family may differ greatly if asset poverty is short lived or persists. The life-course lens can help us to recognize these differences.

A challenge for future research examining asset holding over the life course is the limitation of existing datasets to facilitate longitudinal analyses that are capable of tracking individuals across an extended time horizon. Theoretically, it is plausible that stages of the life cycle and the timing of particular life events in relation to these stages affect asset building, but little is known regarding the magnitude of these effects and their varying dynamics. Beyond describing correlations between asset holdings and life-course stages there is much to learn, especially regarding the impacts and timing of unexpected events such as illness and job loss. Similarly, further exploration will be required to clarify how changing conceptions of retirement may affect asset-building activities over the life course. Longer life spans and shorter employment careers may affect both accumulation and consumption strategies in ways that have yet to be examined.

Determinants of Asset Holdings

The conceptual framework offered in the analysis of what determines asset building is based on an emerging institutional theory of saving and asset accumulation. In this framework, both individual and institutional constructs affect saving and investment, which in turn lead to asset accumulation. Individual constructs include economic resources and needs, informal support for saving, financial knowledge, and psychological variables, such as future orientation and saving-related attitudes. The framework emphasizes the role of seven institutional constructs: (1) access, (2) information, (3) incentives, (4) facilitation, (5) expectations, (6) restrictions, and (7) security. In the "real world," these constructs tend to exist in "bundles" rather than in isolation. These bundles, often supported through public policy, tend to be delivered through employment settings and through the tax system, which means that a household's ability to access these institutional supports depends substantially upon its employers' decisions and on its level of income.

Research on determinants of saving and asset accumulation is extensive and informative, though still insufficient for policy purposes. There is fairly strong evidence that certain institutional mechanisms, such as automatic enrollment in savings plans and the existence of a match, increase participation, but most constructs remain understudied. More research is needed in the very promising areas of eligibility and default enrollment (access) and automatic saving and automatic increases in saving (facilitation). Another revealing line of experimental or quasi-experimental research with policy implications would involve match structure—both match rate (incentives) and match cap, especially when the match cap becomes an expectation. Future research that examines the effects of financial education (information) and the effects of easing asset tests on saving and asset accumulation (reducing disincentives), as well as research on specified uses of accounts (restrictions), could be helpful for policymaking.

Of course, institutional determinants, while very useful for policy, cannot tell the complete story. Individuals and families are embedded in social structures that affect asset holdings and potential. (See the large body of work of Wolff [2004] in documenting asset holding by income level and the groundbreaking work on assets and race by Oliver and Shapiro [1995], and Conley [1999].) Also, kinship networks may affect asset holdings (e.g., the study of African American households and assets by Chiteji and Hamilton [2005]). Because of deeply embedded sociological realities, there will be particular value in research that includes low-income, racial, and ethnic populations.

The Role of Welfare Program Rules

Means-tested public assistance programs are believed to lower saving rates among poor households because they guarantee a certain level of consumption and have restrictive asset tests. Early empirical studies support this hypothesis, especially for asset-test effects. However, evidence is mixed on whether recent policy changes liberalizing asset-limit rules have achieved the goal of increasing low-income households' asset holding. Current asset policies are often confusing for current and potential participants, which could limit the effects of liberalizing them. Asset tests vary widely across government social programs, further contributing to confusion and to administrative costs. The rules could be clarified and simplified by making them more consistent across means-tested programs, across states, and across similar asset types. The recent Farm Bill is a step in the right direction in that it treats similar asset types more consistently. The Farm Bill exempts all tax-preferred retirement and education accounts, where previously 401(k) accounts were exempt but individual retirement accounts were not.

Asset limits are in place to ensure that families with moderate wealth do not use transfer programs. Given other program rules, asset limits may do little to prevent the less needy from participating, yet they make eligibility determinations more burdensome and costly. The costs of mistargeted benefits are not well understood but are an important factor to consider if asset limits are perhaps someday to be eliminated. Further research is required to determine the magnitude of these costs and compare them with the benefits of eliminating asset limits.

Effects of Asset Holding

The potential positive effects of asset holding represent the primary rationale for this body of research and policy. Research yields several significant findings concerning relationships between asset holding and economic well-being, child well-being, and health and psychological well-being. There is substantial evidence that asset holding, especially in the form of homeownership, is positively associated with economic outcomes and child well-being. However, these associations may differ by race, income group, and location, and some economic benefits of homeownership appear to be weaker for low-income and minority families than for moderate- and high-income families. A small number of studies move beyond association and try to document causal links between assets and positive social and economic outcomes.

The body of knowledge on asset effects is still in an early stage of development, especially with regard to effects on low-income families. Several directions for future research may be promising. Especially important will be attempts to measure, analyze, and assess potential causal relationships between asset holding and outcomes. Further research is required to examine the link between assets and household economic stability and development, to measure the effects of asset holding on social well-being and civic participation, and to consider different types of assets when measuring effects. For example, future research measuring financial returns to homeownership could be improved by considering appreciation, implicit rent, mortgage costs, tax implications, and forced savings, as well as rent and housing risk. This work may be particularly relevant to inform effective policies for lower-income households.

Challenges in Using Existing Datasets

Data limitations currently impede the study of assets. The appendix identifies the Survey of Consumer Finances, the Survey of Income and Program Participation, and the Panel Study of Income Dynamics as the most informative and reliable data sources for understanding low-income households' assets and liabilities. The appendix also presents a range of options to improve their usefulness in the future. To take one example, it is important to collect information on dynamics of asset accumulation to understand how asset holding changes over the life course.

Surveying household assets examines just one aspect of financial status and condition. Because of their intimate and interacting relationship, it is preferable to assess both assets and liabilities. This perspective is sharpened significantly when using a "portrait approach," in which several classifiers are used in combination to identify distinct household types. Often the pattern of distribution of some asset in the general population looks different from its distribution in a specific "portrait" group. While such portraits are useful analytical tools, they paint incomplete pictures. Until more asset data are collected and become available over time for groups and particular households, answers to many pertinent questions—such as how assets are accumulated over the life course and passed across generations—will remain obscure.

The lack of homeownership and pension or retirement account ownership among most low-income families goes a long way toward explaining their low asset holdings. Furthermore, acquiring an asset often entails assuming a debt or liability. Importantly, not all debt is created equal. Patterns of asset holding can be related to patterns of debt holdings and to the terms and conditions upon which debt is acquired. For example, the distinction between secured and unsecured debt is meaningful. Unsecured debt, such as credit card bills, can be a long-term drain on assets. The prevalence of this type of debt in asset-poor households often indicates financial drain, affirming the importance of a holistic consideration of a family's balance sheet.

Regarding data availability, still unknown are the roles that different types of assets and debts may play in overall asset accumulation, upward mobility, and the long-term well-being of low- and moderate-income families. Research does provide evidence that assets may matter for household well-being, though at present little is known about the dynamics of how, why, when, and for whom they matter. Moreover, the relative newness of applying an assets perspective to social policy creates opportunities for additional studies.

Advancement in data availability on assets and liabilities in existing longitudinal datasets will be an essential foundation for continuing to develop this body of knowledge. Fortunately, this is gradually happening. While income has been the primary focus for assessing household well-being, there has been more attention paid to assets over time.

Research Strategies Going Forward

Many other research approaches will be needed as well. Especially valuable will be large-scale applied research, including experiments that use random assignment, to test many of the hypotheses on determinants and the effects of asset holding. The American Dream Demonstration (ADD) of individual development accounts (IDAs), a study of matched savings in low-income households, has been productive, especially in helping specify determinants of saving among a low-income population. An experiment in ADD has found a positive impact on homeownership (Mills et al. 2008), but it is uncertain what has happened to this key impact during the subprime mortgage crisis. Anecdotal information from the field suggests that most IDA homeowners have been successful in holding onto their homes. If so, this is perhaps because of the financial education that is required with IDA participation or the oversight of the homebuying process by a community organization. But this has not been confirmed by quantitative measures. A fourth wave of the ADD experiment goes into the field as this book goes to print, and we hope will know more about ADD impacts as we go along.

Another large applied research project is the SEED initiative (Saving for Education, Entrepreneurship, and Downpayment), which also includes an experiment. The SEED for Oklahoma Kids (SEED OK) experiment tests the concept of universal and progressive child development accounts. The SEED OK experiment randomly selects newborns across the entire state of Oklahoma to receive an account or participate in the control group. In other words, this is an experiment in a full population, without selection, which is uncommon in social or health research. Account holders receive an initial $1,000 deposit and savings are matched progressively. Accounts are held in the Oklahoma College Savings Plan. This experiment rolled out in the spring of 2008 and is scheduled to continue at least until 2014. The experiment is set up so that other researchers can track the SEED OK account holders and control subjects even after 2014, ideally until they reach their college and young adult years. We anticipate that the SEED OK experiment will generate policy-relevant knowledge for many years to come.

The newness of the asset field and the extensive knowledge bases in related fields together call for a more integrated approach to studying assets. Currently housing, credit, retirement, tax, and health experts tend to work in isolation. But these fields can inform one another and together can build policy-relevant knowledge that may enable households to have stronger and more diversified asset portfolios.

In taking stock of all of the chapters in *Asset Building and Low-Income Families,* it is clear that theory and evidence to date are sufficient to merit more attention to the assets perspective by researchers, practitioners, and policymakers alike. Accumulation of assets may enable households to maintain their consumption patterns and keep from falling into chaos, even when incomes decline. Saving for a rainy day prepares a family to weather both unexpected events that cause income fluctuations and more predictable life-course events, particularly retirement. Thus, approaching assets through a consumption lens will remain a valuable perspective. It will always be the case that declining consumption is linked with declining utility for the vast majority of individuals and households.

There is also promise in extending the conceptualization of assets beyond their potential to facilitate consumption. Over the long term, other factors contribute to a family's well-being. Linking assets narrowly with consumption may miss important parts of the story, perhaps particularly for lower-income households. People seek to accumulate assets to improve themselves, to move up economically (e.g., saving for education or a small business), to improve their social standing, or to create opportunities for their children. The accumulation of assets has developmental consequences because it provides access to opportunities to build capacities and maximize life chances (Sen 1999). Initial inquiry has shown that, controlling for other factors, assets are positively associated with a range of well-being indicators at the household level, though the underlying nature of these relationships may be often bidirectional (e.g., wealth affects health and, also, health affects wealth) and complex in other ways as well.

Regarding development, although most policy discussions lump low-income households together, they are in reality a diverse group. Recognition of this diversity can lead to a greater understanding of how different households value, hold, and build assets. Similarly, given preliminary findings regarding asset effects, it is reasonable to anticipate that impacts of assets may vary by household type as well.

A comprehensive perspective is also valuable when looking at asset effects. To date, positive correlations found between asset holdings and a range of outcome measures at the household, community, and even societal level is compelling but preliminary. Causality among assets and these outcomes remains mostly in the hypothesis stage and should be subjected to further research to learn more about these relationships.

Much of the research on asset effects has focused on homeownership. This remains a worthy subject of inquiry given its central role in American social philosophy and the American psyche, and its prominence in the financial portfolios of many households. But while homeownership is clearly a promising explanatory variable, it is just one of the various forms that assets can take, and for many households, homeownership is the culmination of a longer-term, asset-building endeavor. In this respect, asset accumulation and wealth building are best conceptualized as an extended process that occurs over time—indeed, over the life course.

One of the strengths of the assets perspective is its connection to the life-course framework as the dynamics of asset accumulation at the individual level change with age. Asset poverty among young adults is less of a social problem than when it persists after those adults become parents and raise children. Similarly, episodic income poverty is distinct from chronic income poverty, often because of the mitigating role that assets can play in offering protection from temporary hardship. The potential security offered by assets—whether they are savings, investments, home equity, or human capital—is that they can work as building blocks over a lifetime. For those focused on retirement security, assets can serve as bridges connecting different stages of the life cycle. Yet for many household types, little is known regarding the role of assets over the life course. Many questions also remain regarding what motivates a family to save and begin the asset-building process.

This underscores the need for a well-specified and policy-relevant theory—along with empirical evidence—on how the process of saving works. A policy-relevant theory is one that considers how individuals interact with the conditions and circumstances all around them. In this respect, understanding how people build assets requires a focus on how individuals interact with institutions in the saving process. An institutional theory suggests that factors other than income, preferences, and other individual characteristics shape saving behavior and outcomes. These factors are external to the individual but are potentially present in the daily environment (e.g., in the form of a 401(k) plan with direct deposit and tax deferment or the home mortgage interest tax deduction).

The identification of factors can be building blocks of an institutional theory in the form of constructs that may affect saving. Key constructs appear to be access, information, incentives, facilitation, expectations, restrictions, and security. While not yet a fully developed and integrated theory, these building blocks and related empirical evidence can inform policy development and future research. It may be that some constructs are mediating to others or some are more important than others. It may be that particular combinations of these building blocks create interactions that are synergistic. This research agenda has the potential to contribute directly to policy.

In the real world, it is already the case that public policies serve to "bundle" groups of these building blocks together in ways that shape the manner in which people save and build assets. In fact, it is quite difficult to isolate any particular one of these elements that contribute to the saving process. These bundles appear in several common forms. For example, there may be a form that provides mostly security in a "rainy day" fund (e.g., a passbook savings account in the private sector). Other forms may have strong elements of incentives, facilitation, expectations, and restrictions designed for long-term asset accumulation (e.g., a 401(k) retirement-savings plan). Thus, some bundles may be better for particular purposes. A conceptual bundle of features can be represented as a policy or program "package." In the context of this discussion, the question remains as to what type of package is most desirable for a particular policy objective.

At this point, there is much more to learn about these issues. More theoretical development and empirical testing lie ahead. But enough is now known to move beyond a narrow focus on individuals to an emphasis on how institutions encourage saving and asset accumulation through interactions with individual behavior. Policy interventions that promote targeted asset building by lower-income households are likely to be more effective if they recognize and build on institutional theory and evidence.

Overall, if these several facets and understandings of asset building are eventually to play a larger role in guiding research and informing policy, a wide range of research programs in different policy fields and academic disciplines will be required. This work is emerging. Especially useful to date have been advances in behavioral economics (e.g., the work on defaults by Besheares and others [2006]), field experiments in saving and asset accumulation (ADD and SEED OK), secondary studies using longitudinal datasets (e.g., Green and White 1997; Shanks 2007; Sullivan 2006), and qualitative studies that can uncover unforeseen dynamics (e.g., Sherraden and McBride [forthcoming] on the qualitative research from the ADD).

This is a large research agenda, and whether an assets perspective on human well-being and public policy continues to develop will depend largely on specified theory, research findings, and their policy and practice relevance. As this body of work progresses, if research knowledge continues to be academically productive and useful in the real world, then the body of work will continue to grow. If not, then eventually it will be set aside. At present, the future for asset-based research looks promising, both intellectually and practically.

REFERENCES

Besheares, John, James Choi, David Laibson, and Brigitte Madrian. 2006. "The Importance of Default Options for Retirement Savings Outcomes: Evidence from the United States." NBER Working Paper 12009. Cambridge, MA: National Bureau of Economic Research.

Carter, Michael R., and Christopher Barrett. 2006. "The Economics of Poverty Traps and Persistent Poverty: An Asset-Based Approach." *Journal of Development Studies* 42(2): 178–99.

Chiteji, Ngina, and Darrick Hamilton. 2005. "Family Matters: Kin Networks and Asset Accumulation." In *Inclusion in the American Dream: Assets, Poverty, and Public Policy,* edited by Michael Sherraden (87–111). New York: Oxford University Press.

Conley, Dalton. 1999. *Being Black, Living In the Red: Race, Wealth, and Social Policy in America.* Berkeley: University of California Press.

Green, Richard, and Michelle White. 1997. "Measuring the Benefits of Homeowning: Effects on Children." *Journal of Urban Economics* 41: 441–61.

Mills, Gregory, William G. Gale, Rhiannon Patterson, Gary V. Englehardt, Michael D. Eriksen, and Emil Apostolov. 2008 "Effects of Individual Development Accounts on Asset Purchases and Saving Behavior: Evidence from a Controlled Experiment." *Journal of Public Economics* 92(5): 1509–30.

Oliver, Melvin L., and Thomas M. Shapiro. 2006. *Black Wealth/White Wealth: A New Perspective on Racial Inequality,* 2nd ed. New York: Routledge.

Sen, Amartya. 1999. *Development as Freedom.* New York: Knopf.

Shapiro, Thomas M. 2004. *The Hidden Cost of Being African American: How Wealth Perpetuates Inequality.* New York: Oxford University Press.

Sherraden, Margaret S., and Amanda M. McBride. Forthcoming. *Saving in Low-Income Households.* Ann Arbor: University of Michigan Press.

Sullivan, James X. 2006. "Welfare Reform, Saving, and Vehicle Ownership: Do Asset Limits and Vehicle Exemptions Matter?" *Journal of Human Resources* 41(1): 72–105.

Williams Shanks, Trina R. 2007. "The Impacts of Household Wealth on Child Development." *Journal of Poverty* 11(2): 93–116.

Wolff, Edward N. 2004. "Changes in Household Wealth in the 1980s and 1990s in the U.S." Working Paper 407. Annandale-on-Hudson, NY: Levy Economics Institute of Bard College.

8

Policy Implications

Reid Cramer, Michael Sherraden,
and Signe-Mary McKernan

As the previous chapters of this book indicate, a new social policy discussion has emerged during the past two decades regarding the conceptualization of poverty and household development. This discussion has emerged from the growing recognition that economic security throughout the life course is intrinsically linked to both income and asset ownership, and building up an asset base can help individuals, families, and communities expand their economic horizons and social protections. At a minimum, there are sufficient research findings to merit more attention to the assets perspective by researchers and policymakers alike.

The assets perspective has given rise to a new area of theory and research in social policy. This is a promising development in that it has provided an additional lens with which to view the issues of poverty and social development in contrast to the more traditional approach, which has focused on income as a proxy for consumption. The emergent focus on assets does not replace but rather complements income as a measure and determinant of poverty and development. The central organizing claim of this perspective is that assets have the potential—when combined with income—to promote welfare in ways that are distinct and potentially more powerful than income alone.

Yet the body of knowledge on asset accumulation and its effects, particularly with regard to low-income families, is still in a formative stage. This book represents an attempt to document and describe the growing body of research that has emanated from the assets perspective and also to identify gaps in the research agenda that must be addressed. While a rigorous research agenda will be required to fill in knowledge gaps, some findings are already suggestive. Despite a growing list of questions that require more empirical work, the research findings that have already emerged offer a broad array of information relevant to crafting public policy. This chapter is our attempt to describe and examine the policy implications for research findings that have emerged from the assets field to date and to identify aspects of a potentially productive policy agenda moving forward. We do not advocate for a specific policy agenda per se, but we examine what the policy frontier looks like given what we have learned from research thus far. We assess whether current initiatives build on what we know and what may be required to improve policies in the future.

Approaching Poverty through an Assets Perspective

Dimensions of poverty and its distribution among different social groups are significantly different when approached from an assets perspective, in contrast to an income perspective. Those with a low stock of resources to draw on in times of need are asset poor. This *asset poverty* may leave them vulnerable to unexpected economic events and unable to take advantage of opportunities offered by a prosperous society. Many families in the United States have little financial cushion to sustain them in the event of a job loss, illness, or other income shortfall. Also, these families' social and economic development may be limited by a lack of investment in education, homes, businesses, or other assets. Understanding how those with low resource holdings can build up their asset bases is likely to become an important policy issue.

In several important respects, an assets perspective is relevant to a reframing of poverty. Since the manner in which problems are defined often leads to a specific policy response, defining poverty as a function of low incomes has led historically to proposals that focus on income maintenance. As most people use their incomes to facilitate current consumption, it makes intuitive sense to focus on income as a key determination of material hardship. However, poverty that extends over time can curtail opportunities for growth and development. Defining the problem in asset terms may give rise to a policy response that considers deployment of resources strategically over an extended time horizon.

The official poverty measure calculated annually by the U.S. Census Bureau poses an obstacle to the consideration of more comprehensive responses to poverty, because it bases its definition of poverty solely in terms of income. First devised over 40 years ago, this metric provides relatively narrow insights to inform the public policy challenge of ameliorating poverty. To be sure, the official poverty measure provides historic continuity—and this is valuable in identifying trends—but there is widespread consensus in the research community regarding its limitations (Citro and Michael 1995). As currently applied, the measure fails to account for in-kind benefits, consumption patterns, differences in regional costs of living, or tax credit transfers such as provided by the earned income tax credit. These shortcomings are compounded by the measure's sole focus on income.

The findings of earlier chapters in this book indicate some of the disadvantages in relying too greatly on income as a definition of poverty, well-being, and economic security. Most fundamentally, well-being is more closely related to consumption than to income, and income is empirically not a precise proxy for consumption. Furthermore, consumption at any particular time is not an adequate indication of long-term hardship. Poverty is a problem as an episodic condition and is still more challenging as a persistent and intergenerational pattern. A family's financial welfare is in many respects better conceptualized as the product of a long-term, dynamic process rather than an accounting of income over a limited period of time.

Assets are more reflective of economic prospects over a longer time horizon, because assets provide stability and create a foundation and starting point from which families can take advantage of social and economic opportunities. This is particularly true in American society, in which even small asset holdings can make meaningful differences in the lives of low-income families. The potential for assets to expand opportunities, as well as to prevent economic hardship, make them a valuable social indicator and a component of a more encompassing definition of poverty.

The importance of a measure of asset poverty has risen as policymakers have considered alternative strategies to encourage savings and asset development to promote economic security and development of impoverished households. This is indicative of the inroads of the assets perspective in influencing policy discussions, proposals, and legislation. For a number of reasons, the idea that low-income people would benefit from asset-building opportunities has made remarkable progress during the past decade and has led to a greatly expanded discussion of asset-based policy options.

Foremost, the distinction between income and assets—as well as the implications of this distinction for social policy—has resonated among policymakers, particularly because the concept of asset building as an antipoverty strategy debuted as policymakers were looking to restructure the federal government's traditional welfare programs. Initial research findings were also encouraging. Demonstration projects offered evidence that low-income people could in fact save under the right conditions. These research results addressed an initial concern with the asset-building approach, which questioned whether the poor, with low incomes by definition, could save.

Income-maintenance strategies remain prominent in antipoverty discussions. Within these discussions, skepticism remains as to whether the assets perspective has substantial policy relevance when most federal antipoverty programs are geared toward facilitating more immediate consumption. The newness of the assets perspective may explain some of the tension, along with recognition of budget-resources constraints. Most asset-based policy proposals are designed to complement antipoverty solutions based on income support. Still, it is a fair assessment that policymakers throughout government and across the political spectrum now seriously consider the "assets perspective" when focusing on the long-term social and economic development of individuals, families, and communities.

The Foundations of Asset-Based Policy

Since assets are accumulated and used by their owners in different ways, it is not surprising that asset-based policy would have many potential meanings that lend themselves to a range of policy objectives. These include policies that promote the accumulation of financial wealth, tangible property, human capital, social capital, civic engagement, cultural capital, and natural resources. While all of these meanings have value, building financial wealth for the purpose of household social and economic development may be a particularly effective strategy in the context of social policy. Contributing to the accumulation of financial wealth is an appropriate public policy goal because it is relevant, achievable, and measurable (Sherraden 2005).

In many respects, there is little that is novel about asset-based policy. America has a long-standing history of promoting ownership and asset development. In fact, it is fair to say that the United States has been particularly successful at generating wealth and that public policy has repeatedly been deployed to support diverse asset-building activities. Landmark legislative efforts, such as the Homestead Act of 1862, the creation of the Federal Housing Administration in 1934, and the G.I. Bill of 1944, have sought to expand opportunity through acquisition of meaningful assets. To this day the public sector remains active in support of asset building on a number of fronts, as reflected in existing policies to promote home and business ownership, investment, and saving.

Many of the policy devices employed in these efforts are embedded in the tax code. In recent years a proliferation of tax-preferred account systems—along with other tax deductions, credits, and deferrals—has subsidized a broad range of saving and asset building. These asset-based policies have grown rapidly in recent years and today represent a significant proportion of overall federal expenditures and tax subsidies. All told, the value of these asset-building tax-expenditure programs is expected to exceed $407 billion in fiscal year 2008, including over $176 billion a year to support homeownership and over $111 billion to subsidize retirement savings (Cramer, O'Brien, and Boshara 2007).

The problem from a policy standpoint is that many low-income families are denied access to these asset-based policies delivered through the tax code. For example, in fiscal year 2005, less than 3 percent of the benefits from federal asset-building programs went to the bottom 60 percent of households as measured by income. The top 20 percent, in contrast, received nearly 90 percent of the benefits (Woo and Buchholz 2007). Lower-income families are less likely to own homes, investments, or retirement accounts, where most asset-based policies are targeted. Even if they own homes or have retirement accounts, those with low incomes receive no or low tax benefits. Moreover, many lower-income families are subject to limits on the amount of assets they can hold and still qualify for federal program assistance, which may function as a disincentive for these families to save. The result is asset-based policy that benefits the nonpoor far more than the poor. In other words, this policy contributes to asset inequality.

These policies should be considered in light of the overall distribution of wealth. Survey of Consumer Finances data show that the top 10 percent of U.S. households ranked by income earn 42 percent of the nation's income, yet they own 67 percent of total family net worth, while the bottom 60 percent earn 18 percent of the nation's income and own less than 10 percent of the nation's wealth (Bucks, Kennickell, and Moore 2006).

If inclusive (universal and progressive) asset accumulation is the goal, structured saving *plans* that represent large bundles of key constructs are likely to be an effective policy package (Clancy, Orszag, and Sherraden 2004; Sherraden 2005). Current savings plans—all of which are created by public policy—include 401(k) plans in the private sector, 403(b) plans in the nonprofit sector, the Thrift Savings Plan for federal employees, and state-run 529 plans for postsecondary education.

While none of these plans reach the entire population, the plans have potential to deliver bundles of services and institutional support structures that can lead to greater inclusion. The bundles could include greater *access* through availability to all, outreach, and ease of registration; greater *incentives* at the bottom through progressive matching and elimination of fees on small savings; greater *information* through financial education; greater *expectations* though higher match limits and target savings amounts; and greater *facilitation* through automatic enrollment and direct deposits.

Savings plans, which can be provided by the private sector, are often supported by public policies. Tax benefits to employers that offer 401(k) plans encourage the provision of these savings opportunities in a fundamental way. Similarly, 529 plans offer families a chance to save for the specific objective of paying for postsecondary education. Additional proposals have been previously made to build on this model and even though they have not been enacted, they reflect the potential of this approach. President Clinton proposed universal savings accounts, essentially an inclusive 401(k) plan for all workers, with greater subsidies at the bottom. And the bipartisan ASPIRE Act calls for creating a universal and progressive children's savings account modeled on the Thrift Savings Plan (Cramer 2006). Such proposals have potential for inclusion that is extremely unlikely for savings products in the private market.

Universal savings accounts, such as children's accounts, can play a powerful role in financial education. These accounts allow families and children to see firsthand the value of compound interest. That alone may improve financial acumen. But combining accounts with some financial training through schools or other programs is proving to be most effective for increasing understanding of finances and financial management (Seidman, Murrell, and Koide 2007).

Packages of Institutional Supports

Currently, asset-building packages tend to be delivered through employment settings and the tax system. For the most part, those who have jobs with benefits, those who are homeowners, and those who are "investors" have access to these packages. The primary institutional supports delivered through employment settings come through retirement benefits—both defined benefit and defined contribution plans. Defined contribution retirement plans especially support asset building in several ways. Perhaps most importantly, they provide incentives for asset accumulation. Employer matches directly increase wealth (unless recipients save less in other forms to offset these matches). When employer contributions require a corresponding employee contribution, they also create potential incentives for saving. The federal government provides an additional subsidy and incentive by deferring employee contributions from income taxation.

These retirement plans also provide facilitation. The use of automatic transfers allows individuals to precommit, and this greatly reduces the mental and physical effort required to save. Automatic-enrollment or "opt-out" plans provide even greater facilitation, by automatically enrolling individuals in voluntary plans unless they elect otherwise. And well-diversified defaults for the accounts help ensure that families maintain a diversified retirement portfolio.

Employer-sponsored retirement accounts are almost always restricted. In many defined benefit plans, funds are not available until workers reach a certain age. In most defined contribution plans, early withdrawals are allowed but are subject to taxation and in some cases substantial tax penalties. Although a sizeable proportion of families do withdraw funds before retirement, especially when changing jobs (see, e.g., Poterba, Venti, and Wise 1995; Samwick and Skinner 1997), these restrictions probably still help protect retirement savings or at least support the accumulation of savings by deferring the consumption of income. Additionally, employees who have access to employer-sponsored retirement plans often have access to financial education as well, especially if they work for medium-size or large firms. These educational initiatives—often newsletters or optional group seminars—attempt to motivate and inform employees.

Incentives, facilitation, restrictions, and information all send the message that saving and asset accumulation are desirable. The terms of matching contributions may also set up specific expectations for saving. If a worker receives the maximum employer contribution when she contributes 5 percent of her earnings to a 401(k), for example, then the plan may create an expectation that employees save 5 percent of earnings. Similarly, the terms of automatic-enrollment plans may communicate specific expectations about saving for retirement. These expectations become saving targets for many participants.

Homeownership also comes with its own set of unique institutional supports. Because homebuying usually involves taking out a mortgage, it brings important aspects of facilitation and restrictions. For example, mortgages represent a contractual obligation to make monthly payments. Portions of these payments go to pay down the principal of the loan and increase the ownership stake in the home. In this sense, the savings happens automatically with little extra effort required; it is facilitated as part of the normal process of owning a home. Indeed, merely holding onto a home that increases in value with inflation while the corresponding mortgage debt stays constant (or declines in real terms) results in a buildup of equity. Also, because it takes a great deal of effort to sell a home, home equity is generally considered illiquid. The high transaction costs of selling a home are the restrictions that help protect home equity.

But as the housing downturn of 2007 and 2008 has confirmed, more is needed to protect home equity, especially for low- and moderate-income families. These families typically pose greater credit risks than higher-income families do (due to less-stable employment and other factors) and so are more likely to finance their home mortgages outside of banks. These alternative lenders originate most subprime loans but receive less federal oversight and supervision than banks—one reason why the current credit crisis originated in the subprime market. Increased regulation of lenders that are not banks will help protect assets (McKernan and Ratcliffe 2008).

In addition to facilitation and restrictions, there are incentives or subsidies for homeownership. For instance, the exclusion of capital gains on the sales of principal residences from federal income tax provides an incentive and subsidy for homeownership. Still, the most recognized subsidy is the ability for some homeowners to deduct their mortgage interest and property tax payments from their incomes when calculating tax liabilities. These tax benefits reduce the cost of homeownership (and send the message that homeownership is "good") and so may encourage people to purchase homes. This is important because, as noted above, home equity is the primary asset for many people. In some time periods, home values in some locations have appreciated dramatically. These high rates of return directly increase wealth, and the possibility of "passive" asset accumulation may serve as an additional incentive for saving in the form of home equity. Of course, recent experience demonstrates that home values can also fall, eroding home equity that has been built up over time.

Despite the risks inherent in potential property value fluctuations, it remains clear that there are inequities in who benefits from homeownership subsidies. Federal spending on homeownership programs was roughly $176 billion in 2007, and 99 percent was in the form of tax subsidies (Cramer et al. 2007). As discussed above, subsidies provided as tax breaks mostly benefit high-income families. Of the two largest homeownership expenditures—the mortgage interest deduction and deductions for property taxes—for instance, 60 percent goes to households in the top 10 percent by income while the bottom 50 percent of households get less than 3 percent (Woo and Buchholz 2007).

The mortgage interest deduction is by far the largest single component of homeownership expenditures, comprising more than 60 percent of federal spending on homeownership subsidies ($89.4 billion in 2007). Tax filers can deduct the amount of interest they pay on their home mortgages from their adjusted gross incomes if they itemize their deductions. Interest paid on mortgages up to $1 million can be deducted from taxable income. Partly because it subsidizes debt instead of assets, this tax benefit has had little effect on homeownership rates, but it has spurred the purchase of bigger and more expensive homes. Low- and moderate-income families benefit less from the mortgage interest deduction because they tend to purchase less-expensive homes and are less likely to itemize their deductions. An alternative approach to make the subsidy more progressive and still promote homeownership is to convert the mortgage deduction to a tax credit. This would make it accessible to all homeowners regardless of their income and tax liabilities.

Finally, a package of institutional supports is available to "investors," that is, to those who hold specific saving and investment vehicles. Of particular interest here are individual retirement accounts (IRAs), such as traditional IRAs, Roth IRAs, and Keogh plans. The most important institutional supports provided by these programs are incentives, restrictions, and expectations. Incentives are provided through the tax system. For example, contributions to traditional IRAs are deductible (although withdrawals are taxable). Contributions to Roth IRAs are not deductible, but earnings and withdrawals after age 59.5 are not taxed. Traditional IRAs and Keogh plans are restricted. For example, withdrawals taken from a traditional IRA before age 59.5 are subject to a 10 percent penalty unless used for higher education or a first-time home purchase, or unless the account holder becomes disabled. The maximum deductible contributions for these individual retirement programs may also set up expectations for saving.

Unlike employer-sponsored retirement plans, participation in individual retirement plans must be initiated and structured by individuals. Nearly half of U.S. workers do not have an employer-sponsored savings plan, such as a 401(k) plan. Employer-sponsored savings plans allow workers to easily save for retirement. Without such plans, workers may find it harder to maneuver the system (say, figure out how to open an IRA). Easy access to a retirement-savings plan could help workers save for retirement and make the post-earning years more financially secure (McKernan and Ratcliffe 2008). This is particularly relevant for low-wage workers because they are less likely than higher-wage workers to have an employer-sponsored retirement plan. Further, retirement saving among low-income families is very low—only 10 percent have any retirement savings.

The main point here is that households with lower incomes and fewer resources are much less likely than others to benefit from a bundling of institutional characteristics delivered as policy "packages." They are less likely to own homes, they have low tax liabilities, and their employers may fail to offer saving opportunities. To overcome these limitations, more inclusive policy interventions will be required, and the impact of these efforts will be more effective if they build on institutional theory and evidence.

The Search for Inclusive Policies

The shortage of asset-building opportunities for the low-income population created much of the impetus for Sherraden's 1991 book *Assets and the Poor*. In this book the idea was introduced of individual development accounts (IDAs), matched savings accounts designed to help low-income families build up their asset bases. IDAs are only one example or mechanism for more inclusive asset building. In the intervening years, the IDA concept has received federal support, been implemented on a modest scale, and led to insights on how to create more comprehensive and larger-scale asset-building opportunities.

Federal policy has expanded IDAs in several significant ways. First, Congress passed the Assets for Independence Act in 1998, which authorized a five-year, $125 million IDA demonstration project, and second, the federal Office of Refugee Resettlement established in 1999 an IDA program for refugees. President Clinton endorsed expansion of IDAs and other matched savings plans. President Bush has repeatedly proposed creating up to 900,000 matched savings accounts for lower-income people, which would provide eligible account holders with a dollar-for-dollar match of up to $500 of savings each year by offering a tax credit to the financial institutions that contribute to the match. Although never enacted, legislation that would further expand IDAs remains pending in Congress with bipartisan support (Cramer et al. 2007).

Even without spurring the creation of a large-scale targeted savings incentive, the IDA experience has been a valuable proving ground for further policy ideas. Specifically, evaluation of IDA programs has allowed for the extraction of a number of relevant research findings that may inform future policy discussions. Moreover, the advent of the assets field creates opportunities for additional studies or large-scale demonstration programs that use random assignment to test many of the hypotheses on the determinants and effects of asset holding.

The key findings of the research presented in this book suggest directions for future asset policy. Four primary conclusions are worth highlighting for their policy implications. The first is that saving is a process shaped by institutions, not merely individual preferences. Understanding the array of institutional factors and constructs that help explain savings outcomes is particularly instructive, because it identifies the components of the savings infrastructure and how public policy has been used to encourage them. Consider, for example, that as many as 22 million families in the United States are "unbanked," and therefore do not have access to a basic checking or savings account with which they can conduct basic financial services (Stuhldreher and Tescher 2005). These families' use of financial services outside of the mainstream limits their ability to begin saving. Most often, these constructs work in tandem with each other; benefits may be bundled together in packages. Opening a bank account with a financial service provider often opens the door to a relationship that may facilitate the delivery of additional information. Once a depositor becomes a customer, she may learn how to take advantage of particular savings incentives, such as those offered by a tax-preferred retirement account. Similarly, a 401(k) plan that combines direct deposit, an employer match, and automatic enrollment is likely to build savings.

These constructs have helped make sense of the IDA experience. Research examining the savings performance of IDA participants has demonstrated that expectations have a large effect, as participants increased their savings 40 to 50 cents for every dollar the target was increased. The savings match and offer of direct deposits have helped people continue to save in IDA programs, though savers have not increased net monthly amounts saved (Schreiner and Sherraden 2007). These particular findings suggest that policies intended to promote savings behavior might be more effective if they identify ways to combine incentives with other institutional supports. Considering how the range of institutional constructs can be bundled together in an expansive delivery system should inform future asset-based policy efforts.

The second conclusion is that homeownership plays a special role in how families build assets. Homeownership is a goal that families often strive to achieve, representing the culmination of a savings process, and also serves as a primary means of possessing and augmenting wealth. Homeownership, therefore, can be a signifier of the asset-poverty threshold and a potential gateway to ongoing and long-lasting benefits. Families often use homeownership to continue wealth building through the accrual of equity and real estate appreciation. Beyond the provision of shelter, homeownership provides access to a bundle of goods and services provided at the local level, such as schools, neighborhood amenities, and social standing. There is evidence that children of homeowners, controlling for other factors, are better off in many ways (e.g., improved educational attainment, decreased teenage pregnancy, improved emotional and cognitive development). Yet for lower-income families, there is still much that can be learned about the benefits and potential pitfalls of homeownership. Owning a home and holding a mortgage create risk and liability that for some households may exceed the positive effects of homeownership. The falling home values and rising foreclosures that began to appear in 2007 reinforce the extent of these risks and should focus the attention of policymakers on how to identify and encourage responsible homeownership. Despite risks and challenges, homeowner-ship deserves a prominent place in any discussion on assets policy in the United States, especially opportunities for first-time homebuyers.

The third conclusion is that private retirement savings are a crucial asset for the typical middle-income family, yet are missing for the typi-cal low-income family. Social Security is the key retirement support for low-income families. Social Security is the major program of social insurance in the United States, and it is enormously successful in pro-viding support in retirement, as well as disability and survivor benefits. But this support is basic. The policy challenge, in relation to this discus-sion, is how to build retirement assets in addition to Social Security for the whole population.

The fourth conclusion with major policy implications is that assets are associated with multiple positive outcomes, and these outcomes extend beyond consumption. Assets are valuable as a source of economic secu-rity, but they also may encourage their owners to plan for the future, make productive investments, and invest in their communities. The association between assets and beneficial child outcomes suggests that "asset effects" may be a long-term phenomenon, best approached over an extended time horizon. The existing evidence on asset effects warrants continued research, especially given potential links between wealth and civic engagement, and the ramifications of these connections for a demo-cratic society. Overall, research linking assets with positive outcomes is suggestive for the poor and nonpoor alike. This evidence, combined with the observation that current policy creates disincentives for many lower-income families to accumulate wealth, provides a compelling rationale for implementing and testing policy options that would make asset building more inclusive.

Characteristics of Inclusive and Integrated Asset-Building Policy

Inclusive and integrated asset-based policy would have several key char-acteristics. First, it could provide the means to reach a large number of people, perhaps even all people. Second, it could occur throughout life and be flexible enough to adjust to changes in an individual's life course. Third, it could consider assets needed over the life course in an integrated fashion—from a bank account to a home or business, through retirement.

Fourth, it could offer greater subsidies to people with fewer resources and greater need. It would provide incentives for building assets to low-income families (not just high-income families) and minimize disincentives—such as asset limits in means-tested public assistance programs. And fifth, it could be large enough to support adequate levels of accumulation in a meaningful way (Sherraden 2005). If inclusive and integrated asset-based policy is useful as a social policy framework, policy-makers may want to explore policy options that support asset building in a manner that is more universal, lifelong, flexible, progressive, and adequate.

There is no single strategy for an inclusive and integrated asset-building approach. Because assets can be held in many different forms over the life course, many policy levers can be used to help families build assets. These range from simplifying and liberating means-tested asset limits, to broadening tax credits and making them refundable so that they reach low-income families, to a reformed pension system that complements Social Security (Cramer, O'Brien, and Lopez-Fernandini 2008; Perun and Steuerle 2008). While financial and tangible assets have been the focus of this book, education and its interaction with asset outcomes is also important. The aim is for lifelong policies that use public resources somewhat fairly.

One specific example of an inclusive policy structure may be an account-based system designed to promote long-term asset accumulation. This is consistent with the growing interest of policymakers to address specific social policy goals through the provision of individual asset accounts. While this approach is attractive to those who argue Social Security is too generous, many advocates of this approach see these account systems as opportunities to supplement a basic level of social insurance. An inclusive account-based policy would provide a platform and infrastructure that would facilitate saving and asset accumulation.

For this platform to be effective, accounts may be offered that are simple, widely available, and portable. Technically, information technology already exists that would enable such a system to be managed efficiently. Financial services are well developed in the United States. Public policy can and should rely on private sector providers. For example, an impressive public-private partnership has already demonstrated ability to run such a large-scale system through the federal Thrift Savings Plan. This experience can be drawn upon in building a larger, more inclusive account system.

As with the current array of tax-preferred savings accounts, the financial services sector should play a primary role because it offers a high degree of security, transparency, and efficiency. These markets can facilitate investment within the framework created by the public sector and will establish the institutional structures that maximize access, provide protections, and minimize costs. Whether the accounts and subsidies are tax preferred, and for what income levels, will have important implications for progressivity (Butrica et al. 2008). A focus of policy deliberations in this area should be the search for the most effective ways to achieve these ends for the greatest number of families.

Extending opportunities for savings and inclusive asset building points to the role of an effective delivery system and underscores the relevance of accessible savings plans. Savings plans, such as those for 401(k) retirement plans or 529 college saving plans, have features that lend themselves to *inclusion*. These include centralized accounting, provision of financial information, low-cost investment options, direct deposit, and automatic defaults. Most plans allow their participants to choose from a range of investment options. Expanding choice, while offering protections through diversification and professional management, is an effective combination. All told, the plan structure presents an opportunity to bundle together many of the constructs that determine saving action and maximize saving performance (Clancy et al. 2004; Clancy, Cramer, and Parrish 2005).

A well-designed, low-cost, inclusive savings plan could have broad benefits by encouraging savings, promoting economic development, and creating a more engaged citizenry. Although many of the challenges in constructing an inclusive account-based system are significant, they can be dealt with during the process of program design. Rules and regulations will be required to clarify eligibility, the role of the private sector, and the delivery of incentives and subsidies. A more fundamental challenge for policymakers may be to identify ways to use the assets perspective to inform ongoing social policy deliberations in ways that both embrace and move beyond a focus on social insurance.

The idea of an inclusive asset-based social policy, seldom discussed 15 years ago, is today ascendant. The language of assets is now part of a bipartisan lexicon and represents an opportunity to establish asset-building policies for the whole population, including lower-income households. The rise of asset-based policy discussion and the introduction of assets into the calculation of poverty have opened up a broader range of policy options. These options include proposals to foster ownership more broadly and to create specific avenues for savings, responsible homeownership, and other forms of wealth building. While there is still much to learn, pursuit of these policy objectives offers considerable potential.

REFERENCES

Bucks, Brian K., Arthur B. Kennickell, and Kevin B. Moore. 2006. "Recent Changes in U.S. Family Finances: Evidence from the 2001 and 2004 Survey of Consumer Finances." *Federal Reserve Bulletin* 92(1): 1–38.

Butrica, Barbara, Adam Carasso, C. Eugene Steuerle, and Desmond J. Toohey. 2008. "Children's Savings Accounts: Why Design Matters." Washington, DC: The Urban Institute. Opportunity and Ownership Project Report 4. http://www.urban.org/url.cfm?ID=411677. (Accessed July 8, 2008.)

Citro, Constance F., and Robert T. Michael, eds. 1995. *Measuring Poverty: A New Approach.* Washington, DC: National Academies Press.

Clancy, Margaret, Reid Cramer, and Leslie Parrish. 2005. *Section 529 Savings Plans, Access to Post-secondary Education, and Universal Asset Building.* Washington, DC: New America Foundation.

Clancy, Margaret, Peter Orszag, and Michael Sherraden. 2004. "College Savings Plans: A Platform for Inclusive Saving Policy?" St. Louis, MO: Washington University in St. Louis, Center for Social Development.

Cramer, Reid. 2006. *Net Worth at Birth: Creating a National System for Savings and Asset Building with Children's Savings Accounts.* Washington, DC: New America Foundation.

Cramer, Reid, Rourke O'Brien, and Ray Boshara. 2007. *Federal Assets Report 2007: A Review, Assessment, and Forecast of Federal Assets Policy.* Washington, DC: New America Foundation.

Cramer, Reid, Rourke O'Brien, and Alejandra Lopez-Fernandini. 2008. *The Assets Agenda 2008: Policy Options to Promote Savings and Asset Ownership by Low- and Moderate-Income Americans.* Washington, DC: New America Foundation.

McKernan, Signe-Mary, and Caroline Ratcliffe. 2008. *Enabling Families to Weather Emergencies and Develop: The Role of Assets.* Washington, DC: The Urban Institute. New Safety Net Paper 7. http://www.urban.org/url.cfm?ID=411734. (Accessed July 30, 2008.)

Perun, Pamela, and C. Eugene Steuerle. 2008. "Why Not a 'Super Simple' Saving Plan for the United States?" Washington, DC: The Urban Institute. Opportunity and Ownership Project Report 3. http://www.urban.org/url.cfm?ID=411676. (Accessed July 8, 2008.)

Poterba, James M., Stephen F. Venti, and David A. Wise. 1995. "Do 401(k) Contributions Crowd Out Other Personal Saving?" *Journal of Public Economics* 58(1): 1–32.

Samwick, Andrew, and Jonathan Skinner. 1997. "Abandoning the Nest Egg? 401(k) Plans and Inadequate Pension Saving." In *Public Policy towards Pensions,* edited by Sylvester Schieber and John Shoven (197–218). Cambridge, MA: MIT Press.

Schreiner, Mark, and Michael Sherraden. 2007. *Can the Poor Save? Saving and Asset Building in Individual Development Accounts.* New Brunswick, NJ: Transaction Publishers.

Seidman, Ellen, Karen Murrell, and Melissa Koide. 2007. *Public Policy Ideas to Improve Financial Education and Help Consumers Make Wise Financial Decisions.* Washington, DC: New America Foundation.

Sherraden, Michael. 1991. *Assets and the Poor: A New American Welfare Policy.* Armonk, NY: M. E. Sharpe.

———. 2005. "Inclusion in Asset Building." Testimony for Hearing on Building Assets for Low-Income Families, Subcommittee on Social Security and Family Policy, Senate Finance Committee, April 28. St. Louis, MO: Washington University in St. Louis, Center for Social Development.

Stuhldreher, Anne, and Jennifer Tescher. 2005. *Breaking the Savings Barrier: How the Federal Government Can Build an Inclusive Financial System.* Washington, DC: New America Foundation.

Woo, Lillian, and David Buchholz. 2007. "Subsidies for Assets: A New Look at the Federal Budget." Washington, DC: CFED.

Assessing Asset Data

Caroline Ratcliffe, Henry Chen, Trina R. Williams Shanks,
Yunju Nam, Mark Schreiner, Min Zhan,
and Michael Sherraden

T he lack of quality data has been a long-standing concern among researchers studying assets. Except for the 1962 Survey of Financial Characteristics of Consumers, no serious efforts were made to collect reliable asset data before the 1980s. In 1983, the Survey of Consumer Finances and the Survey of Income and Program Participation were the first to ask respondents detailed questions about asset holdings. Another major dataset, the Panel Study of Income Dynamics, added a wealth supplement in 1984 (Spilerman 2000). The availability of data on assets stimulated asset research and increased interest in asset-building policies as an antipoverty strategy and drew attention to the widening economic gaps that had developed since the 1980s (Sherraden 2001; Spilerman 2000). With available data, researchers started to examine the distribution of assets, test theoretical models and hypotheses, and develop new concepts and theories on assets.

Currently, numerous datasets provide information on households' assets and liabilities. These data sources differ along multiple dimensions and have different strengths and weaknesses. This appendix identifies and describes the datasets that provide the most informative and reliable information about low-income households' assets and liabilities. In describing limitations of these data, this appendix presents means for improving asset data.

Datasets Identified and Criteria for Assessment

Based on a review of the literature, survey data, and demonstration data, 12 datasets have been identified as having the potential to provide valuable information for studying the assets and liabilities of low-income households.

1. American Dream Demonstration Account Monitoring (ADD-AM) data
2. American Dream Demonstration Experiment (ADD-E) data
3. Assets for Independence Act (AFIA) Evaluation data
4. Consumer Expenditure Survey (CEX)
5. Current Population Survey (CPS)
6. Health and Retirement Study (HRS)
7. Home Mortgage Disclosure Act (HMDA) data
8. National Longitudinal Study of Youth 1979 (NLSY79)
9. National Survey of Family and Households (NSFH)
10. Panel Study of Income Dynamics (PSID)
11. Survey of Consumer Finances (SCF)
12. Survey of Income and Program Participation (SIPP)

Of these 12 datasets, 8 are based on large-scale national surveys and 4 are generated from demonstration and administrative data. To identify the datasets that have the greatest potential to provide informative and reliable asset and liability data, they were evaluated against four criteria: relevancy, representativeness, recurrence, and richness of correlates. Although we pay special attention to each dataset's ability to provide information on assets (relevancy) among the low-income population (representativeness) over time (recurrence), we also consider the correlates datasets provide (richness of correlates) and thus their ability to answer other important research questions, such as the effects of assets on outcomes. Based on these four criteria, three datasets are identified as having the greatest potential for future asset research: the SCF, the SIPP, and the PSID.[1]

Details on these three datasets are provided below. For each dataset, a brief overview is presented, followed by a discussion of the survey's content (i.e., assets, liabilities, and their correlates), dataset quality, and strengths and limitations. Table A.1 presents a summary of the three key datasets. Further, a summary of the asset and liability questions is presented in table A.2 and a list of correlates is presented in table A.3.[2]

Table A.1. Summary of Primary Datasets

	Survey of Income and Program Participation	Panel Study of Income Dynamics	Survey of Consumer Finances
Unit of observation	Individual	Individual	Family
Sample size[a]	46,500 households	8,002 families	4,522 households
Years available	Individual panels starting 1984–1993, 1996, 2001, and 2004	Ongoing: 1968–2005	Ongoing: 1983, 1986, 1989, 1992, 1995, 1998, 2001, 2004
Longitudinal data	Two- to five-year panel survey allowing for examination of changes in asset holdings over time	38-year panel survey allowing for examination of changes in asset holding over time and intergenerational analyses	Cross-sectional data that does not allow for examination of changes in asset holdings over time
Frequency of asset data collection	Annual	Once every five years from 1984–1999 and biennially since	Once every three years
Broad asset topics	(1) Home; (2) vehicles; (3) farm or business assets; (4) interest earning banking assets—savings accounts, interest-earning checking accounts, money market deposit accounts, certificates of deposit; (5) interest earning nonbanking assets—municipal bonds, corporate bonds, U.S. securities; (6) equities—stocks and mutual funds;	(1) Real estate; (2) vehicles; (3) farm or business assets; (4) stocks, mutual funds, and investment trusts; (5) checking, savings, money market funds, IRAs, CDs, savings bonds or T-bills; (6) other investments in trusts, bonds; (7) net wealth excluding home equity; (8) net wealth including home equity	Financial assets: (1) CDs, transaction accounts, savings and other bonds; (2) value of stocks, IRAs, Keogh accounts, 401(k)s, and 403(b)s; (3) participation in a defined benefit private pension plan; (4) life insurance, other managed assets, loans made to others

(continued)

Table A.1. Summary of Primary Datasets *(continued)*

	Survey of Income and Program Participation	Panel Study of Income Dynamics	Survey of Consumer Finances
	(7) other assets—mortgages, other investments, noninterest-earning checking accounts, savings bonds, proceeds from sales of businesses or property; (8) personal retirement—IRA and Keogh accounts; (9) Employer-provided retirement accounts—401(k), 403(b), and Thrift Savings Plans		Nonfinancial assets: (5) Vehicles; (6) farm or business assets; (7) real estate; (8) other nonfinancial assets—artwork, jewelry, precious metals, antiques, hobby equipment
Broad limitations	Does not measure retirement annuities such as Social Security and defined benefit pensions	(1) Asset-related questions not asked at every interview (only in 1984, 1989, 1994, 1999, 2001, 2003, and 2005), (2) does not measure retirement annuities such as Social Security and private pensions	(1) Cross-sectional, (2) does not measure the value of future payouts from Social Security and defined benefit private pensions, (3) small sample size when analyzing by subgroups such as race or education

a. Sample size is for most recently available data (2004 SIPP, 2005 PSID, and 2004 SCF).

Table A.2. Asset and Liability Question Coverage by Dataset

	PSID	SCF	SIPP
Financial assets			
Bank accounts			
Ownership	X	X	X
Value	X	X	X
Other interest-earning assets			
Ownership	X	X	X
Value	X	X	X
Stocks and mutual funds			
Ownership	X	X	X
Value	X	X	X
U.S. savings bonds			
Ownership	X	X	X
Value	X	X	X
Other financial assets			
Ownership	X	X	X
Value	X	X	X
IRA and Keogh accounts			
Ownership	X	X	X
Value	X	X	X
401(k) and Thrift accounts			
Ownership		X	X
Value		X	X
All retirement accounts, IRA and 401(k)			
Ownership	X		
Value	X		
Other quasi-liquid pensions		X	
Life insurance		X	
Overall financial assets			
Ownership			
Value			
Nonfinancial, tangible assets			
Residence			
Ownership	X	X	X
Value	X	X	X
Nonresidence real estate	X	X	X
Vehicles	X	X	X
Businesses	X	X	X
Jewelry, art, collections, etc.		X	
Durable goods ownership			X

(continued)

Table A.2. Asset and Liability Question Coverage by Dataset *(continued)*

	PSID	SCF	SIPP
Liabilities			
Secured liabilities			
Mortgages on residences	X	X	X
Mortgages on nonresidence real estate	X	X	X
Vehicle loans	X	X	X
Business debt	X	X	X
Margin and broker accounts		X	X
Loans secured by retirement accounts		X	
Unsecured liabilities			
Credit card debt			
Ownership		X	X
Value		X	X
Bank loans		X	X
Other unsecured liabilities (private loans)		X	X
Total unsecured liabilities (credit card and private loans)	X		

PSID = Panel Survey of Income Dynamics

SCF = Survey of Consumer Finances

SIPP = Survey of Income and Program Participation

Note: If ownership and value are not subheadings under an asset and liability question item, then a check (x) indicates the survey provides both ownership and value information unless otherwise noted.

Survey of Income and Program Participation

The SIPP is a panel study that focuses on the income and program participation of households and individuals, and is administered by the U.S. Census Bureau. From 1984 to 1993, panels began annually; additional panels took place in 1996, 2001, and 2004. A 2008 panel is planned and a redesign of the SIPP instrument is underway.

SIPP respondents are interviewed every four months about the previous four months, a period referred to as a wave. Information about each member of the household over the age of 15 is collected. In cases where a member of the household is not available to be interviewed, the head of the household, known as the reference person, provides information about that individual. Each panel generally lasts between two and four years, with more recent panels lasting three to four years. The sample size has varied across panels; the 1996 panel includes 36,800 households, the

Table A.3. Correlates Provided by Dataset

	PSID	SCF	SIPP
Demographic characteristics			
Age	X	X	X
Race	X	X	X
Sex	X	X	X
Marital status	X	X	X
Number of children	X	X	X
Household size	X	X	X
Educational attainment	X	X	X
Household expenditures	X		X
Employment and income			
Current employment	X	X	X
Total income	X	X	X
Earned income	X	X	X
Unearned income	X	X	X
Employment history	X	X	X
Program participation/utilization of tax credits			
Current enrollment			
TANF	X	X	X
Food Stamps	X	X	X
SSI	X	X	X
Medicaid	X	X	X
Social Security (OASI)	X	X	X
Unemployment compensation	X	X	X
EITC			X
Saver's credit			
IDA participation			
Program participation history			
TANF	X		X
Food Stamps	X		X
SSI	X		X
Medicaid	X		X
Financial system use/attitudes			
Use of financial institutions		X	
Attitudes toward credit		X	
Material well-being			
Ownership of consumer durables	X		X
Quality of home	X		X

(continued)

Table A.3. Correlates Provided by Dataset *(continued)*

	PSID	SCF	SIPP
Material well-being (*continued*)			
Quality of neighborhood	X	X	X
Financial stresses faced by household	X	X	X
Child well-being			
Interaction with parents	X		X
Extracurricular activities	X		X
Academic achievement	X		X
Emotional and behavioral problems	X		
Health and familial well-being			
Household stability	X		X
Residential stability	X		X
Health status	X		X

PSID = Panel Survey of Income Dynamics

SCF = Survey of Consumer Finances

SIPP = Survey of Income and Program Participation

2001 panel, 35,100 households, and the 2004 panel, 46,500 households. Only noninstitutionalized civilians are included in the sample.

Each SIPP panel consists of a core questionnaire, administered in each wave, and topical modules, which collect supplemental information on a variety of topics. The core survey questionnaire collects information about labor force status, earned income, income from assets, educational attainment, and family structure, among others. Most core variables are collected for each of the prior four months. The number of topical modules and the topics that they cover vary by wave. Examples of topical modules are assets and liabilities, retirement and pension plan coverage, and adult well-being. The time frame for topical module questions varies. For example, the asset and liability topical module asks respondents about asset holdings and liabilities at the time of interview. In contrast, the employee benefits topical module asks about benefits received from employers over the entire calendar year.

One benefit of the SIPP is that several SIPP panels can be matched with administrative data.[3] SIPP data can be matched to Internal Revenue Service (IRS) and Social Security earnings histories, which can be used to understand the relationship between individuals' earnings histories and asset levels. Additionally, these data can be used to identify the extent to which individuals have contributed to the Social Security system, as Social Security contributions can be thought of as investment and have important implications for individuals' well-being in retirement. The SIPP can also be matched with the U.S. Census Bureau's Longitudinal Employer Household Dynamics (LEHD) data, which includes longitudinal individual-level employee and employer information such as quarterly earnings data and employer-provided benefits.[4] The LEHD data, when combined with demographic and asset and liability information available in the SIPP, provide researchers the opportunity to examine important topics such as the impact of employer pension plan policies on asset accumulation.

Content

The SIPP's detailed information about a wide range of financial and non-financial tangible assets makes it a strong choice for studying the asset holdings of low-income households. Asset-related questions are included in both the core questionnaire and topical modules. The core questionnaire asks about asset *ownership* and the income generated from asset holdings. More detailed asset and liability questions about the *value* of asset holdings and liabilities are asked in the asset and liability topical module. Recent panels have collected asset and liability data annually. The topical module provides information for all individuals in the household over the age of 15, which means SIPP asset and liability data can be analyzed at the individual level or aggregated and analyzed at the household or family-unit level.

The SIPP asset and liability topical module contains very detailed financial and nonfinancial tangible asset holdings information. Financial asset holdings include checking and saving accounts; CDs and money market deposit accounts; IRAs; Keogh, 401(k), and Thrift accounts; corporate and municipal bonds; U.S. savings bonds; stocks; mutual funds; the value of loans made to others; and other financial investments. Nonfinancial tangible asset data cover personal residences, other real estate, three motor vehicles, and farm and business equity. This topical module also provides information on households' liabilities, including home mortgages, other mortgages, vehicle loans, margin and broker accounts, credit card and store credit debt, other bank loans, and other unsecured liabilities.

The adult well-being topical module provides information about ownership of durable goods, including a washer and dryer, refrigerator, telephone, television, and personal computer, at the time of the interview. However, the survey does not ask respondents about ownership of tools that can be used in self-employment, such as sewing machines and gardening equipment.

Detailed information covering both assets and liabilities allows researchers to calculate important wealth and well-being measures that take into account both assets and debt. These measures include home equity, vehicle equity, and net worth. These data also provide researchers with the opportunity to create portraits of asset and liability holdings.

The SIPP's core questionnaire also provides a wide range of correlates beyond demographic characteristics, which provide information about respondents' household composition, employment (e.g., hours worked per week, weeks worked, wage rate, occupation), income (e.g., earned and unearned income, income sources, and investments), educational attainment, and program participation. These correlates allow researchers to identify low-income subpopulations of interest such as single parents and high school dropouts. The topical modules supplement the core questionnaire on topics including employment benefits, adult well-being, child well-being, taxes, recipiency history, and child support agreements. The information in these modules allows researchers to study the links between asset holding and well-being and the effects of tax credits, aid recipiency, and child support payments or agreements on asset holding (and vice versa).

Data Quality

Many characteristics of the SIPP play a role in affecting the quality of the data. These include response rates, imputation procedures, and design of response brackets. SIPP response rates vary by wave and generally decrease as the panel progresses. The 2001 panel had an 87 percent response rate in its initial wave, and a 68 percent response rate across the full panel.[5] In terms of *item nonresponse,* researchers found that in the 1996 SIPP panel, nonresponse for some asset and liability items was very high. One study examined 47 asset and liability items in wave 9 of the 1996 SIPP and found that only three asset and liability items have nonresponse rates lower than 20 percent (Czajka, Jacobson, and Cody 2003). The median nonresponse rate for these 47 items is 38 percent, with common items like home value being imputed less often and less-common items being imputed frequently (Czajka et al. 2003).

High rates of nonresponse pose a problem because item nonresponse requires imputation or "filling in" of missing values. The Census Bureau uses a "hot-deck" procedure to impute most missing values. This procedure matches records with missing values for the item of interest with records that have a value for the item of interest. The value in the matched record then substitutes for the missing response. Matches are made based on similarities in nonmissing variables. These methods do not perform as well when variables have high nonresponse rates and matches are more difficult to find (Czajka et al. 2003).

If respondents are unable to provide the value of an item, they are given the option of providing a range in which the true value of an item falls. This range is then incorporated into the imputation procedure for that item, in theory making the imputation more precise. Research indicates that SIPP response brackets could be improved if the Census Bureau were to increase the number of available brackets and reduce the width of each bracket (e.g., replace one bracket ranging from $10,000–$20,000 with two brackets that range from $10,000–$15,000 and $15,001–$20,000). An additional improvement would be to increase the top value of the brackets. Analyses of SIPP data show that the median value of many assets often falls just inside the upper boundary of the top bracket (Czajka et al. 2003). These two changes would make SIPP brackets more similar to PSID response brackets (Czajka et al. 2003).

Research also indicates that the correlation between assets and liabilities has declined markedly between the 1993 and 1996 panels (Czajka et al. 2003). This decline in correlation has not been noted in other datasets (such as the SCF) and is consistent with changes in the imputation procedure across these panels.

Maintaining correlation between specific assets and their associated liabilities (e.g., home value and mortgage value) is important because the distributions of measures such as net worth are jointly determined by assets and liabilities. Czajka and others (2003) and Toder and others (2002) suggest that a change in the procedures for imputing missing variables may have contributed to the decreased correlation between assets and liabilities in the 1996 SIPP. Czajka and others further note that this change in procedure may not be the root cause or the only cause. It is important that any imputation procedure of assets takes into account liabilities and vice versa.

Strengths and Limitations

The longitudinal nature of the SIPP provides researchers with the opportunity to examine changes in wealth over time. In addition, its large sample size allows researchers to make estimations for detailed subpopulations. For instance, one could study the assets and liabilities of Hispanic households headed by single mothers. The SIPP also includes a rich set of complementary correlates, which allows researchers to study the relationship between assets and liabilities and measures of well-being, school performance, program participation, and household stability. Furthermore, the SIPP can be merged with administrative data from multiple sources (e.g., historical earnings).

Most importantly for asset-related research, the SIPP has coverage of enough of the major asset and liability categories that generating portraits of the asset holding of low-income households is possible. Past analysis suggests that measurements of wealth using the SIPP should do a relatively good job of capturing the wealth and net worth of low-income households.

Survey of Consumer Finances

The SCF provides information about the finances, wealth holding, pensions, and income of families in the United States, as well as their use of financial institutions. This cross-sectional dataset, sponsored by the U.S. Federal Reserve Board of Governors, has been administered every three years since 1983.[6] The most recent SCF data available are for 2004.

Each SCF administration consists of a single questionnaire. The survey collects information about assets and liabilities, attitudes toward financial institutions and credit, and income (pension and nonpension), occupation, and demographic information. All civilian noninstitutionalized households are eligible to be sampled. The sample size is approximately 4,500 families—the 2001 survey includes 4,449 families, while the 2004 SCF includes 4,522 families.

The survey employs two types of samples to obtain estimates of aggregate wealth ownership in the United States. The first sample, an area-probability sample (a type of geographically based random sample), is designed to provide representation of common characteristics that are broadly distributed across the population, such as car and homeownership. Approximately 66 percent of the 2004 SCF sample came from this subsample (Kennickell 2006). The second sample, a list sample (a sample based on a specific list of units), is designed to oversample wealthier individuals, since wealth is highly concentrated within a small subgroup of the population. The cases in the list sample are derived from individual income tax returns. Access to this information is provided by the Statistics of Income Division of the IRS. Approximately 34 percent of the 2004 SCF sample comes from the IRS list subsample.

The SCF surveys the economically dominant individual or the most financially knowledgeable member of the economically dominant couple in a household. This individual is surveyed about the asset holdings of all persons economically interdependent with the financially dominant person or couple. This group of people is referred to as the primary economic unit (PEU). With this design, detailed family-level asset and liability information is available only for the PEU. A relatively short section of the interview deals with the finances of household members outside the PEU. One drawback of this design is that substantial analysis at the individual level is possible along only a few dimensions, such as employment and designated retirement assets belonging to the respondent or, when relevant, that person's spouse or partner. A second drawback of this design is that subfamilies in a household (such as a single mother and her children living with her parents) cannot be examined as closely as the primary family in the household.

Content

The SCF contains very detailed financial and nonfinancial tangible asset-holdings information and is the most detailed among all of the datasets reviewed. Financial asset holdings include checking and savings accounts, CDs and money market deposit accounts, stocks, mutual funds, corporate and municipal bonds, U.S. savings bonds, IRA and Keogh accounts, 401(k) and Thrift accounts, other quasi-liquid pensions, cash value of life insurance, value of loans made to others, annuities, trusts, and other financial investments. Nonfinancial tangible assets include real estate, motor vehicles, business equity, and other assets such as jewelry, collections, art, precious metals, and cemetery plots. The SCF contains liability information on mortgages, vehicle loans, margin and broker accounts, credit card and store credit debt, other bank loans, other unsecured liabilities, and secured debts.

The detailed asset and liability information provided by the SCF allows researchers to calculate wealth and well-being measures that take into account both assets and debt. These measures include home equity, vehicle equity, and net worth—the sum of all assets minus their associated liabilities. These data provide researchers with the opportunity to create portraits of families' asset holdings and liabilities.

A novel feature of the SCF is that it asks respondents about their use of and attitudes toward financial institutions and credit. Questions cover a broad range of topics including from whom individuals receive financial advice, the extent to which they use computers for financial purposes, and how individuals interact with financial institutions—in person, online, through ATMs, and so on. The credit and credit card questions ask about frequency of credit use, creditworthiness, size of credit lines offered, and balances. These questions provide a unique window into U.S. households' credit use and attitudes toward financial institutions.

Although the SCF provides a large number of correlates related to its central mission, the set of variables available for the study of other areas, including low-income families, is more limited, as compared with the SIPP and the PSID. Most demographic characteristics are restricted to the head and his or her spouse (or partner). The SCF also collects information about the head and the spouse's current job and employment status over the past year. Sources of and the value of family income received in the past calendar year are also collected. These income variables allow researchers to determine past-year program participation (e.g., Temporary Assistance for Needy Families, Food Stamps, Medicaid, Social Security, and unemployment compensation), but no program participation history is available. The family roster provides information on family structure so low-income subpopulations, such as single-parent families, can be identified. However, because the SCF collects asset and liability data at the family level, if a single mother is not the economically dominant individual, then only limited information on the single mother's own assets and liabilities is available.

Data Quality

The 2004 SCF has an overall response rate of 45.2 percent, which is considerably lower than both the SIPP and the PSID. However, this rate reflects in large part the design of the list sample that oversamples wealthy families. The 2004 response rate for the area-probability sample was 68.7 percent, while the response rate for the list sample (wealthy household oversample) was 30.2 percent. Members of the list sample, unlike the area-probability sample, are given the opportunity to opt out of being interviewed before an SCF interviewer first approaches them, by returning a postcard to refuse participation. Although the SCF has lower overall response rates, SCF respondents provide answers to asset and liability questions more often than SIPP respondents. Czajka and others (2003) find that imputation rates in the 1998 SCF were one-half to two-thirds the imputation rate for associated variables in the 1996 SIPP. The PSID has the lowest item nonresponse rates of the three surveys, which may be due to the long history that PSID respondents have with the survey.

To impute missing values, the SCF uses a complicated model-based procedure, which is different from the procedure used for the SIPP and the PSID. For nearly every variable, missing values are imputed five times, and these five values are stored in the final SCF datasets. These five imputed values are obtained by drawing repeatedly from an estimate of the conditional distribution of the data. Because families have five values for each answered question, the data may initially be more difficult for the novice to use. Although multiple imputations may initially seem cumbersome, they allow for more statistically efficient estimates. In addition, they make it possible to quantify the amount of uncertainty introduced by missing data, thus enabling more scientific calculations of statistical significance.

As with the SIPP and the PSID, if respondents are unable to provide the exact value of an item, SCF respondents are given the option of choosing a range from a selected set of ranges or providing a range in which the value of an item falls. This range is then incorporated into the imputation for that item.

The Federal Reserve goes to great lengths to ensure that they are providing the general public with high-quality data. The computer-assisted personal interview instrument employed by SCF interviewers uses extremely careful wording and logic checks. Interviewers also record their comments about the interview and any responses that might require clarification. Interviewers are also required to complete a debriefing questionnaire after each interview. When the data arrive at the Federal Reserve, they are extensively checked using automated computer programs and are edited using interviewer notes to resolve inconsistencies when possible (Athey and Kennickell 2005). Because the main objective of the SCF is to obtain accurate information on assets, liabilities, and net worth in the United States, evaluations of other datasets' asset and liability information is often based on comparisons to the SCF.

Strengths and Limitations

The SCF is the most focused survey on asset ownership available. It provides the most detailed questions about assets and liabilities, and unlike surveys such as the SIPP and PSID, which do not focus solely on assets and liabilities, it is clear to those administering the SCF and to respondents that the main goal of the survey is to get the most accurate depiction of the family's balance sheet possible. The SCF makes a concerted effort to provide an accurate estimate of aggregate net worth in the United States through its sampling procedures—oversampling the wealthy who own a large proportion of the nation's assets—and its sophisticated imputation procedures. Nevertheless, the SCF is not without weaknesses that can limit its usefulness as a survey for studying the assets and liabilities of low-income households.

Compared to the SIPP, the SCF has a relatively small sample size that may make it difficult to study low-income subpopulations such as single mothers. For instance, the 2004 SCF includes only 120 black single mothers and 47 Hispanic single mothers. Small sample sizes make it difficult (and in some cases impossible) to generate national estimates for subpopulations or to estimate econometric models. Further, because the SCF focuses on families, not individuals, it is not possible to identify the assets and liabilities of all family members who live in complex family structures.

Like the SIPP and PSID, the SCF does not provide direct estimates of the value of respondents' defined benefit pensions. The SCF does, however, ask respondents a number of detailed questions about the defined benefit and account-type retirement plans to which individuals might have rights.

Another drawback of the SCF is that it does not provide an accounting of households' ownership of consumer durables.[7] Finally, the limited number of correlates for the study of low-income families and the cross-sectional nature of the SCF interviews since 1989 may limit its usefulness for many asset-related studies. Researchers who use the SCF are not able to track changes in net worth because measures of assets and liabilities are made at a single point in time. Furthermore, the SCF provides little information about dependents in the household; for example, the survey does not provide information on the well-being or education level of children in the household. While the SCF is a very useful tool in generating portraits of asset holding, it may not be as useful for studying the effects of policy changes on asset ownership.

Panel Study of Income Dynamics

The PSID is a longitudinal survey conducted by the University of Michigan's Institute for Social Research, which follows individuals and their families over time. The study has been ongoing since 1968, beginning with two independent national samples, one a cross-sectional sample of about 3,000 families and the second a low-income sample of about 2,000 families.

Individuals still living in the original core-sample family and family members who left the household to form new households were interviewed annually from 1968 through 1997 and have been interviewed biennially since 1997. Two additional changes occurred in 1997—an immigrant sample was added to refresh the sample and reflect changes in the U.S. population, and a portion of the low-income sample was dropped due to budget cuts.

The PSID sample tends to increase over time, as children move out of their parents' household and set up new households. For example, the 2001, 2003, and 2005 surveys include 7,406 families, 7,823 families, and 8,002 families, respectively. Although representative of the population when the appropriate family weights are used, the sample is too small to provide specialized measures for many subgroups (Kim and Stafford 2000). The PSID sample includes only noninstitutionalized civilians.

In each interview, information about each member of the family is collected and a core set of questions is asked to maintain comparability over time. This includes detailed information on income sources and amounts, employment, and family composition. As a long-running longitudinal survey of the same families across 34 waves, one unique feature of the PSID is that it is possible to construct histories for individuals and across generations.

Content

Beginning with the 1984 survey, grants from the National Institute on Aging have allowed the collection of detailed data about individuals' assets and liabilities. Questions on housing and the value of the primary residence (if owned), however, have been included in the PSID survey since it began in 1968, as has ongoing documentation of mortgage details. In 1984, the PSID began asking seven additional questions on the value of assets and two questions on the value of liabilities. Three of the asset questions cover financial assets: stocks, mutual funds, investment trusts, and stocks held in IRAs; checking and savings accounts, CDs, Treasury bills, savings bonds, and liquid assets in IRAs; and bonds, trusts, life insurance, and other assets. Four cover tangible assets—primary residence, other real estate, vehicles, and farm or business ownership. One liabilities question covers mortgages while another question asks about all other debt including credit cards, student loans, medical bills, and personal loans. Unlike the SIPP, the PSID does not collect information about the ownership of consumer durables.[8]

While this asset and liability information has been collected since 1984, it was only collected every five years between 1984 and 1999 (in 1984, 1989, 1994, and 1999). Since 1999, these questions have been included as part of every survey. The asset and liability data are cleaned and summarized to create net worth variables, with and without home equity. In 1999, a new module on pensions was added that collects data on employer-sponsored retirement plans, whether defined benefit or matched contribution. In addition, a series of active savings questions traces flows of money in and out of assets, such as when a house is bought or sold, money is put into the stock market, or an annuity is cashed in. These savings questions were asked in 1989, 1994, and in every wave since 1999.

The PSID provides a wide array of demographic correlates that allows researchers to create specific subsamples of the population (e.g., subsamples based on family composition or poverty status). The PSID also tracks monthly receipt of public assistance and has detailed information on employment status, work, unemployment, vacation and sick time, occupation, industry, and work experience. A recently introduced event history calendar increases the quality of reporting. In addition, the PSID provides information about housing, general health, geographic mobility, family composition changes, and demographic events. There is also sociological and psychological content that is asked in special supplemental modules. Recently this has included information about housing and neighborhood quality, estimating risk tolerance, child development, time use, wealth, financial distress, and bankruptcy.

Data Quality

The PSID has a high response rate of 94 to 98 percent between waves, but the cumulative nonresponse over the 34 waves since 1968 is substantial (over 50 percent). By keeping track of children and other family members over time, the sample remains similar in composition over time. Attrition rates from year to year are typically small, so the sample size tends to increase. In multiple comparisons with the Current Population Survey for income and its correlates, the PSID is found to be equivalent to a nationally representative sample (see Becketti et al. 1988; Fitzgerald, Gottschalk, and Moffitt 1998; Kim and Stafford 2000; and Gouskova and Stafford 2002).

The PSID has the lowest *item* nonresponse rates of the three surveys, which may be due to the long history that PSID respondents have with the survey. The PSID has little missing data for its asset questions and can provide a good accounting for the major components of net worth. However, it is more limited in scope than other datasets, such as the SCF. Because the PSID began with a core set of families in 1968 and does not oversample high-income households, it misses the upper end of the wealth distribution. In addition, the PSID asks questions in significantly fewer topic areas pertaining to households' assets and liabilities than the SCF (12 compared to 30), so it is less precise in certain subcategories such as business equity. In 1989, the value of farm and business equity in the PSID is only 57 percent of that found in the SCF. The largest disparities come in the catch-all "other assets" category, where the PSID only captures 24 percent of SCF estimates. The SCF asks multiple memory-prodding questions, while PSID respondents may leave out some items, such as a piece of art. Despite this, analyses suggest that the PSID does a relatively good job of capturing the wealth of households in the bottom 30 percent of the wealth distribution (Curtin, Juster, and Morgan 1989).

Data from the wealth sequences of the PSID are collected using the interviewing technique of "unfolding brackets" when a respondent would otherwise refuse to respond. If respondents are unable to give an exact dollar amount to the initial question, they are routed through a sequence of ranges, beginning with whether the amount falls above or below a median value. Based on the information provided by the respondent, the missing value is imputed with a hot-deck method within the fairly narrow range offered. In general, for income and all other measures, imputation of missing and nonresponse data is rarely used. Typically PSID flags extreme or fragmented inputs and attempts to edit from survey notes and past responses rather than assigning uncertain values. This is labeled "informed calculation" based on interview notes and complex aggregation rules. Otherwise, an approach that makes extensive use of cross-sectional imputations might invite huge errors in change measures (Kim and Stafford 2000).

Strengths and Limitations

The PSID is a strong dataset for examining assets and liabilities, as it has high-quality asset data and follows the same families longitudinally over several decades. This allows for intergenerational analysis, trend studies, and examining the influence of family histories. The PSID is well suited to study the low end of wealth and income distributions, because income data for the bottom of the income distribution seem to be improving over time and the original set of 1968 core families includes an over-sampling of low-income households. The rich array of correlates allows for detailed analyses across an array of topics, from health to child well-being to time usage.

Unfortunately, wealth questions do not start with the 1968 cohort and were only administered once every five years from 1984 to 1999. Only recently have asset questions been included as a part of each biennial survey. Furthermore, the sample can become relatively small, particularly to exploit multiple panel years, so it is difficult to analyze subpopulations. Compared to the SCF, the PSID uses relatively broad asset categories, which make its wealth estimations less accurate for the upper 5 to 10 percent of the wealth distribution and for particular subcategories such as business and farm equity and "other assets."

Summary Comparisons

The SIPP, SCF, and PSID are all strong datasets for examining the assets and liabilities of low-income households but are not without their weaknesses. Comparisons of (1) the SIPP to the SCF and (2) the PSID to the SCF suggest that both the SIPP and the PSID do a relatively good job of capturing the wealth of lower-income or -wealth households, which is the focus of our evaluation. This is important because the SCF is often used to benchmark the quality of asset and liability information in other datasets.

A comparison of the SIPP's wealth distribution with the SCF's suggests that the SIPP does a relatively good job of capturing the wealth of low-wealth households (especially in pre-1996 panels) and would do even better with the addition of a few questions. While analyses of the 1990–1993 SIPP and the SCF show that the SIPP and SCF datasets have similar wealth distributions up through the 80th percentile (Rodgers and Smith 2000), a comparison of the 1996 SIPP to the 1998 SCF finds that SIPP net worth falls short of SCF net worth across the entire distribution (Czajka et al. 2003, table II.5), most notably in the upper tail. Czajka and others (2003), however, find that the 1996 SIPP panel does reasonably well accounting for the assets and liabilities of the subgroup of families with income below 200 percent of the federal poverty level. For these low-income households, average SIPP net worth was 89.5 percent of SCF net worth. This shortfall of SIPP net worth for low-income households appears to be attributable to SIPP's not covering certain asset and liability items. When items excluded from the SIPP are excluded from calculations of net worth using SCF data (to get an adjusted SCF measure), the mean SIPP net worth for low-income households was 100.2 percent of adjusted SCF net worth (Czajka et al. 2003, tables III.6 and III.7). The SIPP performs quite well in measuring the net worth of low-income households, but adding questions to the SIPP (i.e., those asked in the SCF but not the SIPP) may allow the data to better capture the net worth of low-income households.

The PSID also does a good job of capturing the wealth of low-wealth households. Comparing wealth distributions, the PSID is almost identical to the SCF up to the 30th percentile, at which point PSID estimates trail the SCF's. By the upper 1 to 3 percentiles, the two surveys begin to diverge more dramatically. For the very wealthy, not having the more detailed questions in the PSID about business equity and other less-common assets becomes problematic (Juster, Smith, and Stafford 1999).

While the SCF provides a detailed and comprehensive accounting of families' assets and liabilities, the relatively small sample of low-income households and lack of disaggregated individual assets in the SCF makes it difficult to study low-income subpopulations—only 1,088 families with income below 200 percent of the poverty level are in the 2004 SCF sample. Another drawback of the SCF is that it is a cross-sectional survey.

Therefore, aggregate changes over time can be studied, but changes in a household's assets and liabilities over time cannot be examined.

Both the SIPP and the PSID provide longitudinal data on assets and liabilities, but neither provides the same level of detail as the SCF. Of these two datasets, the SIPP has substantially more detailed asset and liability questions than the PSID. A significant strength of the SIPP, in comparison to both the PSID and SCF, is that the large sample size (roughly 46,500 households in 2004) allows for detailed subgroup analyses of the low-income population. The SIPP does have a relatively high nonresponse to asset and liability questions, although research suggests that this nonresponse has, at most, only a small effect on the asset and liability data for low-wealth households. The PSID has many fewer asset and liability questions and a smaller sample size than the SIPP, but the response rate to asset and liability questions is significantly higher. One important benefit of the PSID is its long panel, which allows for studies over long periods and intergenerational studies.

The SIPP, SCF, and PSID do not provide direct estimates of the value of respondents' defined benefit pensions, which is a drawback since the value of a defined benefit pension is an asset to families. Placing a valuation on the present value of a defined benefit pension is difficult, however, as it requires detailed information about respondents' pension plans and assumptions about lifetime earnings, inflation, discount rates, and mortality. Information on the value of respondents' future Social Security benefits is also not directly available in these three surveys. While not directly available in the SIPP, links between the SIPP and administrative data on Social Security–covered earnings do allow researchers with access to these administrative data to estimate the value of Social Security benefits. Currently, the PSID and SCF are not linked with administrative data on Social Security–covered earnings, so these types of calculations are not possible.

In terms of understanding the detailed asset holdings and liabilities of the low-income population, the SCF allows one to paint the most detailed portrait. The SIPP also provides a great deal of detailed asset and liability information to paint a portrait. If one wants to examine a larger sample or paint a portrait for a subgroup of the low-income population (e.g., low-educated minorities), the SIPP provides the richest data for doing so. Finally, if one wants to examine changes in assets and liabilities across multiple years and across generations, the PSID stands out as the best dataset.

Means for Improving Asset Data

Based on our evaluation of asset and liability data, there is room to improve the quality of these datasets. There are hundreds of types of assets with variation in liquidity (from checking accounts to homes), function (short-term savings such as checking accounts to long-term savings such as retirement accounts), risk, and tax treatment of savings (401(k) accounts versus regular saving accounts). The values of some types of assets (e.g., business assets and real estate) are difficult to estimate even in the best of circumstances (Juster et al. 1999). Item nonresponse rates are higher for assets and liabilities than for other economic variables in most survey data. Low response rates may be explained partly by respondents' unwillingness to disclose financial information and partly by their lack of knowledge of their current asset holdings (Curtin et al. 1989).

This section examines general and specific means for improving asset data. The options are put forward in the interest of enhancing the usability and quality of the data, although they have not been assessed for cost, feasibility, and difficulty of implementation. Also, options are not mutually exclusive; any one or all of these options could be adopted. The decision to implement a particular option (and not another) should be based on goals for the survey.

General Means for Improving Asset Data

Option 1. Collect information on the dynamics of asset accumulation. The asset-accumulation process could play a crucial role in social and economic development since individuals may be empowered and inspired through the process of building assets. Therefore, the asset-accumulation process may be as important as asset possession in understanding determinants and effects of assets and liabilities among the low-income population. Existing data focus mainly on the possession of assets and pay little attention to the asset-accumulation process, such as frequencies of savings deposits and portfolio changes. The PSID collects information on flows of money in and out of assets (e.g., when a house is bought or sold, money is put into the stock market, or an annuity is cashed in), and therefore, has the potential to provide a more dynamic picture of the asset-accumulation process than most datasets. Similarly, the 1989 SCF included questions on major changes in asset holdings since 1983, such as purchases and sales of property, financial assets, and business interests.

None of the existing national datasets, including the PSID, however, provide detailed information on saving patterns such as saving and withdrawal frequencies.

Thus, an option for improving asset data is to include questions related to the asset-accumulation process in existing national datasets. This could be particularly valuable in longitudinal datasets such as the SIPP and PSID. Since the SIPP collects data more frequently (every four months for core questions and every year for wealth questions) than the PSID (every two years), it may have less measurement error due to memory lapse. However, the PSID has an advantage of observing the same households over a longer time period and, therefore, would enable study of changes in saving and asset-accumulation patterns over the long term. Careful assessment of the 1989 SCF shows that asset data collected retrospectively are noisy (Kennickell and Starr-McCluer 1996), probably because the 1989 SCF collected data covering six years (1983–1989). Accordingly, it is recommended that questions be asked about the asset-accumulation process in panel studies with a shorter interview interval. In this regard, the SIPP and the PSID seem better candidates than the SCF.

Another way to collect information on the asset-accumulation process is to include questions about saving behaviors. For example, the cross-sectional SCF asks a question about saving habits and spending relative to income, which allows categorization of saving and spending patterns (Kennickell 1995). Two advantages of such questions are relative ease for respondents in answering the questions and simplicity of processing and analyzing cross-sectional information. This approach, however, has a disadvantage in relying on respondents' subjective judgment of their own behaviors.

Option 2. Encourage survey respondents to use financial statements when answering asset and liability questions. The use of financial statements could increase both the accuracy of responses and item response rates. During the 1998 SCF interviews, interviewers encouraged respondents to refer to their financial statements. As a result, 34 percent of respondents referred to their financial statements at least once while 6.8 percent referred to them on a frequent basis (Kennickell 2000). This approach may be used effectively by other surveys, especially panel data that have successfully built long-term relationships with respondents (e.g., the PSID) because respondents may save their financial statements as preparation for upcoming interviews. Using financial statements may, however, affect the length of the interview. Empirical analyses have not been conducted to test whether encouraging respondents to use financial statements improves the quality of self-reported asset data.

Option 3. Assess the quality of asset data collected with survey methods using other sources, particularly for assets that are difficult to value. The SIPP and the SCF, for example, collect information on automobile makes, models, and years, and then use Kelley Blue Book® prices to calculate the value of automobiles, instead of directly asking respondents about the values of their automobiles. This provides a consistent means for obtaining vehicle values. Other surveys could benefit from similar procedures. It is often mentioned that respondents tend to overestimate housing values. The House Price Index, collected by the Office of the Federal Housing Enterprise Oversight, provides information that could be used to obtain estimates of housing values in the same way the Blue Book provides information on automobile values.[9] However, housing value may have a greater idiosyncratic variation than vehicles. In addition, the reliability and validity of using this index to estimate individual housing values have not been empirically tested.

Option 4. Collect data on assets among crucial subpopulations. For example, little is known about asset accumulation among Native Americans, those who have been incarcerated, or immigrants and refugees. Our limited understanding of these subpopulations is partly due to the scarcity of reliable data. For example, none of the datasets examined include a subpopulation of Native Americans that is large enough for separate analyses. National surveys rarely provide information on those who are incarcerated or identify those who were previously incarcerated. In terms of immigrants, the PSID added 441 immigrant families into its sample in 1997, but the sample size may be too small to substantially advance our understanding of immigrant households. The SIPP has a sizeable immigrant subpopulation in its sample but does not have detailed information on immigration status; it does not have a refugee status variable and does not distinguish permanent residents (green card holders) from other immigrants (i.e., those with visitor, student, and working visas).

Information on subpopulations can be collected as part of an existing national survey (as in the case of the immigrant subsample in the PSID). To obtain a large sample of Native Americans, a survey could oversample individuals living on reservations, although this approach is not able to cover those living off reservations. To obtain a large sample of individuals who have been imprisoned, researchers may have to rely on the Department of Justice's database of prisoner records. Another option could be to field a new survey that focuses specifically on these subpopulations. It would facilitate comparisons if a new survey used survey instruments similar to those employed in national surveys (e.g., PSID or SIPP).

Option 5. Collect data on respondents' experiences with saving-incentive programs beyond retirement-savings accounts. Collecting this type of information would provide a broader understanding of low-income households' savings patterns and responses to savings incentives. Compared to their long-standing interest in retirement accounts, existing datasets provide little information on respondents' experience with other types of saving-incentive programs, such as college savings strategies (e.g., educational IRAs and 529 plans), individual development accounts (IDAs), the small saver's credit, and efforts to promote saving through the earned income tax credit. These saving mechanisms have steadily expanded over the last two decades and may affect asset accumulation within the low-income population. For example, since their inception in the early 1990s, IDA programs have expanded to more than 400 programs currently operating in the United States. In 1998, the Assets for Independence Act (PL 105-285) created a federal IDA program for low-income individuals and families.[10] Except for the datasets specifically designed to evaluate IDA programs, no existing datasets collect information on IDA program participation. Accordingly, little is known about the effects of these programs on low-income households in general.

Collecting data on individuals' experiences with saving-incentive programs from a nationally representative sample would provide information on what percentage of eligible households participate in these various programs and the value of financial assets participating households have accumulated through these programs. Although the SCF provides valuable information on college saving plans, the SCF includes limited information on correlates of interest (e.g., child outcomes) that are needed to understand determinants and effects of these programs. The PSID collected detailed information on college savings in the 2002 Child Development Supplement. This survey supplement provides information on college savings for one year (2002) and covers a subsample of families with children 5 to 18 years old in that year and those interviewed when the first Child Development Supplement data were collected in 1997. Collecting data on college savings from every household with children, including college-aged children, would significantly enhance the PSID data.

Questions on asset-accumulation programs could be added to existing datasets. Because the PSID and the SIPP contain a wide range of correlates (e.g., public assistance history and child outcomes), they are ideal candidates to collect information on asset-building interventions for low-income households.

Specific Means for Improving Asset Data

Survey of Income and Program Participation

Option 6. Collect information on quasi-liquid financial assets (e.g., pensions and life insurance), other tangible assets (e.g., jewelry, cemetery plots, art, and collections), and other secured debt. Collecting this information could improve the usefulness of SIPP's asset data as it would capture a wider range of individuals' assets and liabilities. For some of these categories, the survey questionnaire could provide guidance to help respondents determine the reported values.

As currently designed, the SIPP asset and liability topical module does not include information on quasi-liquid pensions such as 403(b)s and other defined contribution pensions, although it is asked in the retirement plan topical module. Incorporating this information into the asset and liability module would provide consistency and may provide more accurate estimations of wealth.[11]

Option 7. Revise the imputation method used to fill in for item nonresponse. SIPP's nonresponse rates are higher for asset and liability questions than for other questions, and data quality could improve if the current hot-deck imputation methods were replaced with a model-based approach, such as the one used for the SCF. Further, the relationship between assets and liabilities should be taken into account in the imputation procedure. There are interactions between assets and liabilities when calculating net worth, so it is important that asset items be taken into account when imputing liabilities and vice versa. This would add complexity to the imputation method and could increase the cost of preparing the survey data for release to the public.

Option 8. Increase the number of response brackets, narrow the width of each bracket, and raise the top code of the asset brackets. As described above, an evaluation of response brackets in the SIPP suggests that replacing the relatively small number of wide brackets with a larger number of narrow brackets and increasing the upper bound of the top bracket will likely lead to a more accurate picture of asset holdings and liabilities among respondents (Czajka et al. 2003). This is a low-cost and straightforward way to improve quality of the SIPP asset and liability data.

Going further, asking for exact estimates by dollar value of assets and liabilities might be just as easy for respondents and would make the calculation of total assets, total liabilities, net worth, and other composite measures both more accurate and simpler.

Option 9. Collect data on citizenship and refugee status more than once during the SIPP panel. Although not directly related to asset data, immigration status can change and this change (e.g., from a permanent resident to a citizen or from a refugee to a permanent resident) may influence asset accumulation. If there is sufficient movement in immigration status over a SIPP panel, researchers could examine how assets and liabilities change with immigrant status.

Panel Study of Income Dynamics

Option 10. Link PSID data with administrative data (e.g., data from the Social Security Administration, the IRS, and the Employer Pension Study), as the SIPP and HRS currently do. Linking administrative data to existing survey data is a low-cost way of obtaining significant information about individuals and households. These administrative datasets provide information on contributions to retirement-savings accounts (e.g., 401(k) and 403(b) accounts), contributions to the Social Security system, and other available financial resources in employment-related pensions. The PSID recently added questions on retirement accounts and pensions, and links to administrative data would provide valuable information. The PSID has built a relationship with respondents through more than 30 years of data collection, and this relationship would likely facilitate collection of respondents' Social Security numbers and their permission for data linking. However, as discussed above, issues around confidentiality may make it difficult for the PSID to obtain clearance to link the data.[12]

Option 11. Add questions about business equity and other assets to the wealth section to strengthen PSID's ability to capture net worth across the entire wealth distribution. Although it is difficult to represent business assets accurately, the PSID makes little effort to address this problem and asks only one question about the total value of farm and business equity. A few additional questions would allow for more precision and accuracy. In addition, expanding the "other assets" section to include separate questions about specific types of assets might help jog the respondent's memory and improve reporting at the higher end of the income scale (Juster et al. 1999).

Survey of Consumer Finances

Option 12. Link SCF data with administrative data, as described for the PSID above. This link would provide additional information about the earnings histories, retirement savings, and Social Security contributions for the SCF sample.

Option 13. Add more low-income families to the SCF sample. Currently, the SCF includes a relatively small number of low-income families (approximately 1,088 in 2004). This limits the dataset's usefulness for studying subgroups of the low-income population. Expansion of the low-income sample should not be at the expense of the high-wealth sample, given the SCF's primary goal of providing information about wealth holdings in the United States.

Option 14. Decrease the lower limit of inter vivos transfer in the SCF. The SCF asks whether respondents' families gave $3,000 or more to other families and whether they received $3,000 or more from other families as a measure of interfamily transfer of assets. The truncation of data at $3,000 is often mentioned as a shortcoming of the SCF in studying interfamily transfer and asset accumulation of the low-income population. Asking whether a family received from or gave to other families gifts or supports worth $100, like the PSID, provides more information and is preferable (Gale and Scholz 1994; Schoeni 1997).

Option 15. Collect data as a panel that includes at least three waves. The SCF provides a great deal of information on asset and liability holdings, but information over time would allow researchers to identify portfolio changes. Panel studies are costly, and this must be weighed against the fact that changes in reported wealth over time are subject to measurement error and regression to the mean (Haider et al. 2000; Toder et al. 2002).

Also, the experience of the 1983–1989 SCF panel suggests that it is very difficult to reinterview the wealthy respondents who are a central part of the SCF sample for other research purposes.

NOTES

1. Details of the rating system used to evaluate the datasets and a summary of the ratings received by each of the 12 datasets are available online at http://www.urban.org/books/assetbuilding/. This online reference also provides a brief description of the 9 datasets not identified as "primary" datasets.

2. A comprehensive list of the asset and liability questions contained in the three surveys is available online at http://www.urban.org/books/assetbuilding/.

3. Access to these administrative data requires approval from the organizations managing the databases, which can be difficult to obtain. Often, researchers are required to work with the data at an approved location.

4. Additional information about the LEHD can be found at http://lehd.did.census.gov/led/ (accessed July 28, 2008).

5. Initial analyses of the 2004 panel indicate that the initial wave had an 85 percent response rate, slightly lower than the 2001 panel. The response rate across the full 2004 panel is not yet available.

6. The 1986 SCF reinterviewed respondents to the 1983 survey. For a number of reasons, this survey was of a notably lower quality than the usual SCF interview. The questionnaire was far less comprehensive, the sample size was fairly small (2,822 observations), and the nonresponse rate was high. The 1989 SCF was a type of overlapping panel cross-sectional design. The 1989 survey included 1,479 respondents selected from the 1983 survey and 1,622 new respondents. Of the panel cases, 849 were also eligible to be included with the new sample for cross-sectional estimation. The experiences of the Federal Reserve with the 1983–1989 panel suggested that it is very costly to collect panel data from a sample like that used for the SCF. In addition, the nonresponse rate was high and the amount of staff effort required to achieve a usable level of data quality was quite high. For these reasons, no additional SCF panel data have been collected.

7. The recent SCF has an open-ended question about miscellaneous assets that allows respondents to identify the three most valuable assets they own not covered elsewhere in the survey. If the respondent identifies a computer, equipment, or tools as one of three most valuable assets they own, then it is recorded in the survey. However, if a respondent's computer, equipment, or tools are not included in their three most valuable miscellaneous assets, these assets will not be recorded.

8. The 2005 survey includes a question about how much was spent in the last year on furniture and equipment.

9. This information is available at http://www.ofheo.gov/HPI.aspx (accessed July 28, 2008).

10. Assets for Independence Act, U.S. Public Law 105-285, 105th Congress, 1998, http://www.acf.hhs.gov/assetbuilding/afialaw2000.html (accessed June 7, 2005).

11. The retirement module and the assets and liabilities modules are currently administered in different survey waves. Therefore, measures of net worth are constructed using nonretirement asset values and retirement asset values from different points in time, which is not ideal because individuals can shift assets from one time period to another. Furthermore, the assets and liabilities module was fielded three times in the 2001 panel while the retirement accounts module was fielded only twice, meaning that less-frequent updates are available for retirement accounts.

12. Also, there is concern that asking for Social Security numbers might negatively impact response rates.

REFERENCES

Athey, Leslie A., and Arthur B. Kennickell. 2005. "Managing Data Quality on the 2004 Survey of Consumer Finances." http://www.federalreserve.gov/pubs/oss/oss2/papers/Athey_Kennickell_101805.pdf. (Accessed July 25, 2008.)

Becketti, Sean, William Gould, Lee Lillard, and Finis Welch. 1988. "The Panel Study of Income Dynamics after 14 Years: An Evaluation." *Journal of Labor Economics* 6(4): 472–92.

Curtin, Richard T., F. Thomas Juster, and James N. Morgan. 1989. "Survey Estimates of Wealth: An Assessment of Quality." In *The Measurement of Saving, Investment, and Wealth,* edited by Robert E. Lipsey and Helen Stone Tice (473–548). Chicago: University of Chicago Press.

Czajka, John L., Jonathan E. Jacobson, and Scott Cody. 2003. "Survey Estimates of Wealth: A Comparative Analysis and Review of the Survey of Income and Program Participation." Washington, DC: Mathematica Policy Research.

Fitzgerald, John, Peter Gottschalk, and Robert Moffitt. 1998. "An Analysis of Sample Attrition in Panel Data: The Michigan Panel Study of Income Dynamics." *Journal of Human Resources* 33(2): 251–99.

Gale, William G., and John Karl Scholz. 1994. "Intergenerational Transfers and the Accumulation of Wealth." *Journal of Economic Perspectives* 8(4): 145–60.

Gouskova, Elena, and Frank Stafford. 2002. *Trends in Household Wealth Dynamics, 1999–2001.* Ann Arbor: Institute for Social Research, University of Michigan.

Haider, Steven, Michael Hurd, Elaine Reardon, and Stephanie Williamson. 2000. "Patterns of Dissaving in Retirement." Washington, DC: AARP Public Policy Institute.

Juster, F. Thomas, James P. Smith, and Frank P. Stafford. 1999. "The Measurement and Structure of Household Wealth." *Labour Economics* 6(2): 253–75.

Kennickell, Arthur B. 1995. "Saving and Permanent Income: Evidence from the 1992 SCF." Washington, DC: Federal Reserve Board. http://www.federalreserve.gov/pubs/oss/oss2/papers/saving.abk.scf92.pdf. (Accessed July 25, 2008.)

———. 2000. *Wealth Measurements in the Survey of Consumer Finances: Methodology and Directions for Future Research.* Washington, DC: Federal Reserve Board.

———. 2006. "How Do We Know if We Aren't Looking? An Investigation of Data Quality in the 2004 SCF." Washington, DC: Federal Reserve Board. http://www.federalreserve.gov/PUBS/oss/oss2/papers/asa2006.3.pdf. (Accessed July 25, 2008.)

Kennickell, Arthur B., and Martha Starr-McCluer. 1996. "Retrospective Reporting of Household Wealth: Evidence from the 1983–89 Survey of Consumer Finances." http://www.federalreserve.gov/pubs/oss/oss2/papers/sv8389.pdf. (Accessed July 25, 2008.)

Kim, Yong-Seong, and Frank P. Stafford. 2000. "The Quality of PSID Income Data in the 1990s and Beyond." Ann Arbor: Institute for Social Research, University of Michigan. Mimeograph.

Rodgers, Diane Lim, and Karen Smith. 2000. "Options to Adjust Asset Simulation and Spend Down." Washington, DC: The Urban Institute. Report prepared for the Social Security Administration.

Schoeni, Robert F. 1997. "Private Interhousehold Transfers of Money and Time: New Empirical Evidence." *Review of Income and Wealth* 43(4): 423–48.

Sherraden, Michael. 2001. "Asset-Building Policy and Programs for the Poor." In *Assets for the Poor: The Benefits of Spreading Asset Ownership,* edited by Thomas M. Shapiro and Edward N. Wolff (302–23). New York: Russell Sage Foundation.

Spilerman, Seymour. 2000. "Wealth and Stratification Processes." *Annual Review of Sociology* 26(1): 497–524.

Toder, Eric, Lawrence Thompson, Melissa Favreault, Richard Johnson, Kevin Perese, Caroline Ratcliffe, Karen Smith, Cori Uccello, Timothy Waidman, Jillian Berk, Romina Woldemariam, Gary Burtless, Claudia Sahm, and Douglas Wolf. 2002. "Modeling Income in the Near Term: Revised Projections of Retirement Income Through 2020 for the 1931–1960 Birth Cohorts." Washington, DC: The Urban Institute. Final Report. http://www.urban.org/url.cfm?ID=410609. (Accessed July 25, 2008.)

About the Editors

Signe-Mary McKernan is an economist with more than 15 years' experience researching access to assets and credit for the poor and the impact of welfare programs on the poor. She leads the Urban Institute's Opportunity and Ownership Project. Prior to joining the Urban Institute in 1999, she worked at the Federal Trade Commission, where she was the lead economist on credit issues. She has also been a visiting professor at Georgetown University (teaching econometrics) and is currently an adjunct professor there. She has extensive experience using rigorous econometric methods and large databases, such as the Survey of Income and Program Participation. Her research has been published in books, policy briefs, reports, and more than 14 journal articles and working papers, and been presented at more than 45 professional conferences and seminars. She received her Ph.D. in economics from Brown University and her B.A. in mathematical economics and Scandinavian literature from the University of California, Berkeley.

Michael Sherraden is Benjamin E. Youngdahl Professor of Social Development and founding director of the Center for Social Development (CSD) at the George Warren Brown School of Social Work, Washington University in St. Louis. His first book on asset-based policy, *Assets and the Poor: A New American Welfare Policy* (M. E. Sharpe, 1991), proposes universal and progressive saving beginning at birth in individual development accounts (IDAs). IDAs targeted toward low-income adults have been implemented in more than 40 states and have been a focus of CSD research. Universal asset-based policies are discussed in a volume edited by Sherraden, *Inclusion in the American Dream: Assets, Poverty, and Public Policy* (Oxford University Press, 2005). CSD research and policy design in this area has influenced policies and programs in the United States, the United Kingdom, Canada, Australia, Taiwan, China, Korea, Uganda, Peru, Hungary, and other countries.

About the Contributors

Sondra Beverly is an independent scholar with more than 10 years of experience researching asset building in low-income families. She has helped design and implement a large quasi-experimental study of children's savings accounts and smaller studies of programs that offer low-cost savings accounts and refund splitting during tax season. She received her M.S.W. and Ph.D. from the George Warren Brown School of Social Work at Washington University in St. Louis and an M.A. in economics from the University of Missouri–St. Louis.

Adam Carasso is chief economist for the House Budget Committee (Democratic staff). Previously, he was a research director at the New America Foundation and a research associate for the Urban Institute. He has written extensively on how federal programs affect the distribution of wealth, income, and taxation. Mr. Carasso's research has been featured on NPR and in the *Washington Post*, *Wall Street Journal*, *New York Times*, and *Los Angeles Times*. He received his master's degree in public policy from the University of Maryland.

Henry Chen served as an Urban Institute research associate from 2003 to 2007. While at the Urban Institute, he was a member of the Opportunity and Ownership Project team. Using large survey databases such as the Survey of Consumer Finances and National Longitudinal Survey of Youth, he has studied the personal finance, employment, and education patterns of the poor. He received his B.A. in economics and mathematics from Northwestern University.

Reid Cramer is research director of the Asset Building Program at the New America Foundation. Recently, he served as a codirector of the New America Foundation's Next Social Contract initiative. Prior to joining New America, he served as a policy and budget analyst in Bill Clinton's and George W. Bush's administrations. Cramer earned his Ph.D. in public policy from the University of Texas at Austin and a master's degree in city and regional planning from the Pratt Institute.

Jin Huang is a doctoral student at the George Warren Brown School of Social Work and a research associate in the Center for Social Development, Washington University in St. Louis. His areas of interest are poverty, asset building, and disability. He has published several articles on disability, asset building, and Chinese social policy. He received his master of social work from Washington University in St. Louis.

Robert I. Lerman, senior fellow at Urban Institute and professor of economics at American University, has published widely and conducted policy analyses on income support, youth development, family structure, and asset building. He formerly served as staff economist for the Congressional Joint Economic Committee and the U.S. Department of Labor. His current research deals with family structure, apprenticeship training, and asset-based policies. Dr. Lerman earned his A.B. at Brandeis University and his Ph.D. in economics at MIT.

Yunju Nam is an assistant professor at the George Warren Brown School of Social Work and a faculty affiliate of its Center for Social Development, both at Washington University in Saint Louis. Her scholarly interests include asset building as a socioeconomic development tool. She has examined the impact of asset tests in welfare programs on low-income households and the roles of assets in children's long-term development. She holds a Ph.D. in social work from the University of Michigan.

Mark R. Rank is the Herbert S. Hadley Professor of Social Welfare in the George Warren Brown School of Social Work at Washington University in St. Louis. His research interests include poverty, social welfare, economic inequality, and social policy. His most recent book is *One Nation, Underprivileged: Why American Poverty Affects Us All* (2005) and is published by Oxford University Press.

Caroline Ratcliffe is an economist and senior research associate at the Urban Institute, where she has worked since 1996. She was recently a visiting associate professor at Georgetown University and is currently an adjunct professor there. Her research focuses on the outcomes and behaviors of low-income families, including their asset accumulation. Her research has been published in reports, policy briefs, and peer-reviewed journals. She earned her Ph.D. in economics from Cornell University.

Mark Schreiner is senior scholar with the Center for Social Development at the George Warren Brown School of Social Work, Washington University in Saint Louis. Along with Michael Sherraden, he wrote *Can the Poor Save? Saving and Asset Building in Individual Development Accounts* (Transaction, 2006), an analysis of the largest demonstration of individual development accounts. He is also director of Microfinance Risk Management L.L.C., a firm that uses poverty scoring and credit scoring to help the poor build assets through improved access to financial services.

Trina R. Williams Shanks is currently an assistant professor at the University of Michigan School of Social Work. She is coprincipal investigator on the SEED impact assessment survey, a quasi-experimental study of children's savings accounts among Head Start families. Her interests include asset-building policy and practice across the life cycle; the impact of poverty and wealth on child development outcomes; and community and economic development, especially in urban areas.

Min Zhan is an associate professor with the School of Social Work, University of Illinois at Urbana-Champaign. Since she joined the faculty in 2001, her research has centered on examining the impact of educational approaches and asset development in the long-term economic well-being of low-income families with children. Her research has been published in more than 20 journal articles, and in book chapters and reports. She received her Ph.D. in social work from Washington University in St. Louis.

Index

class differences. *See also* social-
    stratification theory
  in how people describe assets, 16–17
Cohen, Stewart, 93
conspicuous consumption, norm of, 93
constraint of matches to set goals, 166
consumer durables, 22–23
consumption, 26
  assets and, 185–87
consumption-floor effect, 116, 161
consumption model, 2–4, 207
  alternative measures in, 6–8
  asset-poverty measures outside, 14–15
  asset-poverty measures within, 13–14
  measures of assets in, 4–5
conversion stage (asset accumulation), 18
countable assets, 5
credit risks, 130
credit worthiness, 129, 130

debt burdens, 55–56, 186
debt holdings, 42, 44–48. *See also*
    mortgages
  family characteristics and, 44–48
  future research on, 209
debt load, 104
developing countries, economic develop-
    ment in, 27n.2
Dewilde, Caroline, 69

earned income tax credit (EITC), 118–19,
    134–37
economic development in poor coun-
    tries, 27n.2
economic downturn, 70
economic mobility, assets and, 201
economic resources and needs, and sav-
    ing and investment action, 102–9
education, 75, 78
  and family assets, 58
  and family liabilities, 58–59
eligibility, 110
employment. *See also* pensions
bundles of institutional supports pro-
    vided through, 127–28
ethnicity. *See* race/ethnicity
expectations, 119–20, 226
expected assets, 21
experimental program designs, 180

facilitation, 117–19, 137, 226, 228
  defined, 117
families. *See also specific topics*
  single-headed, 59
family characteristics
  asset holdings and, 36–43
  debt holdings and, 44–48
  net worth and, 51, 52, 61
family life cycle, 69. *See also* life course
family structure, and asset building
    across life course, 78–79
family transfers. *See* intergenerational
    transfer of assets
Federal Housing Administration (FHA),
    133
Federal Reserve, 253
fill-the-gap approach, 6–8
financial (liquid) assets, 19
financial literacy, 105–7, 202
Food Stamp program (FSP), 153, 155,
    156, 159–60
forced savings, 188, 189
fungible worth, 6–7
future orientation, 107–8

general linear model (GLM) regression,
    179–80
goal contagion, 95
gross financial assets, 5
Gruber, Jonathan, 5

Hacker, Jacob S., 71
Hansen, W. Lee, 6
head-start assets, 15, 24
health. *See also* medical expenses
  asset accumulation and, 183
  IDAs and, 198
health insurance coverage, 103
  increasing, 62
Hirschl, Thomas A., 80
Hispanic families, assets of, 59–60
Hochschild, Jennifer, 75
HOME Investment Partnerships Pro-
    gram (HOME), 132–33
homeownership, 11, 12, 15, 40–42,
    61–62. *See also* housing
  economic returns to, 190